European Top Gun

European Top Gun

The Tactical Leadership Programme: NATO's Advanced Aircrew Training School

Salvador Mafé Huertas & Rafael Treviño Martínez

AIR WORLD

First published in Great Britain in 2025 by
Air World
An imprint of Pen & Sword Books Limited
Yorkshire – Philadelphia

ISBN 978 1 03612 179 2

Typeset by Mac Style
Printed in the UK by CPI Group (UK) Ltd, Croydon, CR0 4YY.

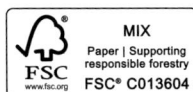

The Publisher's authorised representative in the EU for product
safety is Authorised Rep Compliance Ltd., Ground Floor,
71 Lower Baggot Street, Dublin D02 P593, Ireland.
www.arccompliance.com

For a complete list of Pen & Sword titles please contact

PEN & SWORD BOOKS LIMITED
47 Church Street, Barnsley, South Yorkshire, S70 2AS, England
E-mail: enquiries@pen-and-sword.co.uk
Website: www.pen-and-sword.co.uk
or
PEN AND SWORD BOOKS
1950 Lawrence Road, Havertown, PA 19083, USA
E-mail: uspen-and-sword@casematepublishers.com
Website: www.penandswordbooks.com

To: Tono Fernández Leonarte, a good friend and a great photographer.

Contents

Introduction

The TLP Programme

The Tactical Leadership Programme (TLP) is an international advanced tactical aircrew training programme established by the agreement of ten NATO member countries (Belgium, Denmark, France, Germany, Greece, the Netherlands, Italy, Spain, the United States and the United Kingdom). Other countries, such as Poland and the Czech Republic, are currently reported to be interested in joining the programme.

The mission of the TLP is to increase the effectiveness of Allied Air Forces by developing the leadership capabilities of their aircrews through

Large TLP emblem that presides over the façade of the programme hangar. (*Salvador Mafé*)

Access door to the TLP hangar decorated with the cockades of the member countries of the programme. Through this gate you can access the hangar and the work offices and relaxation areas of the crews participating in the courses. (*Salvador Mafé*)

The TLP hangar is decorated inside with this large panel that includes the flags of the member nations of the course. (*Salvador Mafé*)

improved mission planning and analysis. It is also the mission of TLP to conduct conceptual and doctrinal initiatives at the Air Force level.

The programme was initially established in Germany in 1978 to promote, in a highly collaborative manner, the understanding of different nations in the employment of Air Forces, through mutual knowledge and the integration of different capabilities.

TLP activity is structured in different courses that are offered to participants from member nations and also from other allied countries. By far the most important and unique

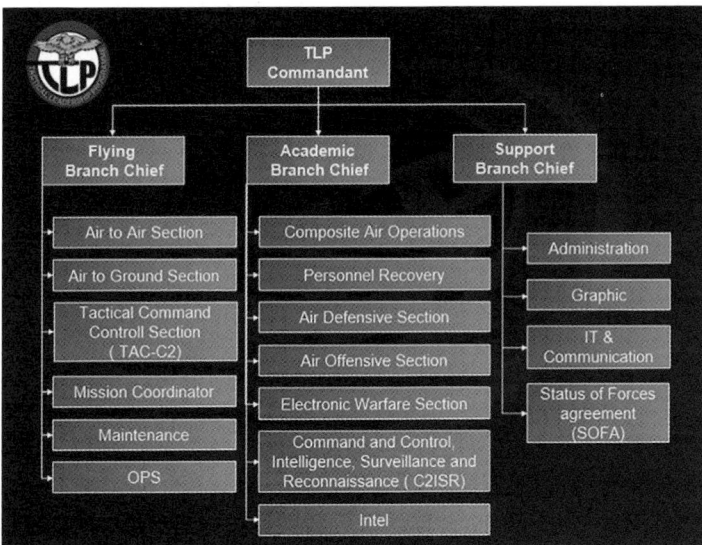

TLP's organizational chart. (*TLP Staff slide*)

Colonel Andrés E. Maldonado, who led the TLP from 2018 to 2020, photographed on 3 July 2018 signing the documents in which he assumed command of the programme. (*Salvador Mafé*)

product of the programme is the Flying Course (FC). The TLP is prepared to hold up to six Flying Courses per year, in which the participating aircrews acquire tactical Mission Commander training, which means that they will be able to plan, organize and conduct a Composite Air Operation (COMAO).

The TLP also offers a series of academic courses, all of which focus on allied air operations (COMAO, Combat Search and Rescue [CSAR]), or on vital capabilities such as tactical intelligence or support assets. The aim of the courses is to show how the different capabilities are optimally integrated to fulfil the mission, in realistic scenarios and with current threats. All of these courses are designed to ensure the success of Alliance Air Forces, success orchestrated by the exercise of leadership and through collaboration and communication among its members.

In the late 1970s, NATO's Allied Air Forces Central Europe (AAFCE) Headquarters set out to promote multinational tactical air operations. The Eastern Bloc threat demanded the generation of a harmonized Allied defence capability through tactical air leadership.

In January 1978, Belgium, Canada, Germany, the Netherlands, the USA and the UK established the Tactical Leadership Programme (AAFCE TLP), which began at Fürstenfeldbruck Airbase, Germany. Initially, two-week courses (seminars) were scheduled in which expert aircrews presented, discussed, formulated and evaluated tactics, techniques and procedures.

In September 1979, the TLP moved to northern Germany, to Jever Airbase, and a flying phase was added to the initial programme, extending the courses to four weeks. At Jever, 71 flying courses were completed, graduating nearly 2,000 pilots and crew members.

In March 1989 the TLP moved to Florennes Airbase (Belgium). In this new stage, the programme took on new tasks and was reorganized, with three Branches: the existing Flying Branch was joined by the studies one, Academics, and the doctrine one, Concepts & Doctrine.

During these years, the TLP recruited new members. In 1989, a liaison officer from the Armeé de l'Air joined the TLP staff and France began to participate actively in the courses. In 1996, Denmark and Italy joined. In 1997, Canada, withdrawing its forces from Europe, decided to leave the Programme, but retains a liaison officer and continues to participate in the courses.

In January 2002, the TLP became a support unit of Supreme Headquarters Allied Powers Europe (SHAPE), which joined as a partner in the programme: the TLP was renamed the Allied Command Operations TLP (ACO TLP). In the same year, Spain joined TLP, and in 2009, France and Greece joined.

The TLP remained at Florennes for 20 years, during which 107 flight courses were conducted and 2,978 participants graduated. During this period, the programme underwent a remarkable development, increasing the number of participating nations and playing a leading role in the adaptation of the Allied Air Forces to post-Cold War missions.

Author's Note

During the preparation of this work on the TLP, the authors have had the opportunity to visit the base where the courses are developed on numerous occasions. The TLP Staff has provided many facilities for photographing aircraft and interviewing pilots and maintenance personnel. Although they have been inflexible in one respect for security reasons; photographs that made it possible to identify the face and name of the participating personnel were not allowed. For this reason, many of the interviews appear under the condition of anonymity of the interviewee. Currently the Antiterrorist Alert Level in Spain is four out of five.

Chapter 1

Flugplatz Fürstenfeldbruck

Before the prestigious TLP moved to its current residence in Albacete (Spain) and before reaching its state of maturity, the programme had travelled a long itinerary in the context of the European Air Forces, having its roots in the Cold War Age and starting its activities in 1978.

From that date onward, the programme has passed through four European military installations of great prestige and traditions and its didactic contents have evolved in accordance with the lessons learned, the

TLP crest. (*TLP*)

Aerial view of Fürstenfeldbruck. (*NATO*)

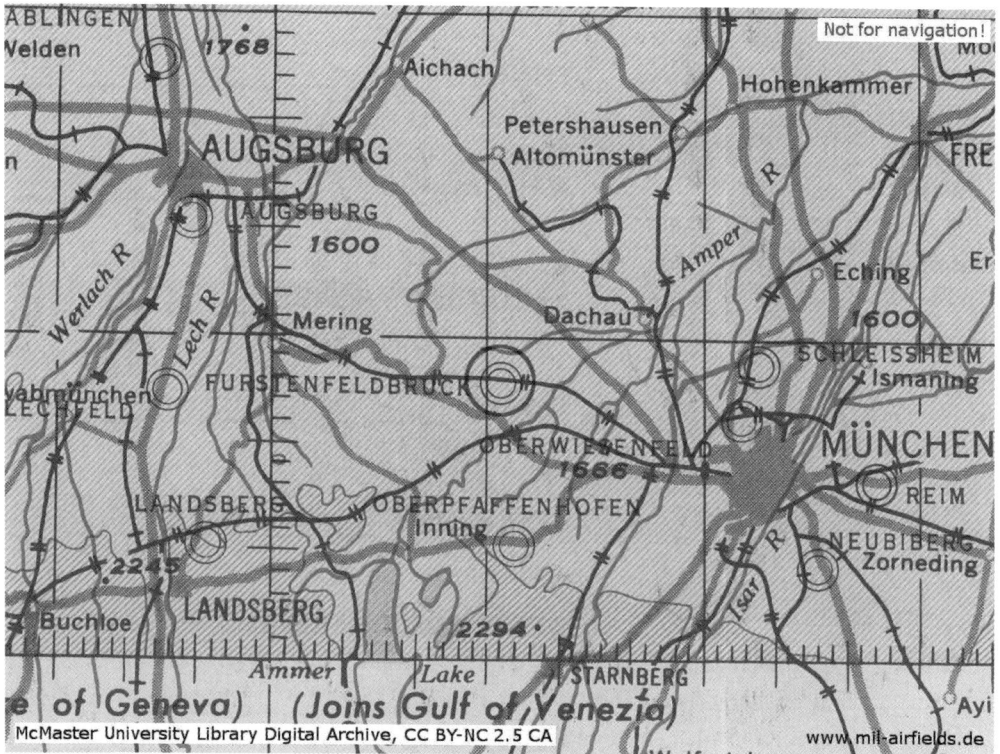

A map dated 1944 showing the location of Fürstenfeldbruck. (*NATO*)

evolution of technologies, techniques, tactics and geo-strategics and political situations. All of these four bases have very interesting histories to tell, but space pressures forces us to simply outline the main events that took place there.

The first airbase in which the TLP began its activities was Fürstenfeldbruck, which is located north of the Bavarian town of the same name and close to Munich. Construction began in 1935 at a cost of 40 million Reichsmark. It was set up from the beginning to be a prestigious military institution with the name of Luftkriegsschule 4 (LKS 4) (Air War School 4), becoming the largest aviation school of the Third Reich during the Second World War. It is said that Hermann Göring himself, the commander-in-chief of the Luftwaffe, took a great personal interest in establishing this training base that ironically was inspired by the training centre of the United States Army Air Force (USAAF) at Randolph Field, Texas. The new airbase was delivered to the Luftwaffe in 1937, and the concrete runway was finished in 1943.

During the war, both the RAF and the USAAF considered that Fürstenfeldbruck was basically being used as a training base and therefore of little strategic value. Consequently, it escaped the bombings until the last stages of the conflict, when Allied attention focused on it, suffering unique but serious air attacks.

In October 1944, Luftwaffe leaders launched a hurried programme to extend the length of the base runways to facilitate the take-off of fighter jets, especially the new

Bf 109F2 Stab. II JG 53. (*Author's files*)

Messerschmitt Me 262s, whose production centres, Lechfeld and Landsberg, were in nearby Munich. The change of purpose, from a training base to a fighter base, caused the only serious raid of Allied bombing on the airfield.

On 11 September 1944, P-51s Mustangs belonging to the VIII Fighter Command carried out a low-level attack, claiming a number of aircraft destroyed on the ground. On 9 April 1945, the base was bombed for the first and only time by 139 B-17 Flying Fortresses and strafed again by VIII Fighter Command P-51s. The bombers dropped some 250 tons of bombs obtaining fifty direct hits on the airfield causing extensive damage to the runway, taxiways, repair shops and other facilities of the base, that were demolished, rendering it practically useless for air operations for the remainder of the war. On 29 April, the airfield was captured by advancing US forces.

F-84E 36th FBW, 1951. (*Author's files*)

Once the base was restored to usable status, the first use during the post-war period was as a centre of acclimatization for occupation troops coming from the USA. Tens of thousands of Army Air Force replacement troops coming from the USA arrived by train from the port of Le Havre where they had disembarked, to be housed in the stone barracks of the base for rest and acclimatization, before being assigned to their final airbases or other destinations. These soldiers were the veterans' replacements being sent home to be discharged also through the Fürstenfeldbruck Replacement Depot.

On 13 August 1948, the 36th Fighter Wing from Howard Air Force Base, located in the Panama Canal area, was assigned to Fürstenfeldbruck. During the first crisis in Berlin, for a short period of time, July–August 1948, the 301st Bombardment Group equipped with B-29s was stationed there.

In November 1953, the 7330th Flying Training Wing was activated in Fürstenfeldbruck, becoming the first unit of the United States Air Forces in Europe (USAFE) to be equipped with the Lockheed F-80 A/B Shooting Star. In May 1949, the USAFE Headquarters authorized the formation of the Skyblazers, an aerobatic air demonstration team for air shows in Europe, the Mediterranean and North Africa.

On 20 January 1950, the 36th FW was redesigned as a Fighter Bomber Wing (FBW) when it received eighty-nine Republic F-84E Thunderjets. The 117th Flying Training Wing of the Air National Guard was deactivated in 1952 and its flying squadrons were transferred to the newly assigned 10th TRW that had already operated from Fürstenfeldbruck as the 10th Reconnaissance Group in 1947. In November 1953, the 7330th Flying Training Wing was activated in Fürstenfeldbruck.

T-33 with the Skyblazers scheme, 1951. (*Author's files*)

F-84G of the Skyblazers demonstration team. (*Author's files*)

In 1955 the French, British and American occupation of Germany ended and the West German Government was granted permission to re-establish its armed forces. On 1 November 1957, the airbase was taken over by the Air Force of the Federal Republic of Germany and was officially handed over on 14 December 1957 but until 1958 become a joint facility between USAFE and German Bundesluftwaffe. This lasted until 1958 with the 7330th Wing, then the organization was renamed as 7376th Training Flying Wing until that activity was terminated in 1960.

In 1961 the base became the residence of nineteen units, including the Flugzeugführerschule (Flight Training School) 'B'. In 1964 the Waffenschule der Luftwaffe 50 (Luftwaffe Weapons School 50 or WaSLw 50) that also moved to Fürstenfeldbruck. Unfortunately, Fürstenfeldbruck became tragically famous, appearing in the headlines of the world press as the setting for the terrorist acts of the 1972 Olympic Games that were held in Munich.

1978 was a year of interesting changes at the base. Fürstenfeldbruck was chosen as the first teaching centre for the future TLP. This base has been considered, practically since its foundation, as a prestigious aeronautical and military training centre, and currently is an inactive German Air Force facility, but is the home of the German Air Force Officers Training School.

In those days, and as an initiative of the Central European Allied Air Forces (AAFCE), six countries belonging to NATO, namely West Germany, Belgium, Canada, The Netherlands, the United Kingdom and the USA, established the first instruction programme in order not only to improve their tactical capabilities, but also to develop common techniques and standardized procedures to be used by pilots that could enhance operations in multinational tactical environments.

On 8 January 1978, members of the six founding countries attended the first theoretical course called Allied Air Forces Central Europe Tactical Leadership Program (AAFCE TLP). The purpose was to improve tactical capabilities, techniques and procedures in joint air operations.

The residence of the incipient TLP in Fürstenfeldbruck was not very prolonged, since in September 1979 the programme moved to the northernmost base in Germany at Jever where the teaching content was also expanded. Until September 1979, another 16 courses were held, attended by 330 crews in total.

Also in 1978, the resident WasLw 50 changed its name, adopting that of Jagdbombergeschwader 49 or (Fighter Bomber Wing JaBoG 40) that was subsequently disbanded in 1994, while the Flight Learning Group was established in that same year and was deactivated in 1997, ending the era of military flights in 'Fursty', as the base had been affectionately called by the Americans. Now the days of Flugpaltz Fürstenfeldbruck are numbered as it seems that by 2023 military activities had ceased.

Chapter 2

Flugplatz Jever

J ever Airbase is the second base on which the TLP courses were developed. It is located in northwestern Germany, in Lower Saxony, near the town of Jever, from which it takes its name. It is very close to the shores of the North Sea.

Jever's story as an airfield can be divided into three historical periods; from the mid-1920s until 1935, as the property of a civil flight club; since 1935 as an operational base of the Luftwaffe and from 1951 onward, as a base of fighters of the RAF and later of the Bundesluftwaffe, a member of the NATO defences.

During the 1920s, employees of Focke Wulf Ag in Bremen decided to form a sports flight club that began with a core of veteran pilots of the First World War. In 1926 they had already organized a thriving club with seven light aircraft, flying from a small airfield located at the edge of the Jever forest.

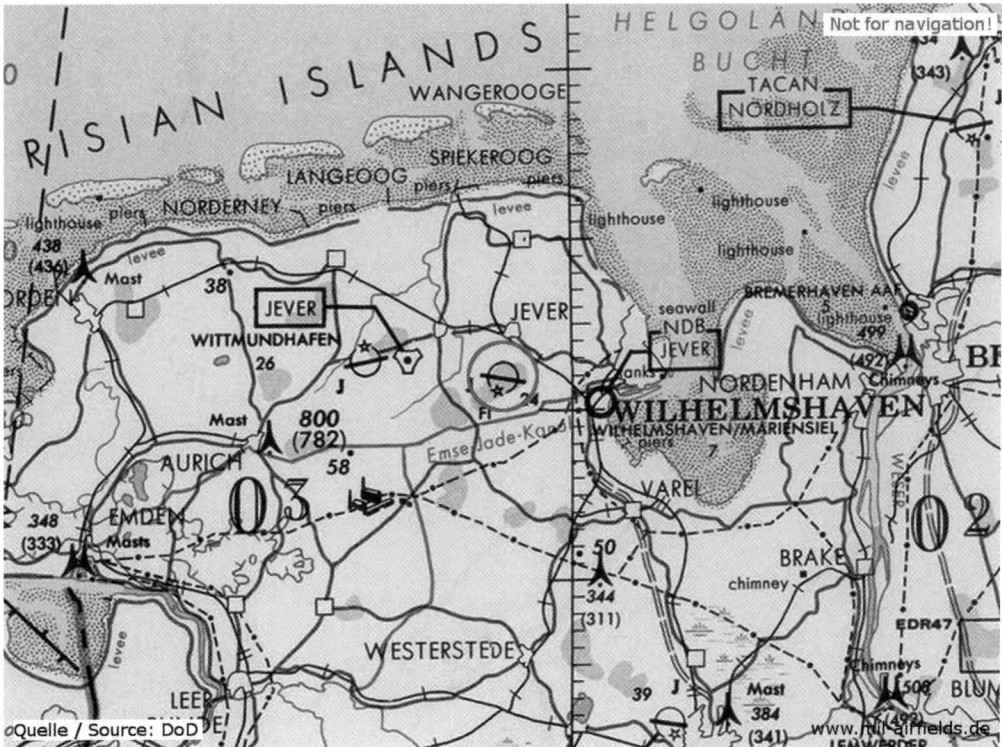

Map showing the location of the Jever base. Note the proximity to the Wilhelmshaven Naval Base. (*University of Texas at Austin*)

In 1935 the Reichlufthartministerium acquired an area of 282 hectares of adjacent land, beginning the adaptation works very quickly by clearing trees. Three-quarters of the space occupied by the base is located in the middle of the forest area called Upjeverschen Forst belonged to a district of the city of Wilhemshaven Upjever. As we have said, the facilities were developed very quickly, so that within a year they were ready for use, but without concrete landing strips. On 1 May 1935, General Erhart Milch took official delivery.

Given its proximity to the coast, the first unit to use it between August 1934 and June 1936 was the Luftdienst-Schleppstaffel Nordsee. This unit was replaced in October 1936 by I. Gruppe der Jagdgeschwaders 136 (I./JG 136), a coastal fighter unit equipped with three Staffeln of Heinkel 51 biplanes that operated until October 1938 with some precariousness. By the Munich Crisis of 1938, the base only had a fighter group equipped with Messerchmitt Bf109Bs.

In November 1938 the I Gruppe der Sturzkampfgeschwader 162 (I.St.G 162) 'Immelmann' arrived, equipped with the famous Junkers Ju 87 Stuka dive bomber, which operated until April 1939. At the beginning of 1939 Jever entered the operational spectrum with the formation of the first Group equipped with Messerschmitt Bf 109s and Bf 110s, that in September were responsible for the heavy losses suffered by fifteen Bristol Blenheims, of which ten belonged, five each, to 107 and 110 Squadrons, based at RAF Wattisham and five others from 139 Squadron based at Wyton. This raid had the distinction of being the first that was organized against German targets during the Second World War and was carried out on 4 September 1939 flying at low altitude against the warships anchored in Schilling Roads. From the beginning of 1940 until July 1941 there were no tactical units in Jever. In July 1941 it became the headquarters of the 2nd Fighter Division and the

A Bf 109 G-6/R6s of 9./ JG 11 seen in Oldenburg during the summer of 1943. Source: JG 11 Gustavs defending the Reich 1943, J. Prien's Jagdfliegerverbände. (*Author's files*)

A Ju 87 Stuka of STG.2 'Immelmann', after a crash-landing in Russia. (*Author's files*)

Heavily-armed Focke-Wulf Fw 190A5/U12 from 2./JG 11 at Holstein, Germany 1944. The aircraft is armed with a Rüstsatz R1WB gondola under each wing, with two 20mm MG 151/20 each. These fighters were used against US heavy bombers. (*Author's files*)

German Bight Fighter Command with a staffel of Bf 109s and two other staffeln on Wangerooge and Borkum Islands.

In 1943 the Stab and the first group of Jagdgeschwader 1 (JG 1) was established in Jever. At the beginning of that year, the US Eighth Air Force commanders were under great pressure from Washington to expand the reach of their raids on the Reich. On 26 February, the Americans launched another attack with sixty-three B-17s and twenty-eight B-24s, against the Wilhemshaven submarine shipyards and again the I./JG, the unit closest to the port took off to make repeated attacks against the formation, downing two B-17s and three B-24s.

During 1943 the base suffered several bombing attacks. In October, the rare 'T' variant of the Bf109, which had been destined to operate from the ill-fated German aircraft carrier, began operating from Jever, assigned to the Jasta Helgoland. From August 1944 until

Focke-Wulf Fw 190A showing its pilot posing proudly and details of its cowling and 2./JG 11 emblem. (*Author's files*)

Side view of a RAF 93 Squadron F-4 Sabre. (*Author's files*)

93 Sqn personnel pose for a photograph in front of F-4 Sabre XB829 'D' at Jever – 3 March 1955. (*Author's files*)

possibly the end of the war, a group of Junkers Ju 52 from the Seenotgruppe 80, Seenotstaffel 80, especially modified with some spectacular magnetic rings for the detection of maritime mines, was added to Jever. Towards the end of the war the fighter formations left Jever being replaced by one equipped with Junkers Ju 188 bombers.

Shortly before the surrender, all aircraft were flown from Leck to Schleswig-Holstein, to be destroyed, consequently when the troops of the 7th Polish Armoured Division entered the base on May 8, 1945, there were no more planes left.

During the war the Luftwaffe did not improve the facilities of the Jever airfield in any way, and so, after the Allied occupation, its relatively primitive conditions meant it was classified as an a landing field without concrete tracks, without radio installations and without illumination. Its grass track was 1,300 yards long. The total field size was 1,800 yards from east to west and 1,000 yards from north to south. Between 1945 and 1951 the base was used to house many of the people displaced by the war.

In mid-1951, the RAF assumed control of the almost demilitarized area and decided to develop Jever as a base for jet fighters, thus beginning the possibly most important period in the history of the base as an operational facility. During that year, as a main need, a concrete track of 1,828m (6,000ft) in length and 46m (150ft) in width was built, radio facilities were provided, underground fuel tanks were added and improvements were made plus accommodation facilities for residents.

No. 4 Squadron was the first of three equipped with Vampire FB5s to meet in Jever from March 1952 and form what was called the 'Jever Wing'. The other two squadrons were No. 93 and No. 112. In March 1954 4 and 93 Squadrons began to re-equip with the North American Sabre F4; the use of this 'second-hand' American fighter was for only

Name board located at the main access gate of Jever Airbase, 1986. (*Author's files*)

a short period. Another unit, previously equipped with Venoms, and now with Hunters, 118 Squadron, was added to the base on 31 July 1955, thus increasing the number of squadrons resident in Jever to five. This conversion was followed in 1956 by a move to the Hawker Hunter F4, 93 Squadron becoming famous during this time having formed a four-pilot aerobatic team, which represented the 2nd at many airshows. As the squadron with the longest service time in Jever, No. 4 received in July 1955 its easy and pleasing to fly Hunters, while No. 93 did not do so until January 1956. In 1958 both squadrons were re-equipped with the Hunter F6.

A new resident in Jever arrived in January 1958, in the form of 2 Squadron from Geilenkirchen equipped with Supermarine Swift FR5s to take on the task of tactical reconnaissance.

1961 was the years designated for the progressive withdrawal of the British Armed Forces Overseas, including the Royal Air Force units framed in the 2nd TAF, in favour of the West German armed forces, which consequently affected the RAF units in Jever.

In February 1961, 2 Squadron began replacing its Swifts with Hunter FR10s, followed by 4 Squadron that was also equipped with the Hunter FR10, which had arrived from Gutersloh. Between March and September, the Hunter F6s of 14 Squadron were based at Jever, developing fighter missions and interception practices, while the tracks of the usual squadron base were repaired.

In mid-1961 preparations began for transferring all the squadrons to Gutersloh, since Jever had been destined to be returned to the Germans. The transfer took place in September, including the 'Cloth Bomber', the 'rag bomber' of the Flight Station; an Avro

Beautiful 'Buntevogel', painted to commemorate the end of the works of Luftwaffenwerft 62 (LIG 21). (*Author's files*)

Anson registration TX160. The British aerodrome period closed on the 8th of the same month. RAF ground personnel remained to hand over to the German Air Force, finally leaving on 10 January 1962.

As we have said, the process of returning control to the German Air Force began in 1961, which resumed air operations in 1964. In the interim period, the 26th Anti-aircraft Missile Battalion equipped with Nike missiles was based there and in 1973 was transferred to Hohenkirchen. The first flight unit of the modern Bundesluftwaffe to use the base was the WaSLw 10 (Weapons Training School Luftwaffe 10) equipped with Lockheed

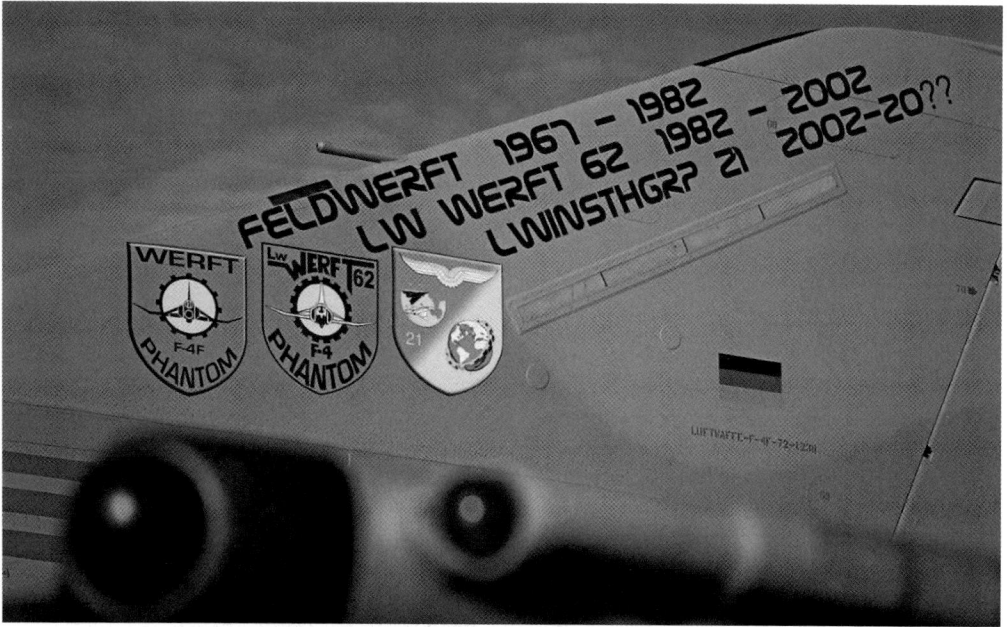

Detail of the vertical fin of Phantom 38+28, displaying a brief history of the unit and badges. (*Author's files*)

F-104G, which was moved from Oldenburg. This unit later became JaboG 38 'Friesland' equipped with Panavia Tornados. JaboG 38 was deactivated in 2008.

In Jever was Luftwaffenwerft 62, the unit in charge of the general overhaul of the McDonnell Douglas F-4F Phantom II that remained in service. Its mission was to recover as much of the usable parts of the aircraft that were decommissioned as possible to support the operation and in-flight maintenance of the aircraft that remained in service. In 45 years at Jever LIG 21 had successfully completed 361 DI inspections (Depotinstandsetzung), 36 HPO inspections and 23 periodic inspections for the benefit of the entire German F-4F fleet. To commemorate the fact, the plane received a special scheme of painting becoming a beautiful 'bunte vogel'. Since 1997 there has been a battalion of the Bundesluftwaffe as the close protection unit.

The TLP arrives at Jever

In September 1979, the TLP moved to Jever, adding a flight phase to its previous activities and extending the duration to four weeks.

If the transfer was completed in a little more than a year and a half, with all the difficulties involved in the construction and reconditioning of facilities in the new destination, it was because from the beginning it was necessary to test the theoretical developments discussed in Fürstenfeldbruck at a practical level. Therefore, the first steps of the TLP were similar to those that a research centre carries out until is able to understand that its theoretic programmes are alive and can evolve quickly towards what we know today.

Personnel of Luftwaffenwerft 62 (LIG 21) photographed as a souvenir in front of 38+28. (*Author's files*)

During this time the participants the flying crews were mainly personnel drawn from the Second and Fourth Allied Tactical Air Forces in Central and Western Europe.

The TLP remained in Jever until December 1988, when the Government of the German Federal Republic requested that the course must leave, not the base, but the country, claiming three reasons:

1st. The increase in flight periods or air activity carried out by the participants in the TLP generated a lot of jet noise in the Jever area and in the areas where it was flown at a low altitude.

2nd. An intensification of low-level flight over Germany due to the presence of Allied air forces based in West Germany.

3rd. The facilities were needed to host a planned ECR Tornado unit in Jever.

As another reason, underlying the aforementioned, one could point to the strong pressure received from the German public and the media, as a result of the fatal accident that occurred in Ramstein during the air show that same year of 1988.

Other reasons support the change of location of these courses, including the prevailing coastal climatic conditions on the north coast of Germany, which often limited flight operations. Also, a diminished perception of the Soviet threat, whose empire was collapsing, aided this decision.

A nostalgic TLP badge from the times when the courses were held at Jever. (*Author's files*)

Consequently, the TLP, taking advantage of favourable circumstances in Belgium, moved to Florennes. When the TLP left Jever in December, a further 71 courses had taken place, with 1,916 graduated crews.

Chapter 3

Florennes Airbase

In March 1989 TLP moved to Florennes Airbase (Belgium). In this new stage, the Programme took on new tasks and was reorganized, with three Branches: the existing Flying Branch was joined by the studies, Academics, and the doctrine one, Concepts & Doctrine.

During these years, TLP recruited new members. In 1989, a liaison officer from the Armeé de l'Air joined the TLP staff and France began to participate actively in the courses. In 1996, Denmark and Italy joined. In 1997, Canada, withdrawing its forces from Europe, decided to leave the Programme, but retains a liaison officer and continues to participate in the courses.

The inauguration of the programme at its current location at Albacete Airbase took place on 1 October 2009. With the new Memorandum of Understanding (MOU) the TLP formally ceased to belong to NATO. The new site was not chosen arbitrarily: cost savings, the expansion of airspace and better weather were decisive factors in the signing in 2006 of the Technical Agreement establishing the bases for the move, which followed the Spanish bid submitted in 2003.

A 370th Fighter Group P-38 Lightning. (*Americanmuseum.com/media/12238*)

On 4 November 2009, the first academic course was held and on 9 November, the first flying course in Spain began. Since then, and in these 14 years in Albacete, a total of 4,584 pilots, interception controllers and intelligence specialists have been trained in 32 flying courses and 121 academic courses.

Under the command of an Air Force Colonel (TLP Commandant), the TLP is structured in three groups: Flying Branch, Academics & Doctrine Branch, and Support Branch. The organization of the programme is fully product oriented, with the Flying Branch being primarily responsible for the preparation and execution of the flying courses, while the Academics Branch organizes and delivers the theoretical courses and leads the initiatives and work in the field of tactical air doctrine. The Support Branch is responsible for providing the means for all TLP activities to be carried out as efficiently as possible, and for coordination with the Albacete Airbase, the host unit whose support is vital to the TLP.

The TLP is manned by aircrews and specialists from member nations, experts in all areas of air tactics, with extensive experience flying different combat aircraft, and who have participated in different operations and major exercises. Having this group of experts in all areas permanently available is the key to the high quality of the courses offered by the Programme.

The Flying Branch has eighteen instructors from the ten nations participating in the Programme, divided into two sections, Air/Surface and Air/Air. The instructors design the flying courses, prepare the scenarios, give the necessary lectures, lead the participants in planning, evaluate the execution, assess the results and draw lessons from each mission conducted.

Academics and Doctrine Branch is composed of two sections: Academic and Intelligence. Its instructors are specialists in Command and Control, Offensive and Defensive Air Operations, Electronic Warfare, Combat Search and Rescue, and Intelligence. In addition to preparing and conducting theoretical courses, the Group is also responsible for work in the doctrinal area, collaboration with other training centres, and attention to new technologies and their applications to air tactics.

P-47 'Razorback' named ASTRA of the 365th Fighter Group (USAAC) warming engine prior to take off. (*Author's files*)

While the Germans were building Florennes airfield, a group of Belgian pilots were operating with the 350 Squadron RAF with Spitfire Mk VBs. Photograph taken at Kenley in 1942. (*Wikipedia*)

Although, as mentioned above, the responsibilities of the two branches, Academics and Flying, are clearly delimited, it is no less true that the interaction and support between them is constant, to the benefit of the whole.

The flying course is the TLP's best known and most popular activity. Up to four courses are scheduled each year, each lasting three weeks. An average of twenty-four combat aircraft participate, plus other support assets (AWACS, Electronic Warfare assets, transports, CSAR helicopters, remotely piloted aircraft-RPAS, etc.), with their corresponding crews and maintenance personnel. The participating aircraft are a broad representation of NATO's current tactical aircraft.

The objectives of the Flying Course are the following:

- Improve the tactical leadership skills of aircrews, and their in-flight application in the management of large aircraft formations.
- Improve the tactical interoperability of air forces to operate with other NATO air forces, integrating different air assets with different capabilities.
- Provide the possibility to validate new tactical employment concepts.

Another objective of the course is to provide realistic training for aircrews within the constraints of peacetime. Participants fly each day in a different tactical scenario, designed to challenge aircrews with situations that force them to approach planning from different perspectives and to work as a team. It is an unparalleled forum to exchange knowledge, tactics and modes of employment, and thus to make the most of the different means at their disposal in COMAO.

Missions are conducted from Albacete, using established training areas, both over land and sea. There may be long-distance missions, and in-flight refuelling means are used in these missions. In this way, the variety of areas and targets to be used is extended. Flying with any kind of real weaponry is not allowed. Weapon launches are always simulated, and are replayed and validated in the briefing room after the mission.

B-26 'Wheels Inc.' with crew. 344th BG 495th BS. (*War Department Official Business*)

The flying course is constantly evolving and introducing new scenarios in order to be prepared for any threat that may arise in the future. Approximately 3,000 NATO air force personnel travel to Albacete each year to participate in TLP flight courses.

The objectives of the Academic Courses are the following:

- To provide a range of theoretical knowledge on tactical air doctrine, weaponry and its effects, weapon system characteristics, surface-to-air missile (SAM) and anti-aircraft artillery (AAA) system capabilities, offensive and defensive air operations, as well as battlefield coordination.
- To increase the knowledge of the participants (aircrew, controllers, intelligence officers, etc.) for the development of their work and to promote a common substratum in all facets of NATO tactical air operations.
- Examine the different concepts of tactical employment of nations and suggest areas for improvement.
- Develop concepts and doctrine for integrated operations and the employment and deployment of NATO combat forces and their weapon systems.

Academic courses are excellent as a first experience for later participation in the TLP flying course. Approximately 400 participants from the air forces of member nations and other invited nations attend the academic courses at TLP each year.

The TLP National Component is made up of a total of sixteen Air Force military personnel, who are assigned to different departments. As Spain is the host nation, in addition to carrying out tasks directly related to the courses, the members of the National Component are responsible for the coordination of TLP flight activities with those of the Air Force, the financial management of the Programme, administration, liaison and coordination with Albacete Airbase, information and communications systems, etc.

The jet era in Florennes began in June 1951 when twenty-one Republic F-84E Thunderjets were delivered, of which only the single-seater version as yet existed. (*Musée Royal de l'Armée et d'Histoire Militaire*)

There are many people who have worked for and with the TLP since its arrival in Albacete, which has been able to count on the participation of more than 150 military personnel from all TLP member countries. Together with them, about 160 civilian personnel have provided their services for the proper functioning and maintenance of the programme. A total of 116 civilian workers (permanent, permanent-seasonal, temporary and contract and service staff) are hired annually by joint venture Copriser-Ucalsa, the company in charge of managing the programme, of which approximately 75 per cent are women. As for the number of companies from Albacete that collaborate with Copriser-Ucalsa joint venture, we are talking about a total of eighty-two suppliers that provide products or services to the TLP.

The future of TLP lies in continuing to be the reference centre for air combat training in Europe. To this end, TLP has identified the following strategic lines: the TLP must remain aligned and relevant in a continuously changing environment.

It must make progress in the development of its five pillars:

- Interoperability between 4th- and 5th-Generation aircraft. The arrival of 5th-Generation aircraft brings with it the challenge of integrating their capabilities with those of existing assets to achieve optimal results. The TLP is working hard to integrate 5th-Generation aircraft into its flying and academic courses.
- Agile employment of combat assets. TLP flying courses offer an outstanding opportunity to implement activities aimed at empowerment and agility in generating combat capability. One example is the cross servicing activities that allow support in maintenance areas between different air forces.

The launch tubes for the GBM-109G being erected. (*Author's files*)

F-16AM of the Belgian Air Component of the Belgian Armed Forces based at Florennes with 2nd Wing. (*Wikipedia*).

- Use of synthetic media. The Modern Air Combat Environment (MACE) simulation room with its thirty cabins enables Live, Virtual, Constructive (LVC) training of participants in flight and COMAO synthetic courses. With this tool, participants can interact virtually and participate in scenarios with real platforms (Live) and even with participants and constructive means operated by the instructors. The evolution of the capabilities of this tool is one of the main challenges and will have to be aligned with the interests and simulation strategies of each of the participating nations.
- High threat scenario operations. The TLP must be able to design scenarios for the participants to train Contested Degraded Operations (CDO). Key elements in these scenarios will be the opposing side's anti-aircraft defence assets or radar and communications disruption systems, among others.
- Multi-domain operations. These operations, also called Joint All Domain Operations (JADOs) are related to the previous pillar because they require the participation of elements from other domains, such as land, naval and even contemplating space and cyber threats for the future.

In addition to the five strategic pillars, the TLP's status as a NATO tactical doctrine 'laboratory' should not be overlooked. Because of the experience accumulated by its staff and the role it plays, the TLP is a centre of reference in the creation and validation of tactical air doctrine.

Without losing sight of its hallmark, which is the quality of its courses, based on the wealth of TLP personnel, with expert instructors from ten nations, as well as course participants, further improvement is needed in the complex and evolving area of air operations.

If necessary, infrastructure investments will have to be envisaged to meet all of the above. TLP staff are proud of the Programme's International reputation as a leading centre for expert pilot and aircrew tactical leadership training, where pilots, aircrew and air operations support personnel have benefited from lessons learned and have established bonds that foster understanding and cooperation between our nations.

A Luftwaffe F-104G Starfighter. (*Luftwaffe*)

Chapter 4

Albacete-Los Llanos Airbase

The Albacete-Los Llanos airbase, where the TLP resides, is the nucleus of what is now called the Albacete Aeronautical Complex. This includes the base, with the three units that reside there, the airport and civil Aeroclub that share the runways, the Airbus helicopter factory and nearby, the heliport of the former civil company INAER.

The airport of Albacete-Los Llanos was created in 1928 for use by the Escuela Civil de Pilotos (Civil Pilots School) by the Compañía Española de Aviación (Spanish Aviation Company). This school opened on 27 April 1929, beginning the training of military naval pilots with AVRO 505J and Bristol F.2B aircraft. In 1932 the school suspended all activities, but the airport maintained all its facilities and equipment.

At the start of the Spanish Civil War in 1936, airmen Lieutenant Captain Padilla and Pina made several flights, using aircraft of this school. After suffering several vicissitudes during the war, on 25 July of that year, the airfield was occupied by the Republican Army

During 2003, Ala 14 spent four months at Vicenza airbase in Italy, patrolling the skies over the troubled former Yugoslavia, almost two years after the Spanish Air Force EF-18 Hornets ceased their operations from Aviano airbase. (*Ala 14*)

141 Escuadrón F1Ms during an exchange with the Aeronautica Militare Italiana. (*Ala 14*)

In June 1975, with tension growing with Morocco, Spain decided to strengthen its Air Force and bought fifteen Mirage F1CEs that were allocated to Albacete AB. In mid-1976 there was still some tension with Morocco, and Algerian and Libyan MiG-25 flights over the Mediterranean, which would lead the Spanish Air Force to purchase ten more Mirage F1Cs and two years later order forty-eight Mirage F1CEs and F1EEs. Some years later Spain also bought twelve F1EDA/DDAs retired from the Qatar Air Force, which also sold some equipment and weapons used by those Mirage F1s. In Spanish service the F1CE was known as the C.14A, the F1EE as the C.14B, the two-seater as the CE.14 and the F1EDA/DDA as the C.14C/CE.14C. (*Salvador Mafé*)

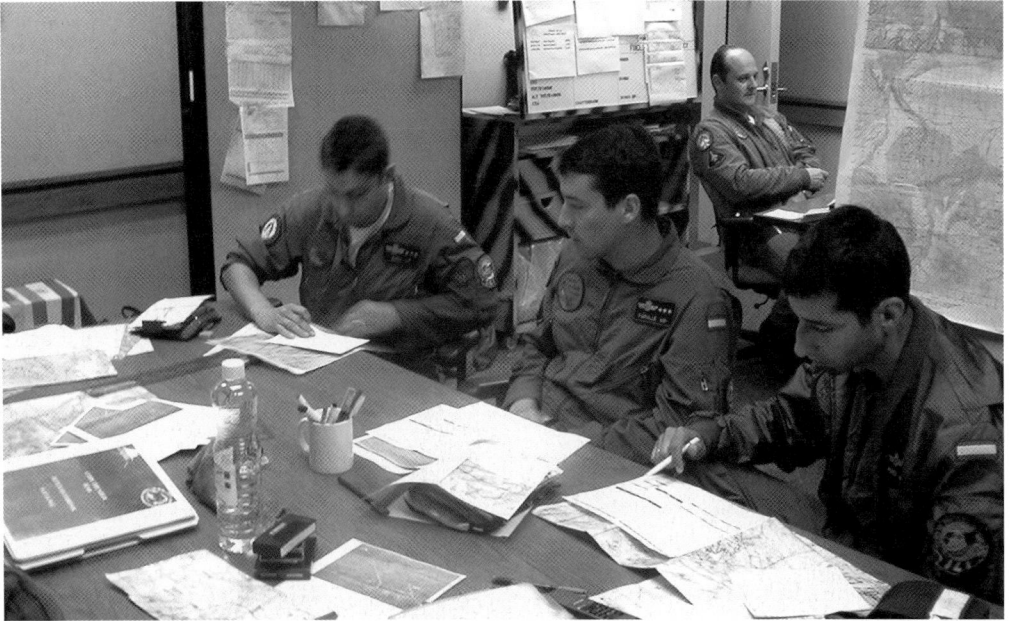

Briefing prior to a mission. (*S. Mafe*)

and turned into an important base for the Aviation Department of the Republicans. On 29 March 1939, the airfield was occupied by the Nationalists.

After the war, on 15 August 1939, the Spanish Air Force took over control of the airport and the 13th Squadron was based here with twenty surviving Tupolev SB-2 strategic bombers, dubbed Katiuskas because of their Soviet origins. In January 1940, it was transformed into the 13th Regiment. Celebrating the close ties between the airport and the city of Albacete, this city handed its banner to the 13th Regiment on 1 August 1943. In 1946 all Katiuska aircraft were decommissioned, being unmaintainable. From 1946, the units operating from the base underwent several changes and reorganizations being equipped with DC-3s as 37th Transport Wing, later changing to Grupo 37, reporting directly to the Chief of Transport Aviation. This situation lasted until 1974, when the base was again reconfigured and modernized for operational use.

The 14th Wing

Due to the base's central position in the mainland of Spain, 14th Wing was commissioned at Albacete-Los Llanos to be equipped with the new Mirage F-1CE fighters, becoming the Ejército del Aire the second air force to order this fighter to equip wing's two Squadrons, 141 and 142. The first arrived directly from Mont-de-Marsan, France, on 18 June 1975. In total Spain received ninety-one Mirage F1 of four variants.

During its years of service the F-1 underwent several upgrades and until the arrival of the EF-18 Hornet, it was Spain's top fighter. After the introduction of the Hornet

Since the Baltic States, Estonia, Latvia and Lithuania are part of NATO, the air defence of these states is the responsibility of the other NATO members. The mission is called Baltic Air Policing and since March 2004 the alliance nations of NATO have policed the Baltic airspace on a three- or four-month rotation. On 1 August 2006 Spain took over the patrol missions from Turkey. Four Mirage F1Ms transferred to Siauliai Airbase in Lithuania together with more than eighty servicemen. The pilots of Ala 14 scrambled three times to intercept undisclosed intruders until the mission was taken over by the Belgians on 1 December 2006. (*Ala 14*)

in 1986, the Mirage F1 still remained an important asset for air defence and ground attack. A substantial avionics and service-life upgrade programme was investigated in the beginning of the 1990s in order to multiple the capabilities of the fighters. Once the specifications of the programme were set, the modernization contract, valued at US$96 million, was awarded to Thomson CSF RCM (now Thales Group) in October 1996. It covered a Service-Life Extension Program (SLEP) and avionics upgrade for forty-eight F1CE/EE single seaters and four F1EB (CE.14) two-seat trainers. As the badge of Esc 142 displays a tiger, it became a member of the NATO Tiger Community in 1986 and consequently organized a Tiger Meet in 1992.

Late in 2011 a total of twenty operational F1 fighters remained, distributed as follows: ten Mirage F1EE(M), with air-to-air refuelling capability, eight Mirage F1CE (M) and two Mirage F1BE (M), although not all operational due to a shortage of engines; also, in December 2011 there were ten pilots to operate them, because the rest were in Morón Airbase doing the conversion course of the Eurofighter Typhoon with 113 Squadron of Ala 11.

The first eight Typhoons with Ala 14 markings arrived at Los Llanos on 1 May 2012, and the four lieutenants who served in 141 Squadron, began conversion to C.16 (the official EA designation for the Typhoon, while CE.16 is for the two-seater) in Morón. However, the two fast jets would coexist for a short period of time in Los Llanos.

Since May 2011, C.14M/CE.14M were operated by 141 Squadron, as 142 Squadron lost temporarily its operational commitments, in order to send (in two batches, May and November 2011) all its pilots to take the course in the Typhoon.

The Mirage F1s were finally phased out in June 2013, and five years later, the twenty-two airworthy jets were sold to Draken International to serve as adversary aircraft in the US.

By 2020 the EdAE had two wings equipped with this advanced 4th Generation fighter, Ala 11 at Morón (Sevilla) and Ala 14 at Los Llanos (Albacete). Since May 2011, the pilots of 142 Squadron, as well as specialists and other technical fields, were in the process of conversion, and ferried the first eight Typhoons to Los Llanos in April–May 2012. The unit participated in several joint NATO exercises, including Cope Thunder in Alaska (USA) to develop air operations with other countries (USA, France, Japan).

Maestranza Aérea de Albacete (MAESAL)

An important unit established at the Albacete Airbase is the Maestranza, better known by its acronym MAESAL. This is one of three similar facilities existing in Spain; Albacete (MAESAL), Sevilla (MAESE) and Cuatro Vientos (MAESMA), each one specializing in a specific type of aircraft. Albacete specializes in combat aviation and the Canadair fleet of firefighting aircraft. Sevilla specializes in transport aviation and liaison light aircraft, and Cuatro Vientos, in helicopters and the C-212 Aviocar.

The Maestranza de Albacete was created by a Royal Decree dated 24 November 1939 being placed in the terrains called 'Casa de la Viña', located a few hundred metres away from the current location. The roles of the Maestranzas Aéreas in modern times were established by a Circular Order dated 3 April 1940 that changed the location from the former 'Casa de la Viña' to its current one.

The responsibility of the Maestranzas is the heavy Maintenance, Repair and Overhaul (MRO) of the aircraft serving in the ranks of the Spanish Ejército del Aire y del Espacio (EdAE). While the three large units that coexist at the Albacete Base, Ala 14, MAESAL and TLP, theoretically work independently and each has a sufficient workload, it is inevitable that they have some relationship and cooperate.

In the evolution of MAESAL four stages can be distinguished. The first one was from 1939 to 1952. During this stage MAESAL accomplished the maintenance of a great part of the EA's fleets, mainly old models dating back the Civil War. More than thirty different models and seventeen engine types can be mentioned that now are part of Spanish aeronautical history: Junkers Ju 52 (T.2), Polikarpov I-15 'Chato', 'Curtis' (C.9), Tupolev SB2 'Katiuska' (B.5), Fieseler Fi 156 'Cigüeña' (L.16), etc. Among the engines it is worth mentioning the Gypsy Mayor Six of the Heinkel He 45 'Pavo', the Walter J-4, of the Heinkel He 46 'Pava', the Whirlwind, installed in the Bücker 131 'Jungmann', and the M100, powering the Bücker 133 'Jungmeister'. These years are remembered as an 'age of miracles', as many of the aircraft supported were no longer in production and the availability of spares was almost zero. So, to keep them flying miracles had to be performed.

The second period was between 1953 and 1968, with the Maestranzas losing its previous territorial character to fit in with EA's new organization. MAESAL specialized during

The Mirage F1 was powered by a single SNECMA Atar 9K-50 turbojet engine, which was capable of providing roughly 7 tonnes-force (69 i; 15,000lbs) of thrust, giving the aircraft a maximum speed of 1,453mph and a ceiling of 65,615ft. *Flight International* described the Atar engine as being 'unexpectedly simple', despite the adoption of an afterburner. An improved engine, initially known as the Super Atar and later as the Snecma M53, was intended to be eventually adopted on production Mirage F1 aircraft, as well as for successor aircraft. (*Salvador Mafé*)

The upgrade for the two-seat Mirage F1BM was minimum, and mainly consisted in the installation of the Spanish-developed and built (by Indra) AN/ALR-300 radar warning & homing receiver, noted by the squared antennas in the leading and training edges of the vertical fin. (*Salvador Mafé*)

The Mirage F1s served mainly as Spain's primary air defence interceptors and interdiction as secondary role until they were superseded by EF-18A Hornets. They operated with Ala 11 in Manises (ex-Qatari planes), Ala 14 in Albacete, and Ala 46 at Gando in the Canary Islands. Ala 46 used their Mirage F1s mainly as air defence planes, using same deep blue colour pattern as French planes. In October 1996, Thomson-CSF was awarded a FFr700 million (US$96 million) contract to upgrade forty-eight F1CE/EE single-seaters and four F1EB trainers to Mirage F1M standard (see below). Ex-Qatar Mirage F1s were left outside the upgrade, as it was a different version, and were the first ones to be retired in 2002. As well as a service-life extension, this improved the avionics and added look down, terrain following capability with a modernized Cyrano IVM radar. (*Salvador Mafè*)

A pair of Ala 14 Mirage F1Ms just before engaging the refuelling hoses of an Ala 31 KC-130H Hercules. (*Ala 14*)

these years in light aviation, assuming the MRO roles for the light aviation including the Bücker Bu-131 (E.3B), Piper PA 23 Azteca (E.19) and Beechcraft B 55 Barón (E.20). etc.

From 1969 to 1981 MAESAL transitioned to medium and heavy aircraft assuming the heavy maintenance of the de Havilland DHC-4 'Caribou' (T.9) and Canadair flying boats for firefighting, now Bombardier CL-215T 'Scoopers' (UD.13). This needed a neat expansion of installations and incorporation of new resources.

The fourth stage started in 1981 and lasted until 2008 and was a real modernization process as MAESAL assumed the Major Inspections (Grand Visit) of the Mirage F1. This was an important step in the evolution of the maestranza requiring a 60 per cent expansion of the hangars' infrastructure and a 20 per cent of increase in personnel, who had to follow an intensive plan of actualization of their technological knowledge. MAESAL's current and always expanding capabilities are to perform Level C maintenance to the following fleet of aircraft: the C-101, F-5M, F-18M, EF-2000 and CL-215T/415.

Generally speaking, the EA organizes the maintenance of its aircraft in three levels or 'echelons'. The first level, or Level A, is that one performed daily on the aircraft, including pre- and post-flight inspections, simple repairs, configuration for the mission and installation and removal of weapons and equipment. In general, those operations that can be carried out within a timeframe of two hours, is performed at the home base of the aircraft that, meanwhile, remain operational.

The second, Level B, encompasses the programmed inspections required by flight hours accumulated or calendar time elapsed. Also includes more complex airframe repairs and inspections/repairs of equipment by replacement of elements. While those inspections

Tiger tail: the scheme applied for the Tiger Meet. (*Tono Fernández Leonarte*)

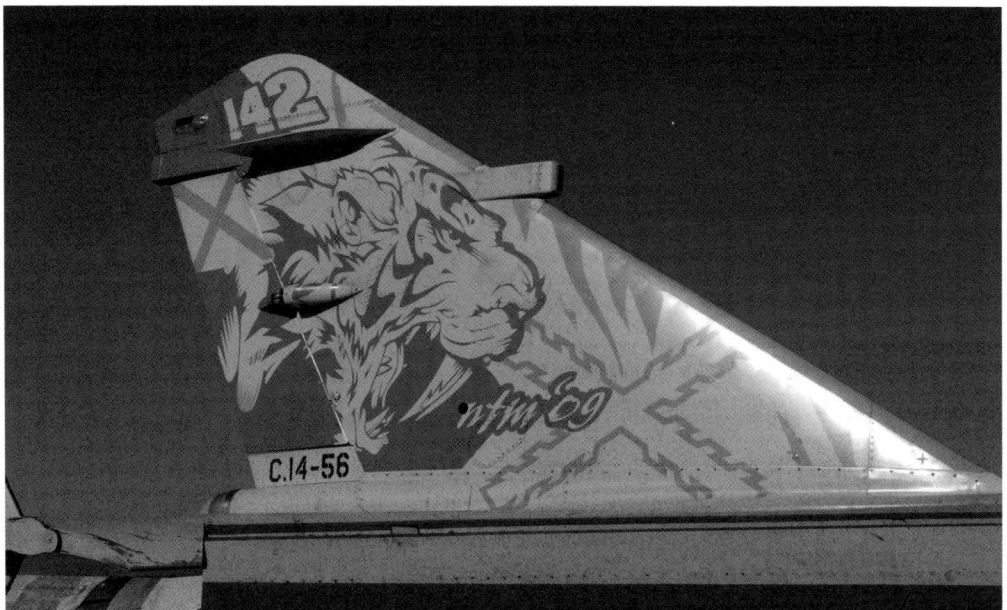

A Mirage F1M (flown by José María Salom, then Ala 14 Operations Commander), and an F1EDA (flown by Major Juan Carlos Raimundo, the 142 Escuadrón C.O.) near the Peñón de Ifach in the province of Alicante, December 1999. (*Salvador Mafé*)

A Mirage F1M flown by Lieutenant Colonel José María Salom, then Ala 14 Operations Commander, photographed near Los Llanos airbase in December 1999. (*Salvador Mafé*)

On 23 June 2013, the Mirage F1s were officially retired from active service, being replaced by the Eurofighter Typhoon. First to reequip was 142 Escuadrón, followed four years later (in 2017) by 141 Escuadrón. (*Rafael Treviño Martínez*)

On Friday 8 September 2018 Draken International closed a deal with the Spanish Air Force, purchasing twenty Mirage F1 fighter aircraft. The supersonic F1s will complement Draken's existing fleet, which is currently flying on contract at Nellis AFB, Nev., supporting the Air Warfare Centre. 'Our mission is to provide the most cost-effective solution to complement organic Red Air assets. We deliver a turnkey solution at a fraction of the cost the Air Force would spend generating the same number of sorties we produce every day. Not only are we generating four to five sorties for the cost of a single F-16 flight hour, each flying hour preserves valuable life on USAF aircraft. Tremendous savings happen when squadrons are not tapped to go TDY away from their families to support Nellis with an already tiring deployment schedule,' said Draken CEO Jared Isaacman. The Mirage F1s are projected to include a helmet-mounted cueing system, infrared missile seekers, data link, and electronic jamming from its radar as well as radar warning receiver capabilities. (*Tono Fernández*)

A section of Typhoons with pilots of the 142 Squadron at the controls. (*Ala 14*)

are made, the aircraft remains grounded for the duration of the operation. Normally this level of maintenance is accomplished also at the home base because are easy and reiterative inspections as the programmed 100 hours (H1), 200 hours (H2) and 400 hours (H3) of the EF-18s.

Finally, the third echelon, or Level C, is the entire responsibility of the Maestranzas.

Other shops

There are no less than twelve specialized shops, the most notable of which are those dedicated to the ejection seats and radars, unique for the maintenance and major repairs of these systems including an anechoic chamber to measure antennas radiation and its radomes. It also has capability to upgrade the EF-18M Hornet fleet's thirty Litening II targeting pods, adding some improvements of the more advanced Litening III.

The Motopropulsion shop has the technologies to apply plasma projection to engines 'combustion chambers in ceramic coatings and the laboratories provided of robotized inspections for non-destructive inspections (NDI).

In addition to the hangars where the aircraft are maintained, there are some other less glamorous shops and activities accomplished within the responsibilities of MAESAL, but vital for the good health of an Air Force, its logistics.

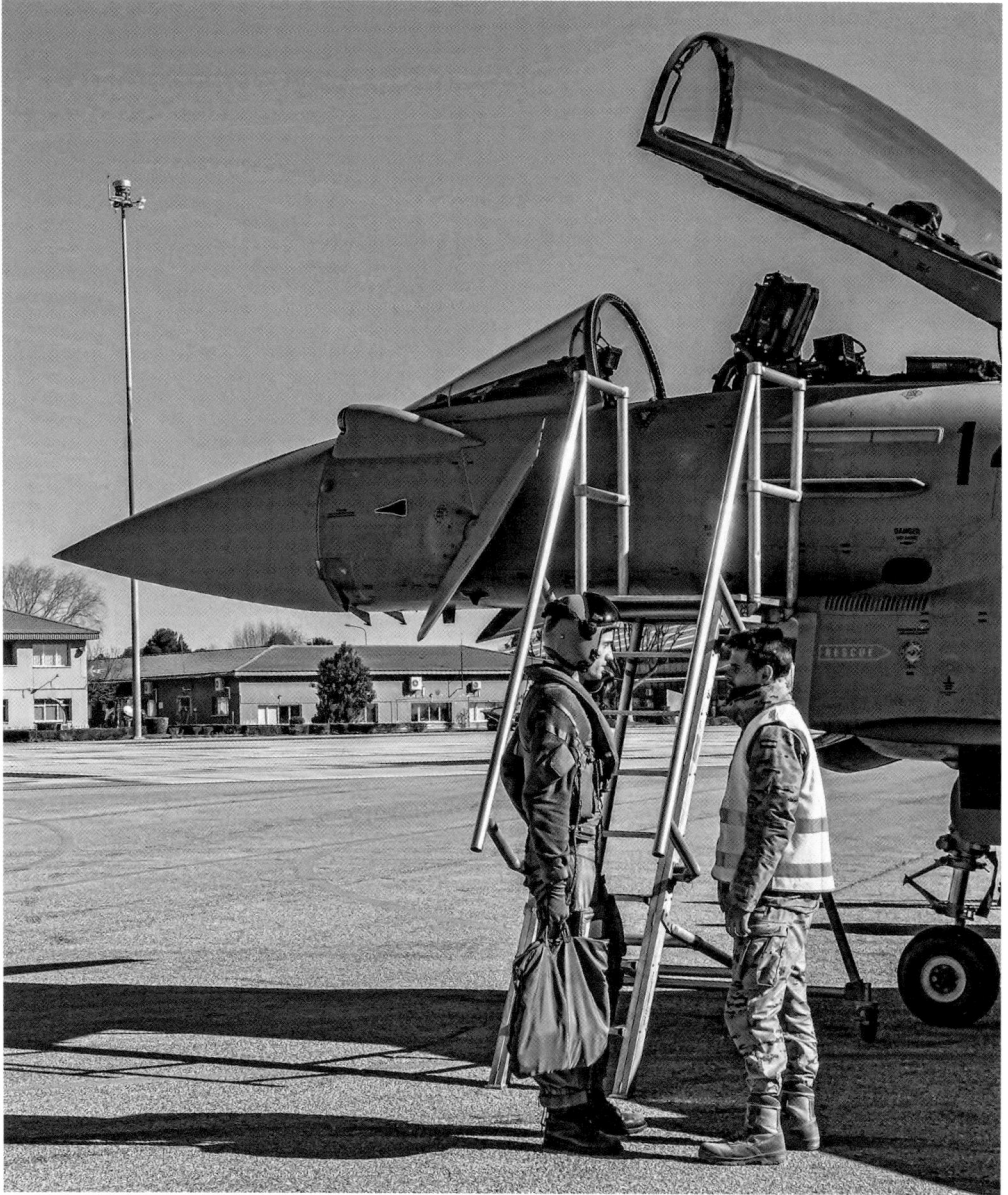

Pilot and crew chief talking after a mission. (*Tony García*)

In MAESAL there is one of the largest spare-parts storage areas of the EdEA and is designated as a Material Management Centre and they work with near half a million catalogue references not just related to the weapons systems, using a system denominated Sistema Logístico 2000 (SL 2000). The system's basic missions are supply, engineering and maintenance of weapons systems. From any terminal it can be ordered a part number, then the systems tell the applicant where is the nearest warehouse where the part is available, how many there are and where is located within the shelves, so it can be ordered.

With the EJ200 at full power, the Eurofighter needs barely 300m to take off. (*Salvador Mafé*)

142 Squadron returned in style to the Tiger Meet. It was at the Zaragoza airbase in 2016, and it was clearly indicated in the drawing of the chosen aircraft, '14-06', that they were back! (*Jorge Portalés*)

For the Tiger Meet of 2018 that took place in Poland 142 Squadron participated with another Eurofighter. The tail fin paint scheme was slightly different. (*Eurofighter*)

On 4 December 2018, the Eurofighter in 'QRA 15', is activated, but finally the mission is entrusted to a pair of Grupo 11 jets. (*Salvador Mafé*)

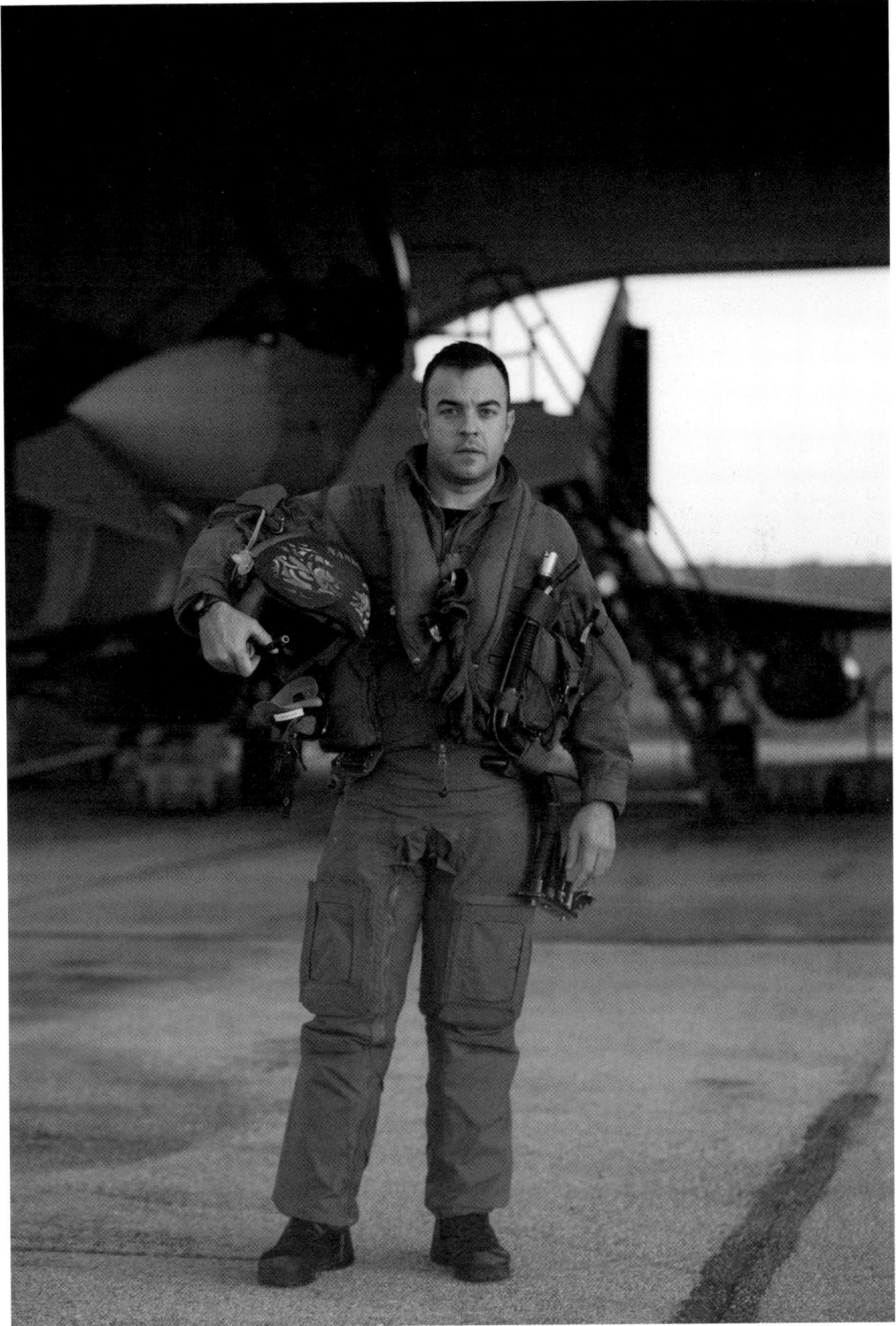

Major Fernando Caballero de Pro posing in full flight gear next to 'QRA 15', 4 December 2018. (*Salvador Mafé*)

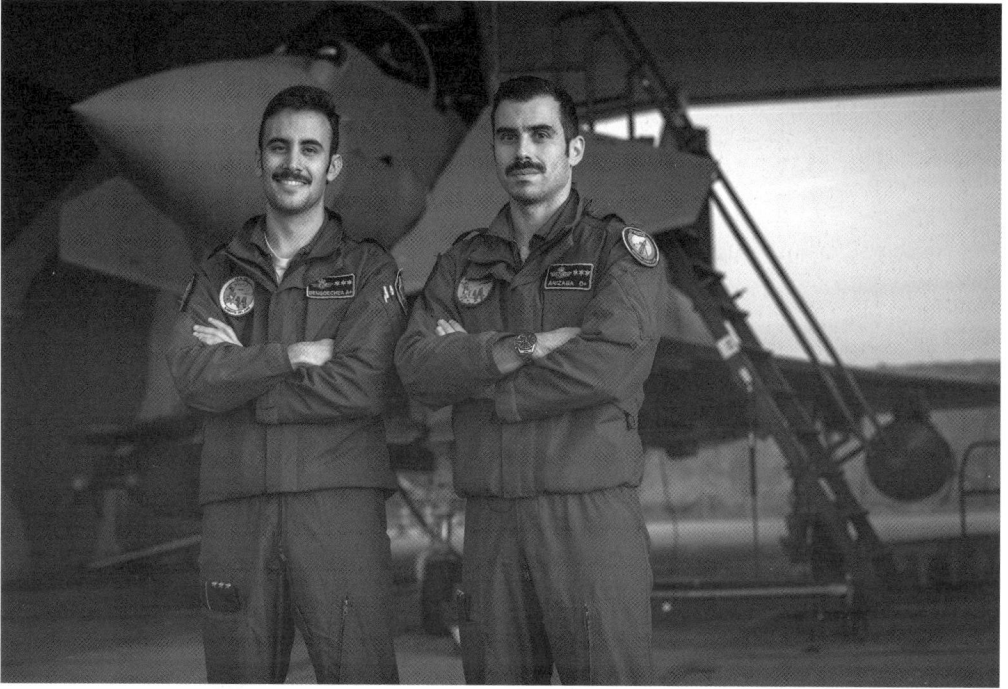

Captain Juan Bengoechea (left) and Gregorio Serrano Arizaga, both of 142 Squadron. The latter is the current Ala 14 display pilot. (*Jorge Portalés*)

C.16 of Ala 14 in 'QRA 15' photographed in a cold night in La Mancha. (*Jorge Portalés*)

In the Red Flag 2017/2, Eurofighter Typhoon fighters from Alas 11 and 14 participated from 27 February to 10 March at Nellis airbase, Nevada, USA. (*Spanish Air Force*)

Eurofighter Typhoon of Ala 14 coming out of its hardened shelter on a training mission. Los Llanos and Gando are the only airbases that have HAS (Hardened Aircraft Shelters). (*Jorge Portalés*)

All of these capabilities are described because, although not directly related to the TLP, on more than one occasion they have been vital to prevent an aircraft participating in the courses from being grounded due to lack of a 'screw, nut or a packing' or a repair beyond the ordinary capacity of deployed personnel. Also the support provided by the neighbouring 14th Wing is vital for the TLP, as described elsewhere in the text.

The TLP arrives

Since 2003, the TLP had been looking for a new base with improved weather conditions and less flight restrictions. Belgium demanded its transfer from the then present Florennes Air Force Base to another country due to problems of air traffic congestion, while the TLP demanded this transfer due to unstable weather conditions. In 2007 TLP announced its new location to be Albacete-Los Llanos, Spain. For its part, the Spanish Council of Ministers approved 2006 the technical agreement on the relocation plans and the general rules governing the establishment of the Tactical Leadership Program of the Allied Command Operations in Spain on 26 October. They proposed Albacete-Los Llanos AFB to host the programme from 2009, based on its lower air traffic congestion, the greater range of facilities and the better weather conditions. Along with the Spanish candidacy, other bases were proposed in Canada and Turkey. The study group recommended accepting the Spanish offer, which was ratified by the other member nations of the programme. Also, part of the agreement were plans, next to the TLP, to create an annual exercise with a simulated air conflict (ACE-Flag), which requires an even greater air capacity. For housing the TLP, an

Ala 14 Eurofighter Typhoon '14-77', flown by Captain Gregorio 'Goyo' Arizaga. (*Tono Fernández*)

investment of around €20.7 million was needed, of which €15.5 million were destined for infrastructures while more than €5 million were for equipment. All these expenses were paid proportionally by all the nations participating in this programme.

Chapter 5

The First TLP Commandant in Spain

With the aplomb that only those who have flown the Mirage III possess, (then) Colonel Ignacio Bengoechea Martí has headed the TLP since its inception in Albacete. Much more than an experienced pilot, flying has been for him not just a profession, but also a way of life. This becomes apparent when speaking with him in the way that emphasizes the importance and virtues of his organization without fear of acknowledging the great challenge at hand, which is to overcome the difficult economic times that have also reached the TLP and it shows that more and more costs to governments, some more than others, devote funds to defence, and in this chapter to something like training, which is very expensive but which results can be seen only in the long term, exemplified by the recently concluded NATO-run Operation Unified Protector.

But Colonel Bengoechea, in addition to being a good professional pilot, is also a good public relations man and is able to convince anyone of something that he is fully convinced, and that TLP is a great school of learning where a pilot and with experience, comes prepared for just about whatever you 'throw at them'.

In addition to the intrinsic quality of TLP from a purely academic point of view, there is a lot in it for Spain is a lot and this must be put in value. On one side is major prestige, of

A pair of Ala 11 Mirage IIIEEs photographed in the early 1980s during a training sortie. After graduating as a fighter pilot, it was the first posting for then Lieutenant Ignacio Bengoechea. (*Salvador Mafé*)

Ala 12 EF-18M Hornet taking-off from Albacete's runway during TLP 2011-1, February 2011. (*J.J. Fernández*)

which Colonel Bengoechea is responsible for the TLP success in Albacete. On the other hand it is very positive for the region, as many personnel move there and generate income and, finally, from a purely military point of view, for Spain to have the TLP 'home' is certainly an advantage to leverage and part of Colonel Bengoechea's work is directed precisely to convince that it is important for pilots of the Air Force and the Navy, which is expected to begin sending its AV-8B Harrier pilots from Novena Escuadrilla for upcoming courses.

To chat with Ignacio Bengoechea is a pleasure and have his opinions in this work is a real privilege that will interest all readers. Colonel Bengoechea thoroughly reviews the most interesting aspects of the TLP. No one better than him to explain.

Interview with Colonel Bengoechea

We begin with a series of questions on general aspects of the TLP.

Salvador Mafé Huertas/Rafael Treviño Martínez (SMH/RTM): Briefly explain what the TLP is and what are its objectives.

Colonel Bengoechea (CB): Tactical Leadership Programme (TLP) is an organization of 10 countries to improve the effectiveness of their air forces by developing the tactical leadership qualities of their crews, planning and execution of complex air missions in a multinational environment. Although all countries in this programme belong to NATO, there is not an organic dependence with the Alliance.

Upgraded F-4E-2020 Phantom from 1 AJU/111 Filo, Turkish Air Force. (*Salvador Mafé*)

SMH/RTM: Could you give a brief summary of how it arose and what specific needs necessitated the TLP's creation?

CB: The TLP was born in 1978 to bridge the gap between the doctrinal concept of COMAO (Composite Air Operations) and the execution of such missions. This type of operation, still in force in the current scenario, is performed by aircraft with very different characteristics. During the Cold War aircraft would take off from multiple airbases located throughout Europe to simultaneously attack a variety of objectives. A detailed coordination of all details of the missions was needed then and still is now. With the creation of TLP the idea was to develop TTPs (Tactics, Techniques, and Procedures) to standardize the way these so-complex missions take place.

SMH/RTM: What experiences are obtained working with pilots and aircraft from different countries?

CB: The experience you get, not only to fly, but especially when planning with pilots from other countries is very enriching for any participant. It allows you to understand what are the tactical capabilities of their aircraft and systems and their different approaches to the same tactical situations. It offers you the chance to see different forms of leadership in a multinational environment, which undoubtedly contributes to the formation of future leaders who will assume greater responsibilities in the coming years.

SMH/RTM: Initially TLP was located in Belgium. How was the move to Spain conceived? Was it a question only of weather? What are the benefits to Spain?

CB: The TLP began in Fürstenfeldbruck BA (Germany) in 1978, then moved to Jever (in Germany) and later to Florennes (Belgium) in 1989. The relocation to Spain is mainly based on two reasons. The first is that the airspace is already very congested in central Europe, which greatly hampers the availability of areas suitable for the simultaneous training of about thirty combat aircraft. The second is the weather.

There is no doubt that in the south of Europe the weather is better than in the north and centre of the continent, helping to reduce the number of missions cancelled by bad weather. In fact, in all flight courses conducted since TLP arrival to Spain, has exceeded 80 per cent of missions flown over those programmed. This underlines the correctness of the decision to move the program from Florennes, where sometimes a course finished with no more than six flight missions!

The advantages of hosting the TLP in Spain are many and significant. Apart from the economic and cultural impact it will have for the city of Albacete and the rest of the community, there are the purely professional advantages. The Spanish Air Force will have great opportunities for training their crews (fighter/attack, transports and helicopters) for the mere fact of being geographically closer to where the missions are done. These possibilities will be extended to intercept controllers (GCI), approach and tower, as well as FACs (Forward Air Controllers), anti-aircraft units and others. Similarly, the Army and the Navy will benefit in their interaction with TLP.

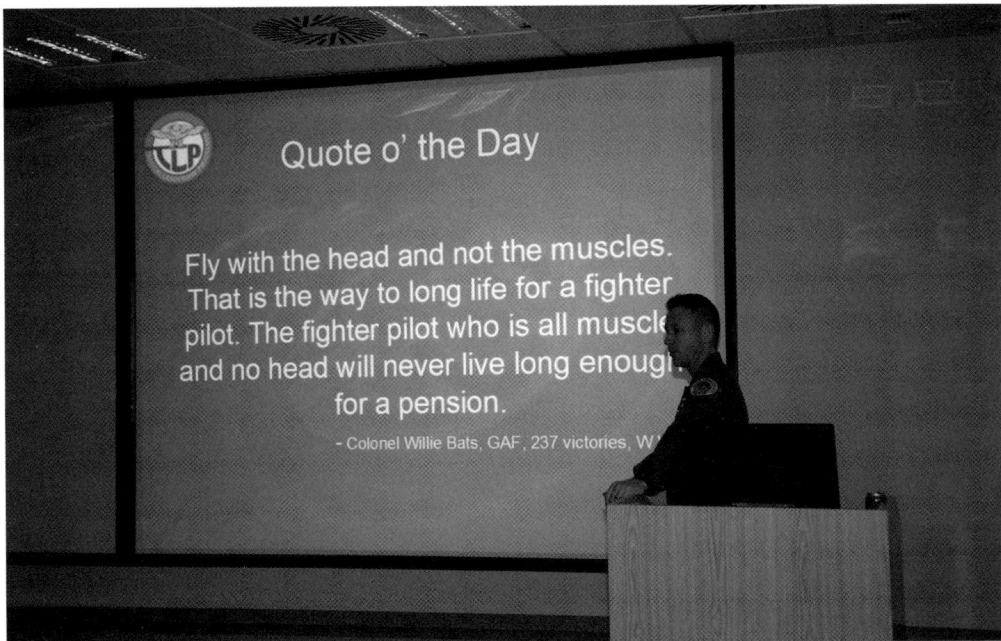

The TLP's briefing room. Note the sentence on the screen, a great truth for fighter pilots! (*J.J. Fernández*)

A Luftwaffe Tornado IDS being readied for a sortie. (*J.J. Fernández*)

On the other hand, to host such a demanding programme in every way, like the TLP, must lead to the reinvigoration, operationally speaking, of many of the procedures currently in use in the SpAF. The flexible airspace management, an agile programming of training missions using the opportunities that TLP will offer, or the implementation of new anti-FOD (Foreign Object Debris) procedures in Spanish airbases are some concrete examples in which the programme can boost this reinvigoration.

Finally, to lead such an internationally recognized program provides an excellent opportunity to give prestige to the Air Force, Armed Forces and Spain.

SMH/RTM:What is expected of a pilot at the end of the course?

CB: The TLP is not intended to teach flying or to carry out simple tactical missions. The crews which we receive are already expert in these endeavours. We seek to develop in them leadership capabilities enabling them to lead as Mission Commander, with rigor and effectiveness, and planning and execution of complex missions in a multinational environment. During the course, to learn the qualities of leadership, tactics, and also to find solutions to specific situations that are present in current conflicts.

What is expected of a pilot after their passage through the TLP is that, on his return to his/her squadron, to implement an effective way to plan and execute any mission with integrity and effectiveness. And, if that is the case, and then should participate in a multinational operation, to be able to lead more complex missions.

Hellenic Air Force F-16C, from 343 Mira. (*Salvador Mafé*)

Spanish F/A-18A Hornets belonging to 462 Escuadrón/Ala 46 at the flight line during TLP 2010-6 in November 2010. In 1994–5 the EdA purchased twenty-four Hornets from US Navy's surplus stocks; actually about eighteen are in service with this Canary Islands-based unit. By 2026 they will be phased out, replaced by Tranche 3 Typhoons. (*Salvador Mafé*)

From my experience in Air Force units, I can assure you that TLP has always achieved this goal with the graduated pilots, and that there is a before and after for those who have had the opportunity to participate.

SMH/RTM: What does it represent for a fighter pilot to lead the TLP?

CB: The TLP is, so to speak, the sanctuary of tactical air training fighter crews. Having the opportunity to lead it is a huge pride for someone who has enjoyed this job during most of his professional life. And it is also a major challenge to live up to the demands and be capable of increasing the international prestige of the SpAF.

SMH/RTM: What did you learn being at the forefront of this organization?

CB: In addition to the tactical concepts and solutions in today's NATO, to be at the forefront of this organization allows you to understand the difficulties and the benefits of coalition work. It also allows you to learn the skills that other countries have and how to use them.

SMH/RTM: Is it difficult to work with so many different people with different idiosyncrasies, different procedures, etc.?

CB: No doubt sometimes integrating different perspectives and procedures is difficult, but also enormously rewarding.

Italian AMX from 51° Stormo, 132° Gruppo during TLP 2010-6, November 2010. (*Salvador Mafè*)

Part of the flight line at TLP 2011-3. Three RNLAF F-16AMs can be seen. (*Tono Fernández*)

SMH/RTM: Colonel, a difficult question: if you had to choose, would you lead the TLP or a Fighter Wing?

CB: Honestly, both. They are two different leadership experiences, each with their difficulties and satisfactions. So far, my professional profile has always dreamed of leading a Fighter Wing of the Air Force with its pilots, their planes and their typical missions. It is the logical culmination and desire for someone who has lived intensely in a combat unit.

To lead the TLP does not allow you to enjoy this experience, but provides the opportunity, as I said before, of being at the head of the sanctuary of fighter aviation in Europe, which is also exciting. Here are other problems, the international projection is very important, and it allows you to improve your professional formation and leadership.

SMH/RTM: Colonel, please explain the different types of missions that are performed and the characteristics and objectives of each.

CB: The mission program of the TLP is long and includes many types of missions: No Fly Zone (NFZ) Enforcement, Anti-Surface Warfare (ASUW) for attacks on ships, Combat SAR (CSAR), Dynamic Targeting, Air Interdiction, Threat Reaction to ground to air threats, High Value Asset (HVA) Defence, Low Level Attack, etc.

SMH/RTM: Is the mission planning always the same? Does it evolve according to different global scenarios? For example, are missions specially developed for the current low intensity conflicts? Who takes the initiative to design a new type of mission?

CB: The method used for the planning of every mission is the same, and passes through a deep analysis of all relevant aspects of the mission, purpose, target, threats, tactics, etc. By always using the same sequence and the same method you can complete an excellent planning regardless of the ultimate objective of the mission.

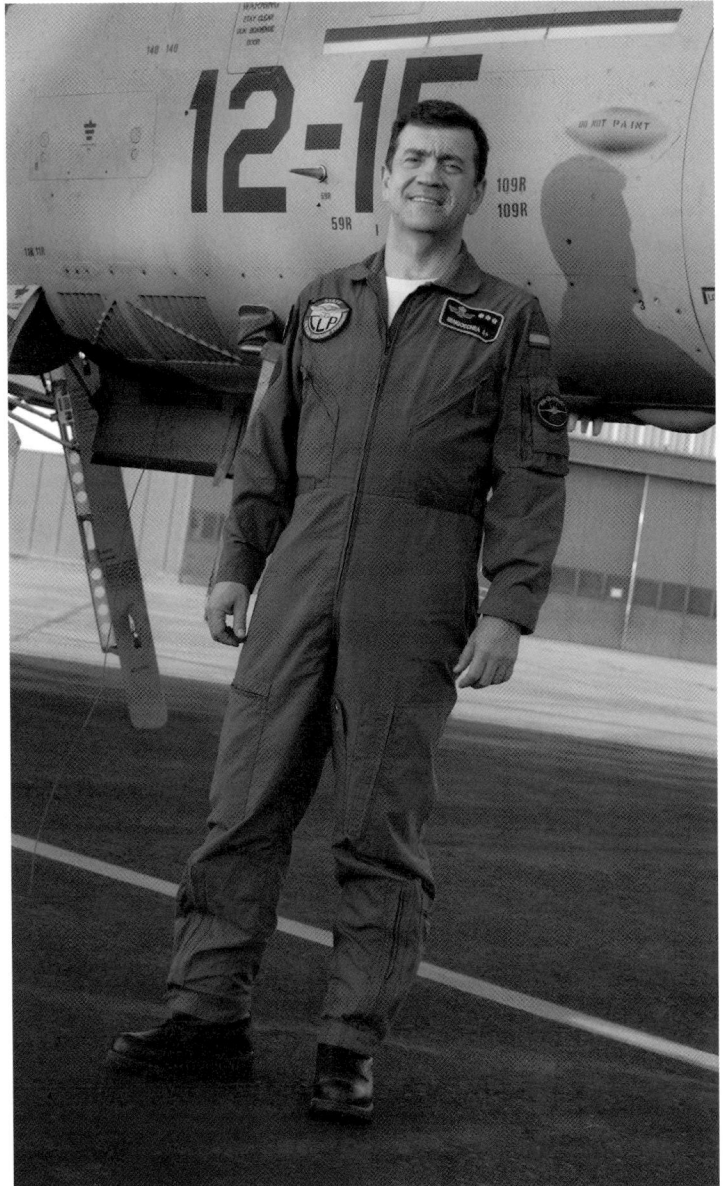

Colonel Ignacio Bengoechea, posing for the author's camera besides an EF-18M Hornet of Ala 12. (*Salvador Mafé*)

For this reason, the TLP does not need to change its missions programme. Whatever the type or pattern of mission being conducted in the real world, it can be planned and conducted in accordance with the method taught in the TLP flight courses. Of course, TLP missions are carried out by incorporating the procedures used in current operations; the CAS is performed such as actually is done in Afghanistan.

What I can say without mistake is that the TLP is for today's and tomorrow's missions at the same time.

SMH/RTM: When helicopters are integrated between units, will specific missions be created, e.g., for SAR combat? How to integrate with other aircraft?

CB: As explained above, the CSAR missions is standard practice in TLP courses, as well as protection of Slow Movers (low-speed aircraft). The integration of these aircraft and the helicopters were performed according to the method of planning taught.

SMH/RTM: How does the TLP coordination and management work?

CB: The TLP flight courses are based on the means by which each country participates, as embodied in an annual meeting held in Albacete. During the meeting, the composition for each course is formed, ensuring that each has the air capabilities necessary to get the best training possible.

My management job is to ensure the courses accurately reflect the wishes of the nations of the programme and carried out in accordance with NATO doctrine.

SMH/RTM: What does the TLP do for the region where it is located? And for the SpAF?

CB: Initially, for the city and the region of Albacete the presence of TLP means the possibility of economic development. But it is not the only way it can benefit. The presence of both foreign staff (around 3,000 people of different nationalities per year for up to one month) would also be a significant cultural development for the inhabitants of the city by their constant interaction with the staff. And that it will also promote the city, region, its cuisine, culture; acquire notoriety in many European countries and even in United States.

About what it will mean for the Air Force, I have to say that, in my view, the TLP offers the option of standing with its allies to lead a program of such international reputation and the opportunity to improve the training of units and to reinvigorate its internal procedures.

And in respect to Albacete Airbase, which is constantly striving to provide us the support we need to operate, I think it will also mean a major boost to its adaptation to the imminent arrival of the Eurofighter Typhoon, and provide an even greater international reputation to that they already have.

Chapter 6

The Way to Albacete

T hose attending to the TLP, either as professionals, press representatives or simply as visitors, will have the impression that everything is running smoothly, and that is true, but to reach such a state, there has been much work behind the scenes from all those involved.

As we have said, the TLP had been running for some 20 years at Florennes AB until the programme moved to Albacete (Spain) in July 2009. There were several reasons to make such a decision. From Florennes, a typical American base with all sorts of facilities and capabilities available, it was possible to organize flight missions over the airspaces of France, Germany, Great Britain, and the Netherlands, allowing practising most of the tactics and scenarios associated to the then current NATO air doctrine. But soon, with the passing of the years, some inconveniences emerged, recommending to the Air Forces involved to look for other locations that would assure the continuity, efficiency and viability of the programme.

Three main reasons to justify the movement were identified:

- **To look for a costs reduction.** The main reason was the cost of the work contracts of more than 100 persons working directly for the TLP at Florennes, not to mention the continuous reduction in defence budgets by the Western European countries.

A Royal Netherlands Air Force F-16AM blasting off from Los Llanos. (*Salvador Mafé*)

Close-up of a Luftwaffe Tornado ECR. (*Salvador Mafé*)

- **Extension for the air space.** By that time, the threat perception had changed in Europe and the strategic situation of the world also. The battle space was no longer only Central Europe but had expanded to other regions of the world. This situation required the use of new tactics by NATO and by its member countries that advised an enlargement of the training areas and more dedication to training for night missions. To this situation was added the increase in air traffic in Central Europe, which increasingly restricted operations in the assigned military flight areas.
- **To look for better meteorology.** The meteorology in Florennes as well as in Central Europe was always problematic, limiting and even frustrating many missions of the courses. Due to the continuous budgetary adjustments experienced by the participating air forces, those nations were forced to make a careful evaluation of the economic risks involved in displacing a contingent of men and material to Belgium due to the possibility of flights being cancelled or limited, making the investment unprofitable. In this respect, fortunately fair weather was almost a given in Spain.

Among other nations, Spain, one of the latest arrivals to the TLP, submitted its candidature to host the TLP in 2003, and after a careful study of all the available options, it was selected as 'Host Nation' in January 2005.

The interests behind the Spanish offer to host the TLP were strategic above all, wishing to improve advanced training of its EdA staff, and the transfer was facilitated thanks to the interest of NATO, that was looking for a location with less civil air traffic congestion, better weather and airspace in which to reproduce possible future scenarios.

An RAF E-3 Sentry landing at Los Llanos. The AWACS are the first to take off and the last to land during the flying courses. (*Salvador Mafè*)

The Defence Ministries of Belgium, Denmark, Germany, Great Britain, Italy, the Netherlands, the United States and Spain signed a Technical Agreement (TA) in which the conditions were established to transfer the TLP to Albacete's Airbase. The initial costs for this movement was calculated at around € 17.5 million, of which Spain had to contribute €1.5 million, corresponding to 8.89 per cent of its participation in the programme. Additionally, and as the 'Host Nation', Spain should add to this investment another € 3.3 million for the improvement of Albacete's infrastructure.

France and Greece would later join this TA, signing an amendment to it, updating the costs of the project, which increased from the initial €17.5 million to €20.5 million and the investment of the Host Nation increased from €3.3 million to €5.5 million.

On 27 October 2006, the Spanish Council of Ministers authorized the conclusion of a Technical Agreement on the relocation plans and the general provisions applicable to the establishment at the Albacete Airbase, starting in 2009.

In June 2008, the JEMA (Jefe del Estado Mayor del Aire – Chief of the Air General Staff) signed Directive 25/2008, dated 26 June, for the Implementation Plan and the creation of the Initial Nucleus of Constitution of the TLP, constituted by a force of ten, thus leaving Spain and the Air Force definitively committed to transfer the TLP to Albacete AB on 1 June 2009, and to officially open the programme on 1 October with the first course beginning on 4 October of the same year.

The first officer to be designated as staff for the Initial Nucleus, depending directly on the Second Air Chief of Staff, was a Colonel (OF-5), in theory bound to be the TLP's

Two Armée de l'Air et de l'Espace pilots walking to their jets. (*Salvador Mafé*)

Beautiful shot of a French Mirage 2000D. (*J.J. Fernández*)

first Commanding Officer, plus a Commander (Mayor OF-3) belonging to the *Cuerpo de Intedencia*, designated as the Financial Officer. Some days later six non-commissioned officers were assigned, who, although destined to occupy specific positions in the TLP, played an extraordinary role in all matters related with the relocation.

At this point we must say that according to the MOU, the TLP is a support element for the Headquarters of the two strategic military commands of the alliance, SHAPE (ACO Headquarters) and SACT (ACT Headquarters). As Commander of the TLP, this officer is responsible only to the SG made up of all participating countries that sign the MOU. To complete the initial nucleus of personnel one lieutenant colonel, to be the Chief of the Support and one commander (mayor), as chief of Air Operations, were progressively added.

If we compare the situation at Florennes, where the TLP moved to an 'American'-style base, with that of Albacete, where except for the terrain and a fighter wing plus a Maestranza units, both busy with their duties, is easy to imagine that raising from scratch such an organization as the TLP would imply many difficulties in the process.

The most complex to solve of the related areas mentioned, were the following:

Infrastructure. In September 2008 the state of the infrastructure was not as expected. The hotel designed to host 500 rooms and the multipurpose building, were only marked on the ground with barely a few foundations and structures visible. The headquarters and hangar had practically not been started and the asphalting of the aircraft parking area and taxiways needed to be improved.

Communications and Information Services (CIS) and Telephony Requirements. TLP had to function as a small NATO Headquarters, with the implication of not belonging to its force structure and also as a small unit of the Air Force with the same problems regarding its organization. Additionally, it had to maintain links with each of the member nations both for communications and for the transfer of operational data.

Among others, the connections for the NATO WAN (Wide Area Networks), the WAN GP (General Purpose) of the MINISDEF, and the WAN of other countries and to the Internet had to be installed, checked, evaluated and finally certified.

The same procedures had to be followed with the following LAN (Local Area Networks):

- LAN NATO Secret
- LAN NATO Restricted
- LAN Internet
- LAN PG for Spanish MINISDEF (Ministerio de Defensa – Ministry of Defence) users

In connection with telephony, it was necessary to install connections to the SCTM (Sistema Conjunto de Telecomunicaciones Militares – Joint System of Military Telecommunications) fixed telephony network, fixed telephony with PBX (Private Branch Exchange) and 650 extensions for national and international calls and Telefónica's mobile telephony through PBX links for the conversion of fixed-mobile calls in mobile-mobile calls.

Mirage 2000C-5. (*J.J. Fernández*)

Finnish Air Force pilot. (*Salvador Mafè*)

Finnish AF F-18C Hornet landing. (*J.J. Fernández*)

A direct connection was also required with the base's Control Tower and the TLP's Headquarters, through two dedicated voice circuits and some telephone booths.

Documentation. At the time of the constitution of the Nucleus, the amendment to the TA and the accessions of France and Greece were not yet signed and the MOU, which according to the TA should have been sanctioned in 2007, was still pending its final drafting and there was no absolute consensus. The Operations Plan (PoO), a document that defined the development of the courses, was a draft, and the Operations Implementation Arrangement (OIA), which marked the relations between Albacete Airbase and the TLP, had not been started.

It was also necessary to adapt all the 'Standing Orders' of the TLP in Florennes to the Albacete base and to make other new ones required by the national operating procedures. In addition to this documentation, essential for the operation of the TLP, the JEMA had to develop and publish an Instruction determining the relations of the TLP with the Air Force (either; operational, financial, of personnel and logistical) and a Ministerial Order for the Creation of the National Component of the Tactical Operations Leadership Program, where in addition to creating the TLP as a Unit, a Status of Forces Agreement (SOFA) section was established.

Integration of Foreign Personnel at the TLP. While initially this issue did not seem that it might present many difficulties, the truth was that it was a matter that required careful attention. In fact, the nations, wanted to have total certainty and guarantee that the rights of both the personnel assigned to the TLP as well as the ones who were temporary detached for the courses would be respected, as well as issues such as the correct application of the international agreements endorsed by Spain, those outlined in the MOU, or those related to taxation, housing, schools, kindergartens, medical assistance, travel, behavioural standards in Spain, and other events of special relevance. Other significant issues that had caused some concern to the nations and that had to be addressed with due discretion throughout the constitution phase, were the more than frequent anti-NATO demonstrations near the base or the concern of certain social communication media outlets, due to the massive arrival of foreign military personnel in Albacete.

Flight Courses Preparation. This was the main reason for moving the TLP from Florennes to Albacete and all nations were very demanding with the quality, safety and possibilities of the new scenarios. In the first place, it was necessary to define a flight zone that was appropriate for the development of the TLP missions. Once agreed with the TLP's nations, the approval still had to be obtained by the Air Staff, and finally coordinated, controlled and supervised by the Spanish Air Combat Command.

As the entire flight zone was the union of several Dangerous Deltas (areas restricted for civilian flight operations), already defined and areas especially activated by NOTAM,

An Ala 15 pilot performing the walk-around before a mission. (*Salvador Mafé*)

it was necessary for the TLP to coordinate with Ente Público Aeropuertos Españoles y Navegación Aérea (AENA – Spanish Airports and Air Navigation Public Entity) to define schedules, priorities, and characteristics of the same. The original air space working areas closer to Albacete, those designated D104, D98, R63 and D26, in 2019 a 45 per cent expansion was requested to allow future operations with F-35s.

Likewise, it was necessary to design the connecting and crossing points of the air corridors to permit the TLP's missions to be accomplished safely and smoothly. It was necessary to specify new departure and recovery points and their associated procedures at the Albacete's AB for all flight conditions. The solution to the problems described was very expensive, since the TLP would require additional duties and work for numerous EdA personnel, especially for the MACOM (Mando Aéreo de Combate – Air Combat Command) and Albacete Airbase, and for those air traffic controllers whose working hours coincided with the TLP's missions.

The control and security of complex missions with the participation of numerous aircraft of different characteristics such as combat, transport, helicopter, anti-aircraft and special operations units, AWACS, ships, etc., belonging to ten NATO nations, together with the combat assets provided by other nations invited to each of the courses, was going to be a new operational experience that had to be faced by a wide variety of civil and military personnel, for which, in principle, they were not adequately prepared.

TLP Comprehensive Maintenance Contract. As has been said, one of the reasons to move the TLP from its previous location was the search for an optimization of costs, thus one of the solutions implemented in Albacete was the adoption of a comprehensive maintenance contract for all infrastructure and other services that had to be provided for the TLP's operation. It must be taken into account that when TLP courses are underway, that part of the base becomes a 'resort', which requires dining rooms, hotels, gardening, cleaning, shuttle services with the nearby city, etc.

With this type of contract, all the personnel employed at Florennes working for the TLP have been replaced and although this expenditure account was and is high, the savings achieved are also notable.

Finally all the problems were solved and on 17 June 2009 (the last possible day for the signing), the MOU was endorsed by all nations. That same day, the official relief ceremony was held in Florennes with the transfer of the flag between the TLP Commander in Florennes and the Colonel Chief of the Núcleo de Constitución. The Spanish JEMA could not attend the ceremony, due to an untimely breakdown of the plane that was to take him to Belgium.

It was instead chaired by the Belgian JEMA, and on the Spanish side by General (OF-6) Francisco Javier García Arnáiz, who some years later also became JEMA between 2012 and 2017, and at that time was assigned as a MIL. REP.

Ala 12 EF-18M Hornet taking off from Los Llanos airbase. (*J.J. Fernández*)

On 22 June, the physical transfer of all the material that had been selected for it began, the first of the transports arriving three days later at Albacete.

The headquarters building was already in quite good condition thanks to the excellent work and disposition of the Mando de Logística (MALOG – Logistic Command) Infrastructure Directorate and the Jefatura de Servicios Técnicos y de Sistemas de Información y Telecomunicaciones (JSTCIS – Technical, Information and Communications Command) staff, it was delivered on time and in the first days of July the furniture purchased for the building adequate for its initial operation was installed.

The work of the TLP Nucleus staff was hard and intense and everyone began to understand that the temperatures in July in Albacete were not the same as in Florennes. If we consider that Spain was selected as Host Nation in 2005, and as acknowledged by the EdA itself, by September 2008 almost nothing had been done, is easy to understand the level of intensity developed to have everything accomplished by the dates scheduled, but ultimately the objectives were achieved and after a summer of intense work, the first meeting of TLP's 'Steering Group' took place on 30 September 2009. The Operation Plan (PoO) and the Operation Implementation Arrangement (OIA), which previously had generated intense debates among the representatives of the various nations, were agreed and signed and a day later, as scheduled, the opening ceremony of the TLP was held. The first flight course started in November 2009 as scheduled.

In general, TLP in Albacete has excellent growth potential and is prepared to host this European training centre of excellence for decades to come.

Definitions

Once transferred to Spain, the nation in which the Albacete Airbase is located became the host country for the TLP, henceforth the terms of reference 'Host Country' and 'Host Base' apply.

The Host Country is to provide a TLP Commander, who is accountable to Participants through the Steering Group, for these to adhere to the TLP Policy, doctrines and tactics of NATO.

The provisions on the Commander's responsibilities are contained in the Plan of Operations (PoO). Subject to subsequent agreements, a NATO Strategic Command will be designated to provide military doctrine and guidelines to the TLP, through a designated International Military Headquarters in cooperation with the participating members and the General Staff.

In addition, the designated NATO Strategic Command may delegate contacts with the President of the SG and the Commander through a NATO International Military General Headquarters.

Chapter 7

TLP's Flying Branch

The TLP's Flying Branch was introduced into the teaching syllabus when the programme moved from Fürstenfeldbruck base to Jever, thus passing from the theoretical approach to a more practical phase. In the more than 40 years of TLP's existence, air warfare the and technologies involved have changed and so have the teachings given to adapt to the new air warfare concepts and aircraft capabilities. What has not changed is the need for the pilots to gain knowledge and practice on large combined operations with the participation of multiple actors of different nationalities. It is therefore fair to say that the Flying Branch is TLP's *raison d'être*.

Thus, the declared purpose of the Flying Branch is: 'To improve the tactical leadership skills and flying capability of front line fighter mission commanders, to improve the tactical interoperability of NATO Air Forces through exposure to other Air Forces tactics and capabilities and to provide a flying laboratory for tactical employment concepts.'

This objective is achieved by holding six TLP Flying Courses (FCs) of four weeks every year until FC 2018-4 which evolved to four courses of three weeks' duration currently. The first, adopting this modality was FC 2019-1, allowed by the introduction of new

A rare sight. The MiG 29s of the Polish Air Force were a welcome participant. Here we see aircraft during TLP 2012-02. (*Salvador Mafé*)

Since the political changes experienced in Turkey the aircraft of the Türk Hava Kuvvetleri are also a rare sight at the TLP. (*Salvador Mafé*)

training technologies. During these courses, up to twenty-four combat aircraft and crews, are allowed in each course.

Spain has granted a permanent diplomatic clearance to overfly Spanish territory to and from Albacete's AB for TLP FCs. All flights included in this Permanent Diplomatic Clearance only have to supply in advance, via diplomatic channels, the Flight Plan form as per requirements by the Spanish Ministry of Foreign Affairs.

Plan of Operations

The Plan of Operations (PoO) is approved by the SG and contains the detailed information of the TLP and is subordinate to the MOU. This PoO is developed and approved prior to the start of TLP operations at the Host Base. The PoO can be modified when required, having been agreed by consensus in the SG. In case of conflict between the MOU and the PoO, the MOU will prevail.

Welcome Package

Upon arrival a welcome package is available for all Detachment Commanders (Detcos). This package contains a valuable information for participants and maintenance crews regarding security, car hire, tax-free purchases, etc, which is delivered to help move in and out the base. The Detcos have to e-mail the TLP Administration, should they wish to receive this package.

While TLP is a very dynamic process, some designations remain standardized. Friendly forces are designated as Blue Air, and opposing forces are Red Air.

A pair of Luftwaffe 'Rhinos' participating in one of the earlier TLP courses held in Spain. These two belong to the Taktisches Luftwaffengeschwader 71 'Richthofen'. Note that both are carrying a AN/ALQ-119GY jamming pod. (*Rafael Treviño*)

Blue Air Aircrew Requirements

The latest requirements for the pilots wishing to graduate as Blue Air Commander are as follows: all participating aircrews must be authorized by their respective commandeers to act as mission commander of large multi-type COMAO formations. Concerning the personal qualifications required, as a minimum, the participants must be Mission Ready, Pairs Lead and qualified to fly missions at 500ft mean sea level/above ground level (MSL/AGL). They should be air to air refuelling (AAR) qualified and current to use the AAR assets that support the course.

The participating aircrews in the Air Defence (AD) role should be Dissimilar Air Combat Training (DATC) qualified, and those participant aircrews during courses involving night flying missions, must be night current. Obviously, the participating aircrews must be current on their aircraft type they are flying for the duration of the course and finally, the participating aircrews in the TLP FC should have a minimum of 500 hours on type and in role.

For those individuals who do not meet any of the above requirements, their Squadron Commander must request an individual waiver from the TLP Commandant, with minimum of 30 days' notice, prior to the beginning of the course.

The course participants should complete Experience and AAR questionnaires, which are available on the TLP Flying Course Joining Instructions web page, and forward them to TLP no later than two weeks before the start of the course.

Red Air Aircrew Requirements

While the purpose of the TLP Flying Course is to graduate Blue Air commanders, the participation of aircrews playing the role of the opposing forces, or Red Air, is necessary and for those also is required to be qualified in the DATC role and, for the courses involving night flying, must also be night current.

Upon arrival, the Red Air participants should report to the Mission Coordinator (MC) in the TLP OPS building. The aircraft playing as Red Air, must be prepared for the TLP assigned missions not later than 12.00 p.m. on the day starting their commitment, as coordinated by the MC.

For both players, Blue and Red Air, to ensure that TLP IFR recoveries are completed in as short time as possible, the preferred recoveries approach to land, are in pairs (formation landing), always given that crosswinds and runway conditions allow. Therefore, if the national regulations of the participants allow them to complete the pairs approach, it must be assured that the pilots are current to carry out this procedure before arrival.

Flying Branch Courses Structure

The courses are structured on a 'Building Block' principle with a progressive build-up of force size and missions complexity. As an example, this approach implies that on the first day of flying, the sorties consist of exercises of dissimilar air combat (DCAT) of one versus one aircraft, progressing through one versus two and two versus four on subsequent days.

The jamming tasks for the benefit of the TLP were later taken over by a Falcon from the British company Cobham. A Cobham Falcon about to touch down. (*Cobham*)

After the Falcons, the jamming jobs were taken over by Learjets of the German company GFD, a subsidiary of Airbus. The furthest Learjet is configured with a pair of AN/ALQ-119GY pods. (*GFD*)

The goal of this approach is to develop effective interaction in training between formations from different air forces and nationalities as a key factor to success in aerial warfare. In the pilots' community, this is referred to as 'establishing mutual support'.

The Spanish Lt. Gral. (OF-8) Ignacio Bengoechea explains that the teaching method employed by the TLP is the so-called four 'Ts', 'Task, Target, Threat and Tactics', pointing out 'that during decades has revealed as a highly effective pattern for tactical mission planning'.

The missions progress from six to eight ship packages, in the early stages, to large fully-integrated composite operations flown against external air defence assets as the course advances. Scenarios include the exposure to a wide range of air-to-air and surface-to-air threat systems. for long endurance missions air-to-air refuelling may be employed, consequently the participants should review the AAR questionnaire for their course. A typical mission may last for 1hr 45 mins from take-off to landing, consequently the aircraft configuration should therefore be considered carefully.

The complete flying syllabus consisted of sixteen missions when the courses lasted for 4 weeks and, cover a broad spectrum of Composite Air Operations). These sorties are aimed at presenting crews with different challenges that will help them to develop their tactical skills needed to plan, brief, fly and debrief a fully integrated multinational formation.

TLP's Operational Assets

TLP owns an Autonomous Air Combat Manoeuvring Instrumentation (AACMI) system, including an on-site support centre manned by Diehl-BGT-Defence personnel.

The system comprises twenty-seven AACMI pods, also referred to as Flight Profile Recorders (FPR), and a workshop with test and repair facilities and a latest-generation ground debriefing station. The attending aircraft will carry FPR pods to the maximum extent possible allowed by availability.

There are mainly two type of pods; the 533.10 (not datalink compatible) and the 533.13 (datalink compatible). Also available are two 533.15 pods for use on Eurofighter Typhoons, which are courtesy of Diehl-BGT-Defence. Consequently the nations operating with Eurofighter Typhoons should, whenever possible, bring along their national pods (e.g. ITAF n533.14 or RAF RAIDS pod).

FPR pods are normally handed out at the Diehl-BGT-Defence On-Site Support Centre (OSSC) located in the TLP hangar. With a few exceptions all nations combat aircraft have clearance to carry at least on pod type (current exceptions without any flight clearance: the JAS-39 Gripen, FAF Rafale and HAF Mirage 2000).

The FPRs are connected exclusively via the AIM-9 Sidewinder umbilical cable (115V connection) and never via the mid-body connection (1760-Milibus). They record nothing but Time-Space-Position-Information (TSPI) data relative to a centre-of-world reference.

Upon arrival at TLP, the pods are handed out to the weapons crews, usually at day course number 2, who will receive a briefing on the FPR, as well as the pilots. It is the weapons crews' responsibility to mount the pod on the launcher/station foreseen in the individual aircraft determined by TLP/Diehl-BGT-Defence. As long as the FPRs remain serviceable, they will stay on the aircraft for the duration of their participation. After the course they have to be returned to the Diehl-BGT-Defence OSSC together with the respective flight hours sheet accomplished by the pod.

One of the ECM configurations used by the GFD's Bombardier Learjets during its participation in the TLP. One AN/ALQ-119GY pod under the port wing and a new Airbus development under the starboard wing. This seems an experimental item because its boxy appearance makes it look unsuitable for supersonic flight. (*GFD*)

Some rare participants in the TLP courses, due to their few jets and many obligations, are the Harriers of the Spanish Armada. This example was photographed in 2014. (*R. Treviño, via EdA*)

During the comprehensive daily debriefs the AACMI system is used to analyse both, air-to-air and air-to-ground results. All aspects of the mission are thoroughly debriefed. All aspects of the mission are thoroughly debriefed and the emphasis at all times is on 'Lessons Identified'.

The last mission is normally flown on the Thursday of the last week. The participants may fly out their aircraft at any time between 07:30 and 14.30 on the following Friday.

A Harrier of the Italian Marine Militare participating in the TLP. (*Salvador Mafé*)

Class Senior

At the beginning of each course, a Class Senior figure is nominated from among the participants and is normally the senior aircrew participant. The Class Senior is required to act as the point of liaison with the Course Leader who is part of the TLP Staff, act as a spokesman for the course participants and coordinate administrative and social activities.

TLP Planning, Briefing and Debriefing Aids

The TLP organization provides briefing/planning areas, planning tables and all maps required during the course. Detachments should bring sufficient planning equipment and expendables for the use in the sixteen scheduled missions.

Participants whose aircraft use Video Cassette Recorders (VCR) are to bring at least two tapes per aircraft for use during the course. HUD, radar and weaponry information is an essential training requirement and tapes will be assessed by a TLP staff member after each mission. Detachment must bring their own VCR recorders.

There is no wet film developing capabilities at TLP. Detachments may bring national planning aids and each nation will be allocated at least one room where planning/debriefing equipment and national documentation may be stored. Keys for those rooms will be issued by TLP on the first day of the course. The following visual aids are available for use during the course:

One of 741 Squadron's C-101s, usually playing as Red Air. (*R. Treviño*)

An RAF AWACS over Albacete. (*R. Treviño*)

- **Video Players:** TLP has several VCRs that can handle most types of videos (UMATIC ¾', VHS½ [PAL SECAM and NTSC], Hi-8/8 Di-8 8 [PAL NTSC]).
- **Training Films:** Participants are encouraged to bring any films, videos and /or briefing materials that they think might be of interest to the course.
- **Presentation Software:** All TLP computers, including those in the briefings rooms, are equipped with MS Office 2003, including MS Power Point 2003. This is the preferred briefing method for all presentations up to and including NATO RESTRICTED. All files must be virus checked by TLP before use on its network.

Flight Information Publications

Participants are responsible for providing their own European Flight Information Publications. TLP holds only a limited stock of these documents, which are for reference only and not for issue. Consequently, if publications are known to expire during the course, units should arrange to have updated publications forwarded to their detachments at Albacete.

In addition to Albacete's AB information, it is advisable to have information about the diversion airfields, which are San Javier (Murcia), Torrejón (Madrid), Zaragoza and Morón (Sevilla).

Joint Tactical Distribution Systems

The Joint Tactical Information Distribution System (JTIDS) is an L-band Distributed Time Division Multiple Access (DTDMA) network radio system, used by the United States armed forces and their allies to support data communications needs, principally in the air and missile defence community. It produces a spread spectrum signal using frequency-shift keying (FSK) and phase-shift keying (PSK) to spread the radiated power

Due to availability, AWACS missions in behalf of the TL are not carried out by E-3s and are replaced, as in this case, by a Grumman E-2C Hawkeye of the French Aeronavale. (*R. Treviño*)

over a wider spectrum (range of frequencies) than normal radio transmissions. This reduces susceptibility to noise, jamming, and interception. In JTIDS Time Division Multiple Access (TDMA) (similar to cell phone technology), each time interval (e.g., 1 second) is divided into time slots (e.g. 128 per second) (Wikipedia).

As mentioned previously TLP uses three network radio systems to support air operations, Havequick, IFF/Mode 4 and Link-16.

- **Havequick** is used on all TLP missions and all participating aircraft should be equipped with this system. FMT Set 2 (Frequency Management Training) is loaded and ODD/EVEN training WODS (Windows Optimized Desktop Scenarios). Training Crypto AMST 3099 (Advanced Military Studies Programme) is also used.
- **IFF/Mode 4:** The Identification Friend or Foe (IFF) Mode 4 is used in all TLP missions, therefore all participating aircraft should be Mode 4 capable and have the appropriated crypto loaded daily. The Crypto Key is AKAT2 3662. According to NATO STANAG 4193, that deals with the 'Technical Characteristics of IFF Mk XA and Mk XII Interrogators and Transponders', the IFF Mode 4 provides a 3-pulse reply, delay is based on the encrypted challenge. IFF/ISF Mode 1, 2 and 3 will be required on all missions.
- **Data Link-16:** Lt. Gral. Ignacio Bengoechea assesses the importance of the new technologies in the formation of tactical leaders. 'If the value of the courses offered by the TLP was amply recognized, now it has been added the possibility of using

One of the 48th FW's F-15Es based at RAF Lakenheath participating in TLP during a take-off. The F-15E is impressive because of its size. The aircraft sports a colourful paint scheme to commemorate the unit's participation in the Normandy campaign. American units participating in TLP courses are very rare in recent times, being busy in other scenarios. (*USAF*)

modern tools that make networking possible.' The training referred to by Lt. Gral Bengoechea is the use of Link-16 to conduct air missions. 'In no other place, so many countries work together with this tool, which will allow not only the development in NATO of tactical air doctrine for the use of Link-16, but will also allow the common formation of its tactical leaders in an environment as complex as this one. 'According to the US Command and Control Missile, Defence definition, 'Link-16 is a Tactical Data Link (TDL) that networks communication between land, sea, and air forces to support joint operations and improve interoperability. The system is critical for interoperability of NATO and coalition forces operating within a single battlespace. It is also used by the US Navy and US Army for air and sea operations, as well as air and missile defence.'

'It allows for real-time transfer of combat data, voice communications, imagery, and relative navigation information between dispersed battle elements, using data encryption and frequency hopping to maintain secure communications. The system facilitates the exchange of data over a common communication link, allowing participants to obtain and share situational awareness information and interoperate within the battlespace. Link-16 also facilitates the exchange of sensor information, enabling command and control centres – either centralized or distributed – to create Common Operating Pictures (COP). Interoperability provided by Link-16 allows each participant in the communication link to electronically observe the battlespace, identify threats, and acquire targets.'

'Link-16 information is commonly broadcasted through radio frequency bearers, but it can also distribute information via landlines, satellites, and serial links. It is a sophisticated radio designed to broadcast omni-directionally, providing maximum interoperability for dispersed and/or fast-moving participants. Messages sent via Link-16 can be broadcast simultaneously to as many users as needed.'

Understandably, in a learning course such as TLP, that promotes the skills in Combined Air Ops, the use of Link-16 is almost mandatory, and its use is emphasized, being one of the most diffused data distribution system. The net currently in use is ESSU0003B. This network is also compatible with ESSU0003A load files. Usually, the host base provides the crypto keys and asks to the participating units to bring the documentation providing evidence of authorization to handle NATO crypto keys.

Aircraft attending the course must have a valid clearance for Link-16 network use and radiation in the Combined Air Operations Centre (CAOC) area involved. It is a nation/unit Joint Data Links Operations Centre/NDLMC (JDLOC/NDLMC) responsibility to obtain appropriate clearance.

TLP employs a ground-based Link-16 system based around a Battlefield Operations Support System (BOOS) terminal during the Flying Course, to provide an enhancement Link-16 training environment. In order to assist in the development of mission scenarios, participants and supporting assets equipped with Link-16 are requested to complete a purposeful form, perhaps too technical to be included here, on which, depending of the aircraft type, is requested the ability to transmit and the ability to receive and display of the J-series messages.

A TLP Operational Tasking Data Link (OPTASKLINK) is published in each flying Course. Copies of the OPTASKLINK can be obtained before the course by contacting by email through the NATO Secret Wide Area Network (NSWAN). The units unable to access NSWAN have another email address as an alternative to obtain the OPTASLINK.

Inter-flight Frequencies

An UHF/VHF inter-flight frequency can be assigned by TLP OPS to each aircraft formation of two ships. Participants must ask for it at least one week before the start of the course, either by fax or by phone. TLP OPS will allocate the available UHF/VHF frequencies and they will be communicated when arriving at TLP.

Intelligence, AWACS and GCI Participants

The TLP courses cover a wide variety of complementary military activities, that include the participation of Intelligence Officers, GCI Controllers and one or two AWACS Controllers. These are full course participants and are used during the course to liaise with external agencies and to brief/debrief aircrew participants. These personnel should also be prepared to give presentations covering their own areas of expertise. Non-flying participants have to fill in the appropriate INT/GLO (Ground Liaison Officer) Experience Questionnaire available at the TLP home page.

Simulated Weapon and External Stores

This is possibly one of the most controversial and misunderstood aspects of the TLP courses, especially for those antimilitarist, ecologist or pacifist organizations, who attack the 'militarization' of Albacete and complain about the use of weapons.

The irony is that no live armament is used during the TLP courses, and those elements capable of causing some harm, such as the flares, are carefully managed to avoid any

Perhaps as a testament to the importance attached to TLP courses, many air forces often send their more ornately-decorated aircraft to participate. (*Rafael Treviño*)

problems. During all the Flying Course missions the use of weapons is simulated by means of stores or pods that simulate the real thing.

Aircraft participating should be loaded with any designation of pod or training weapon that would allow the simulation of the full range of stores available for the related aircraft. Every opportunity is given to use these stores and evaluate their effectiveness during the TLP missions. However, participants are advised that the facilities or spaces available within the TLP hangar for storage of simulation pods and training rounds is severely limited. Detachments planning to bring pods and training weapons should coordinate their requirements with the TLP Maintenance Coordinators.

For mission evaluation purposes, aircrews normally are permitted to simulate only those weapons and weapons loads that are declared to NATO by national air staffs. In certain circumstances however, the TLP staff may allow, on a day-to day basis, the employment of peculiar weapons or weapons loads held by their national air forces, but not declared to NATO.

There are no missions during which inert or training ordnance are dropped. Concerning the use of chaff and flares, those may be used over sea and some overland missions subject to certain restrictions. Flares may only be used over water. Detachments should bring enough chaff for six missions, and flares for three missions. While not in use, flares are not allowed to remain installed on the aircraft. Therefore, after a mission, they must be removed and stored in the base's powder magazine. When the course ends, if any of the participant units still have some unused flares, those cannot remain at the host base and must return to the unit's home base.

Electronic Warfare Equipment

One of the most normal occurrences to be encountered while operating in today battlespace, is to find a strong electronic jamming environment, and consequently one of the aspects that is practised in the TLP courses is the conduction of air operations with jamming interferences. With this purpose in the past, TLP had the collaboration of a Falcon aircraft operated by Cobham Aviation that was charged to provide threat simulation at various stages of the TLP missions.

Today this aircraft has been replaced by a Learjet 35A/36A operated by the German company GFD GmbH which is equipped with two AN/ALQ-119GY pods.

Eurofighter EF-2000 of the Italian Aeronautica Militare decorated with 'Il Cavallino Rampante', emblem of the First World War Italian ace Francesco Baracca, which also inspired the Ferrari emblem. The difference lies in the position of the horse's tail; lowered for Baracca and raised for Ferrari. (*R. Treviño*)

While it is true that many very colourful aircraft participate in the TLP, it is also true that others with very flat, grey colours also participate. A Saab JAS 39 Gripen of the Hungarian Air Force. (*R. Treviño*)

The use of two pods is necessary to have an almost 360° coverage around the carrying aircraft, because the fuselage interferes with the pod's emissions whose beams are more effective towards the external sectors of the aircraft.

The Learjets participating in the TLP have been seen with two jamming configurations; two AN/ALQ-119GY or one AN/ALQ-119GY and one new jamming pod developed by Airbus. According to Airbus Defence and Space in a communication dated October 2014 they

have already delivered four jammer systems to GFD (Gesellschaft für Flugzieldarstellung mbH). The multi-frequency jammer systems based on DRFM technology (DRFM = Digital Radio Frequency Memory) simulate electronic jamming attacks, with the help of which, for example, processes can be developed to protect aircraft from radar-guided missile attacks. Conversely, operators of air defence radars train to combat such jamming attacks in order to keep air defence systems functioning despite electronic countermeasures (ECM).

At GFD, the jammer systems are housed in a pod positioned under the wings of Learjet aircraft. The jammer systems can be integrated into other flying platforms at any time.

Portugal became a TLP member early in 2025, and its first flying course was FC 1/25. (*Salvador Mafé*)

AN/ALQ-119 GY Pod

The Westinghouse AN/ALQ-119 is the jammer pod of choice for many air forces and carried by many combat aircraft. This noise/deception jammer covers three frequency bands. Current AN/ALQ-119 maintenance activities include programming of new threats and techniques to the system, system performance laboratory testing, threat and weapon systems analysis and technique development, and field support for various range testing of the system.

The ALQ-119 was the first jamming pod to incorporate modular construction, flight-line programmability and a single driver and dual mode Travelling Wave Tubes (TWT) emitters and analogue technology incorporated into its production, which uses more than 200 factory-set potentiometers to establish operational characteristics. This pod's single driver and dual outputs provide dual-mode noise and repeater jamming outputs. It was designed to be a 'full-capability' self-protection system operating against Vietnam-era Soviet-designed threats, but has gone through several upgrades to improve and update performance. It served as a test bed for components and subsystem developments later used in the ALQ-131 which was to become, for a time, the USAF's standard jamming pod.

The German Air Force has developed and produced modification kits which will increase the frequency coverage and improve the jamming techniques the ALQ-119 can produce. The pods are jamming technique software programmable. These are recognized by the designation AN/ALQ-119GY, as those carried by the Bombardier-Learjets 35A/36A, that usually participate as jammer aircraft in the TLP courses.

These Learjets are operated by GFD GbmH, which is an AIRBUS subsidiary. The company, which has its headquarters on the Hohn NATO airbase in Rendsburg, currently employs a workforce of around 180 people at different locations throughout Germany,

Not well perceived from a distance, but this Polish F-16 has a curious and humorous protection for the ram-air pitot intake. (*Salvador Mafé*)

of which over 80 are former flight crew members of the Air Force and Navy, who are deployed at GFD as Learjet pilots or operators as well as civil simulator instructors for the Eurofighter and Tornado simulators of the German Air Force. This company's military aviation expertise is unique in Germany and ensures that a high quality and reliable service is provided by its two divisions, GFD Aviation and GFD Simulation.

The GFD Aviation division concentrates mainly on the field of aerial target simulation with tactical training scenarios for the German armed forces as well as flight inspection operations at German military airfields. GFD accomplish operations for Government departments, the defence industry and NATO partners as well as civil contracts for research institutes.

GFD's Aviation division has a fleet of fourteen specially-equipped 35A/36A Learjets providing JTAC training, live Eloka (electronic warfare) training, target simulation with or without towed targets, fighter control training, Red Air presentation and naval ship attack profiles throughout the world. Its large body of experienced former military pilots enables it to deliver training solutions tailored to the needs of their clients on a day-to-day basis for the optimal completion of their missions. These capabilities are used by the TLP for training in jamming environments.

The units participating in the TLP that are capable of modifying their radar warning receiver (RWR) and the electronic countermeasures (ECM) pods according to NATO ground threats as Patriot, HAWK, Rapier, NASAMS, Crotale, Aspide, Skyward, SPADA

Close-up of the protection for the ram-air pitot intake of the Polish F-16. (*Salvador Mafé*)

2000 etc., are encouraged to do so. The Russian-built threats or emulators may also be used throughout. Their transmissions will provide threat simulation at various stages of the TLP. Their transmissions will provide a generic threat (Ground or Air) which will be briefed to aircrews by intelligence personnel on the day of a mission. Participants are provide with a form and requested to incorporate a series of settings (Frequencies, PRF/PRI, PW, SCAN [Self-Correcting Automatic Navigation/Simulated Comprehensive Air Navigation]) into their PFM (Precision Flight Modes), if possible prior to attending the course.

Daily Activities During the Course

Once the previously-described conditions have been reached, the daily development of the course for the attending crews are as follows:

Participants should be seated in the TLP Main Briefing Room not later than 08:55 on the first Monday of the course's first week, as the first briefing will commence at 09:00. With this purpose and to avoid delays, a seating plan is normally available and displayed by the door of the briefing room.

Each detachment will be required to give a presentation on their aircraft capabilities during the first two days, before the flying activities begins, and some participants would be asked to give an additional brief on its specialised weapons systems and tactics. As all the participants are supposed to be combat-ready front-line aircrews, so, a certain level of knowledge is assumed. In particular participants must be familiar with NATO procedures and the following documents are considered essential reading:

The Westinghouse AN/ALQ-119 is the jammer pod of choice for many air forces and carried by many combat aircraft. This noise/deception jammer covers three frequency bands. Current AN/ALQ-119 maintenance activities include programming of new threats and techniques to the system, system performance laboratory testing, threat and weapon systems analysis and technique development, and field support for various range testing of the system. (*Salvador Mafé*)

AIRNORTH MANUAL 80-06.
SUPPLAN 26416M 'COPPER CANYON' or 45610M 'DELIBERATE IMPACT'.
SUPPLAN 24600D 'CONSTANT EFFORT' or 45600D 'DECISIVE GUARDIAN'.
ATP-33/AJP-33 (NATO TACTICAL AIR DOCTRINE).
ATP-3.3.4.2(b) AIR TO AIR REFUELLING.

The first mission is flown the third day of the course initiation, consequently the aircraft must be readied to fly at not later than 14:30 on Tuesday of the first week, and must be fully prepared for the TLP mission not later than 12:00 on the following day.

The participating aircrews are involved in academic lectures during the first two days of the course, so it is a normal practice for the units, to fly-in of the aircraft using additional aircrews, Exceptionally, and because it imposes an additional workload to the base's personnel, the participating aircrews may fly the aircraft into Albacete's AB from 12:00 on the Sunday of the previous week of course initiation. If this is not possible, units have to notify the TLP through their SNRs for alternative arrangements. For non-MOU nations participating as invited, this notification has to be managed through TLP's OPS section.

Missions may be flown on most weekdays, although further academics days are normally scheduled during the course. During the flying phase, the working day for the participants will normally start with a Meteorology Brief (MET Brief) at 10:00 and debriefs may, and

The Bombardier/Learjet 35A/36As that participate in the TLP courses uses the 'GY' version, that is a German derivative pod incorporating programmable jamming technique software. One of the pods used by the Learjets has a very worn-out appearance, while the second one looks much more smartly painted in blue, including a tiger image. (*Salvador Mafè*)

often do, last until after 22:00 even on Fridays. When the course involve night flights, the MET brief will start at 14:00 and a debriefing ending no later than 02:00 the next day.

Crew duty considerations are strictly adhered to and participants are always guaranteed at least 12 hours of rest. The Chief of the Flying Branch reserves the right to schedule academics on the Sunday prior to the last week of the course.

Each flying day, a different crew leads the others through all phases of missions that grow in complexity as the course progresses. The missions are flown departing from Albacete's AB and using both overland and overseas training areas (DELTAS).[1]

When long distance or the endurance of missions imply a high fuel consumption, these are done with the assistance of air-to-air refuelling and also could imply operating in the adjacent nation's air space. This ensures a wide range of ground targets to diversify the training.

Normally the missions are daylight missions, but three times a year, TLP includes Night Operations. The goal is to practice COMAO operations at night and experience the different challenges that the planning and operations at night presents to the aircrews.

As the TLP is NATO's air doctrines laboratory, the staff is always keen to be at the forefront of developing tactics for NATO Air Forces and consequently the courses are developed to include a wide variety of mission profiles. With this philosophy, new scenarios are continuously developed and tested in each course, with the aim of keeping abreast of developments around the world and transfer this knowledge to the crews.

In order to provide realistic training for all those involved in air warfare and within the limits of peacetime regulations, participants are presented with a new scenario each day. Those scenarios cover all the aspects of modern air warfare, intended to be challenging and aimed to trigger the imagination of the participants. To achieve this objective, participants

---

1. A Danger (DELTA) area is an airspace of defined dimensions within which activities dangerous to the flight of aircraft may exist at specified times (ICAO Annex 11: Air Traffic Services).

   Most danger areas are operated by military authorities. The vertical and lateral dimensions of danger areas are publicised in national Aeronautical Information Publications (AIPs) together with the hours of operation where applicable.

   Danger areas are established around areas where hazardous operations are likely to take place. These include, for example, military exercises involving live firing, parachute dropping, violent and unpredictable aircraft manoeuvres, or the use of unmanned aerial systems (UAS).

   Normal practice is to include a buffer zone around the planned area of activity within the physical dimensions of the danger area. Usually, the danger area is monitored by the responsible authorities who cease operations if unauthorized penetration occurs. However, it is the responsibility of pilots to avoid penetration of danger areas.

   Historically, many danger areas and Restricted Areas have been inactive for much of the time for which they have been notified as being active. This has led to the development of the Flexible Use of Airspace (FUA) Concept to optimise the use of airspace within Europe.

   With the application of the FUA Concept, airspace is no longer designated as 'civil' or 'military' airspace, but considered as one continuum and allocated according to user requirements.

   The FUA Concept allows the maximum shared use of airspace through enhanced civil/military co-ordination. The application of the FUA Concept ensures that any airspace segregation is temporary and based on real use for a specified time period.

are confronted with situations that are not normally encountered during their routine training missions at home.

Another interesting aspect of the courses is that they enable the free exchange of information on weapons, tactics and capabilities between participating nations. The course is an environment that encourages the discussion and development of multi-national tactics, and participants are trained to find the best ways to employ to full advantage the different aircraft capabilities of the multinational forces during COMAOs.

The Flying Branch, as said, is chaired by an officer who is responsible to the TLP's Commandant. The positions of the Flying and Academic branches chiefs, have a maximum duration of 2 years and 6 months. The other positions do not have specific durations.

Lieutenant Colonel (OF-4) Sebastián Salgues (EdA), now Colonel (OF-5), who has been Chief of the Flying Branch (CFB), provides the following information regarding the practical aspects of what it is like running the FCs.

The FC commanding officer has two sections under his control, namely Air-Air and Air-Ground, and is assisted by an officer that coordinates the missions or Mission Coordinator (MC), an Operations Officer and a maintenance and coordination team.

The MC's role is ensure the coordination between the different nations participating in the programme and in the FCs, to ensure the good balance in their distribution and composition. He is also in charge of coordinating the assistance, both of the participating pilots, as well as of the great variety of mandatory support personnel and assets for the development of the FCs, such as the Red Air pilots (or Bad Guys), AWACS, transport

Another view of the colourful AN/ALQ 119 GY jamming pod as installed on the Learjet 35A/36A. (*Rafael Treviño*)

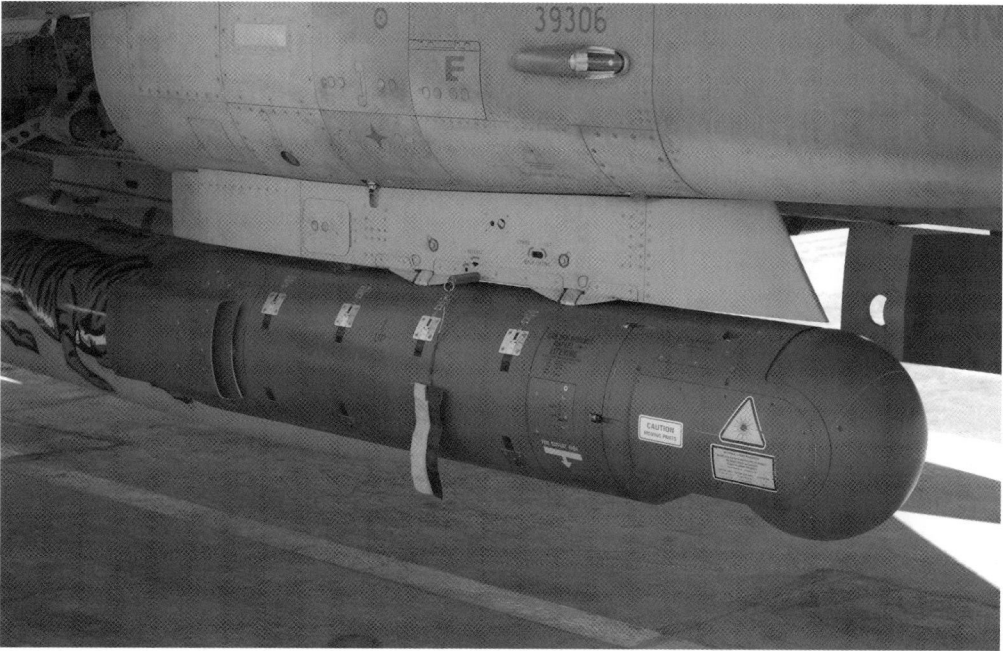

The Rafael Litening advanced targeting pod, in its different versions, is an almost standard fitting for all the combat aircraft participating in the TLP courses. This one is fitted to a SAAB 39D of the Hungarian AF. This targeting pod delivers real-time, forward-looking infrared (FLIR) and TV HD colour camera imagery 24/7. Its high-resolution sensors and effective EO design ensure reliable operation at stand-off ranges. (*Salvador Mafé*)

planes, helicopters, Ground Based Air Defences (GBAD) systems, Forward Air Controllers (FAC) teams, extraction teams, electronic jammers, refuelling planes, ships, SOFAs (Status of Forces Agreement), etc. These really are very complex courses.

The Operations Officer, as chief of the Operations Office, is entrusted with coordinating with the participating nation and the host base all the support needed for the FC, such as reservation of air space, control of services and procedures, documentation of the participants, etc.

The maintenance and coordination team is made up of four non-commissioned officers, who coordinate the maintenance staffs of the squadrons and whose activities we review in more detail separately. They have a great responsibility since they must coordinate with the participating nations and the host base all the deployment and distribution of the aircraft in the parking areas (which is more complicated that it seems), and associated logistics, as well as guaranteeing daily activity and maintenance operations on the ramp and hangar of the TLP, not only during the flight windows, but also before and after.

The fundamental basis of the Flight Branch is the two Air/Air and Air/Ground sections, which are made up of seventeen experienced instructors, with extensive training in operations: 90 per cent of them are fighter pilots, while the rest are controllers.

Two instructors of those sections are responsible for preparing and briefing he missions that the participants will take charge of during the FC, according to the plan and

Tiger detail painted in the Hungarian Litening pod. (*Salvador Mafé*)

programming of the FC. The objectives of the training are reviewed annually in order to keep them updated for future needs of the participants during the operations. in their squadron units and in their air operations centres.

Mission Construction

For each mission, there are two main instructors in charge of designing and adapting the mission to the number of participants. These two instructors are named 'General of the Day' (GOD) and 'Colonel of the Day' (COD). The previous day, both met with the Academic Branch Intelligence Officer, who provides support to the course, and with the Ground Based Air Defences (GBAD) Instructor, to update the latest changes, perfect the training tasks and objectives, according to the progression plan of the participants and mission finalization. In parallel and throughout the day, the participants of the intelligence team are working on their side to provide the best information that will be necessary for the participants of the following day.

The mission is presented at the end of the day to the TLP Commandant and the Flight Branch Chief or CFB for final approval, All necessary materials such as maps, paper orders, scripts, coordinating documents, etc. are prepared and arranged for the next day.

On D-day, the GOD, COD, MC and CFB meet at 09:30, to receive the weather update. The departing outflow and recovery option are decided later (whether it will be visual or instrumental).

At 10:00, all the personnel gather for the last presentation of the mission and at 10:30, the mission for the participants begins effectively, reviewing the intelligence situation, the GCI (Ground Control Intercept) training, the meteorological update and the recapitulation of the training rules.

After this first intense session, they move to the planning room, where the GOD transfers its position to the participant who has been designated as Mission Commander for that day. This must organize, lead, direct and coordinate the participating team to carry out a firm, successful and sure plan that takes charge of the assigned task. The MC has approximately three hours to do it. Meanwhile the GOD and the COD make sure that the participants 'are on the right track'.

Another ten members of the staff are in charge of closely supervising any part of the mission: upkeep of the plan, the route, the objectives of the attack, the weather, the communications plan, the OCA (Offensive Counter Air) plan, and SCAR/TST/CAS, the Suppression of Enemy Air Defence, (SEAD) plan etc. All instructors are attentive to take note of all errors or issues susceptible for improvement. TLP personnel only intervene to ensure safety. The plan must be absolutely safe in order to be allowed to fly later.

Around 13:00 the collective instruction begins, in which the commander of the day's mission, explains in detail and depth to all the participants the plan of the day. At 14:00, the Standardized Tactical Entry Point (STEP) instruction is carried out by the operations officer. This provides the latest weather update, recap of alternative airfields, as well as the latest advice from the COD, GOD and CFB.

Throughout this planning phase, for their part, RED Air opponents set their plan according to the objectives set by the COD. These are supervised by a staff member named RED COD, in order to make sure that the plan manages to achieve the training objectives of the day.

At this point, the reader can see that from 09:30 in the morning till past 14:00, the participants' timetable is very tight and intense. The authors, when invited to visit the TLP, have been able to verify as the pilots attending the canteen to quickly take a bite, what becomes real 'fast food', because they have to quickly board their aircraft as the mission take-offs begin immediately at 15:00 or a bit later. Although the pilots have preference, when it comes to serving the meals, some do not have time even to finish that meal, as there is also an overbooking of the other staff who want to eat at the same time. Actually, the participation in the TLP courses for the future graduates is not 'a paid vacation'.

Take-off Time

The first take-offs of the day start at 15:00, although there is usually some flexibility and sometimes the start is delayed by a few minutes. The planes take off in pairs and with two minutes' separation between each pair.

The full sequence of take-offs, depending on the number of aircraft that participate, takes up to an hour and it is always noisy and spectacular, especially when twin-engine fighters

such as Typhoons, Hornets, Rafales or the 'old dinosaurs', like Tornadoes or F-15s take-off, fully loaded with fuel and with their afterburners on. And yes, this is noisy, but we should remember the old adage: 'Is the sound of freedom'.

In the TLP, the operations command is led by the GOD and the COD and the GBAD and GCI instructors. The mission is monitored and listened to live in a room equipped with large screens through a real-time monitoring system and executed by Spanish operatives of the MALOG Command and Control System located in Torrejón AB. Additionally, the CFB has the option to fly with one of the packages on board of one of the two-seat aircraft provided with this purpose, to overview directly the development of the mission.

Litening pod installed on a veteran Italian AMX ISAF which took part as an ISAF asset in Afghanistan. (*Salvador Mafé*)

This centre interacts with the participants, adding some data to evaluate and monitor their reactions.

There is a place for data Link-16, as the TLP considers it vital to train participants in this regard. In addition, the Tactical Leadership Program is the best environment to integrate, evaluate and improve the Link-16 environment that participants will have to assimilate during future real operations, such as in Libya, Afghanistan, Mali, the Middle East and the new scenarios.

Between 17:30 and 18:00 the last planes return to Albacete, but the day is not over yet. After the return from the mission comes the time on when each participant prepares his own report on the mission to discuss it and learn the appropriate lessons. Thus, another long, but necessary, session begins on the mission report. Once landed, the participants provide the history that will be used to rebuild the mission. This part is carried out by the TLP's contractors of the debriefing system.

Subsequently, the participants report their shots in the presence of a specialized instructor. Often this is an instructor belonging to one of the participating nations. These shots are entered into the TLP's shooting record system and are used during Air Combat Manoeuvring Instrumentation (ACMI) mission reports.

In parallel, the Mission Commander is preparing his mission report, while the GOD and COD and intelligence personnel are putting the finishing touches on his planning report, according to all the points collected by the instructors in charge of supervision during the morning planning phase.

Around 19:00 the mission's debriefing begins. The mission commander collects his points from the morning planning phase and the GOD, COD and the intelligence staff, also provide their respective issues. During this time, a figure called the 'Flowmeister', who is the ACMI debriefing instructor, and the RED COD, complete the preparation of their ACMI report that is taking place around 20:15.

The ACMI debriefing is the time when participants report on the execution of the flight. Each of the flight events is reported and analyzed; taking into account security, procedures, shots, tactics, etc. The duration is approximately one hour, depending on the number of events that occurred during the mission.

The instructors write down all the points that can be improved, the errors or positive points. After the ACMI debriefing, the GOD and the COD meet to collect their points, while the Mission Commander is preparing his execution report based on what he has observed during the ACMI debriefing.

At around 21:30, the execution debriefing begins, which is the last part of the mission. Mission Commander, performs a debriefing on his vision of the flight while the GOD and the COD do it on the air performance of the team, according to the annotations given by the other instructors.

At 22:30, the day ends if no problems appear. After that, everyone marches out to take a well-deserved rest in order to be prepared for the new mission the next day.

Litening pod installed in a Greek F-16 with a very eroded nose radome, probably because is installed very low in the belly of the aircraft and receives the impacts of small debris loose on the runways. (*Salvador Mafé*)

TLP's Flying Courses Update

As described previously, the TLP courses and its contents have changed over the years to accommodate new situations, new national budgets and new teaching technologies introduced during the period 2018–19. Thus, some modifications have been included in the TLP training plans.

The courses that now involve flying missions are:

The COMAO Flying Course (reduced from four to three weeks long)
OPFOR Training Programme (two weeks long)
TLP RMC (Rescue Mission Commander) Flying Course (two weeks long)
C2/ISR Course (two weeks long)

Currently the COMAO Flying Course is the one that takes less time, three weeks instead of four, while retaining the same philosophies of the past, but has included the use of synthetic teaching assets that have permitted the reduction of the previous four weeks' duration of the courses and sixteen flying missions to the current syllabus that include:

Three Synthetic Missions: planned as real-life sorties but flown in the TLP Synthetic System for plan validation. These missions aim to familiarize the participants with the planning process and COMAO procedures, start building up leadership skills and enhance teamwork and cooperation among aircrews.

Nine Live Missions: these missions aim to challenge the participants to develop the tactical leadership skills necessary to plan, brief, fly, and debrief fully integrated multi-national formations.

In this way, the duration of the course has been reduced by a week and the number of actual flight missions from the nominal sixteen to nine, reducing the expenses in fuel consumption, the wear on the aircraft and the days the detachments must remain displaced from their home bases.

The first week includes all necessary academic lectures and the three synthetic missions, followed by two weeks filled with nine consecutive live missions. The second Saturday of the course is a working day. Aircraft should be ready to fly on the second Monday of the course and the last Friday is reserved for redeployment.

COMAO Synthetic Course syllabus example

The synthetic courses are not as such, but require the presence of the student. There is a specific room within the TLP building, configured for this type of training.

Basically, it is a system that is used to support several courses, including flight courses and COMAO academics. The system consists of portable computers configured and interconnected with software that allows basic replication of mission execution. Each

Litening pod installed on a Spanish EF-18. (*Salvador Mafé*)

laptop can be configured as a participating aircraft, GCI station, RED participants, threat control, etc. and also has audio software to be able to adequately replicate communications and radio channels. The goal is not to seek the realism of cockpits, flight models, visual environments, etc as in the usual simulators, but it is oriented to the basic aspects that allow all the participants of the mission to execute and test the planning carried out.

The table below includes the list of lectures imparted and exercises practiced during COMAO course

Academic Lectures
COMAO Concept and Doctrine
Mission Commander Duties
COMAO Mission Planning (The Four Ts)
Precision Guided Munition Attack Planning
Collateral Damage
Close Air Support
Strike Coordination and Armed Reconnaissance
Dynamic Targeting
Joint Munitions Employment Manual
AEW and C2
Suppression of Enemy Air Defence (SEAD)
Force Protection
Slow Mover Protection
ISR and ELINT
Unmanned Aerial Systems
Current Operations Briefings
Participant System Capabilities Briefing
Exercises and Practice
COMAO Brainstorm Demonstration
COMAO Planning Exercise 1
COMAO Planning Exercise 2
COMAO Planning Exercise 3
COMAO Planning Exercise 4

As in the previous format, the lectures and missions are designed for the junior tactical aircrew or individuals with limited COMAO experience, typically at the senior First Lieutenant/young Captain (OF-1/2) level with more than 500 flight hours on type/in role.

Actual course length may be adjusted to account for other TLP requirements and/or Spanish national or regional holidays that may disrupt course continuity.

The TLP COMAO Flying Course fly-window retains the usual one wave in the afternoon. This allows an additional 'shadow wave' in the morning or at night if appropriate 'Flowmeister' agreements with Spain are coordinated.

TLP 2019-1. A Litening pod prominently installed on a Luftwaffe Tornado. (*Salvador Mafé*)

The logical progression of the TLP course attendance is the Support Course, followed by the COMAO Synthetics Course and finally the COMAO Flying.

The secondary target audience is support personnel likely to be involved in a COMAO in the future, including intelligence officers, fighter controllers and C2ISR operators.

The TLP, under normal circumstances, is in very high demand, consequently those nations wishing to send pilots or other military personnel to the courses should plan in advance. Thus slot allocation will be coordinated during the annual Scheduling Conference for the following calendar year.

The maximum number of participants for a flying course remains as in the past: twenty-four jets (twelve pairs) with their respective aircrews, five GCI/C2ISR participants and six INTEL participants.

OPFOR Training Programme

The TLP OPFOR Training Programme offers RED AIR participants the opportunity to participate in the TLP COMAO Flying Course. It aims to improve the skills of the tactical fighter aircrews in the replication of adversary tactics.

The programme primarily intends to educate tactical fast jet aircrews or individuals with limited OPFOR experience, typically at – but not limited to – the senior First Lieutenant/ young Captain level (OF-1/2). The secondary target audience is intelligence officers, fighter controllers and C2ISR operators.

A CATM 2000 practice guided missile installed on a Spanish EF-2000. (*Salvador Mafè*)

Flare launcher (IR decoys) installed on a Spanish Eurofighter 2000 seen by the side of the MLG leg. The aircraft has another pod under the left wing. (*Salvador Mafè*)

The course also enables a free exchange of information on weapons, tactics and capabilities between the participating nations. By providing an environment that encourages the discussion and development of multi-national tactics, participants find the best way to employ the differing aircraft capabilities of the multi-national forces in an OPFOR environment.

The programme is run by a dedicated team within TLP who specialize in OPFOR fighter tactics and Surface Based Air Defences (SBAD) employment with support from Intel and Air C2 (Command and Control) specialists.

During each course, a building-block approach is used to progress the crews through nine carefully structured sorties. These sorties are aimed at challenging the participants to develop the tactical leadership skills necessary to plan, brief, fly, and debrief fully integrated multi-national formations in the OPFOR role. Each day a different crew leads the others through all phases of missions that grow in complexity during the course. Missions will be flown from Albacete and will use both over-land and over-sea training areas. Long-range missions may use air-to air-refuelling and enter the adjacent nation's airspace.

While the TLP maintains a rather open policy towards the public the TLP OPFOR Training Programme syllabus is not releasable to the internet. Please contact TLP to obtain a copy through authorized channels.

Course length and start/finish of course is two weeks. The TLP OPFOR Training Programme begins on the second day of the first scheduled course week, typically a Tuesday. Participants will graduate on the completion of two weeks' training, either in one period or split over two courses, however the maximum benefit would be gained when attending for two weeks of continuous training. Actual course length may be adjusted to account for concurrent flying/academic courses and/or Spanish national or regional holidays, instructor availability and other TLP requirements that may disrupt course continuity.

TLP RMC Flying Course

The TLP RMC Flying Course aims to teach the technical and tactical skills and develop flying capabilities of Rescue Mission Commanders (RMCs) and to provide NATO Air Forces a pool of experts able to conduct such sensitive missions in symmetrical and asymmetrical conflicts. This course was previously considered as a lesson 'within a course', but now has evolved into a specific course as described further as this type of courses is taking much attention during the last times.

The course focuses on weapons employment, survivor/s location and protection tactics, and coordination and protection of mixed-type packages including fighter aircraft, rescue and combat helicopters and C2 or AEW from different nations.

By providing expert knowledge and detailed teaching and debriefings, the RMC flying course will graduate each participant as a reference in Combat Search and Rescue (CSAR) missions, allowing them to spread this expertise through their unit and country.

This specialized area of the TLP COMAO Flying Course aims to educate and graduate tactical fast jet aircrews as RMC leads (Salty 1/3 equivalent) or RMC wingman (Salty 2/4) in the joint environment of CSAR COMAO with the participation of other already qualified units such as Survival, Evasion, Resistance, and Escape (SERE) Team, Extraction Forces and Rescue Vehicles.

The lectures and missions are designed for the advanced tactical aircrew instructors and if possible TLP COMAO flying course graduates, with more than 500 flight hours on their platforms. The secondary target audience is support personnel likely to be involved in CSAR operations in the future, including non-combat ready aircrews, fighter controllers, intel, and C2ISR operators

The logical progression of the TLP course attendance is the RMC academics course, followed by the TLP COMAO flying Course and finally the TLP RMC Flying Course.

This course uses a building-block approach through seven live missions: these step-by-step missions teach the participants from basics of CSAR up to a variety of CSAR missions including multi-survivor, non-conventional Search and Rescue, Immediate and on-call CSAR.

As for the Blue Air course, each day a different crew leads the mission as Rescue Mission Commander, or 'Salty 1' through all phases. Participants will be exposed to Salty 1 to 4 specificities and responsibilities in low to medium intensity conflict scenarios. Missions are flown from Albacete and use surrounding over-land areas.

Nominal course duration is two weeks or nine working days. The TLP RMC Flying Course begins on Monday of the first scheduled course week. The first week includes all

A Raytheon AN/ALQ 184 jamming pod (left) and a SAAB BOZ 107 EC pod (right) waiting to be installed in a Luftwaffe's Jabo 33 Tornado seen in the background. Note that the pods are painted in green while the aircraft is painted in grey. (*Salvador Mafé*)

necessary academic lectures and the first three missions, followed by one week with four consecutive live missions. The Saturday of the course is a working day. Aircraft should be ready to fly on the first Wednesday of the course and the last Friday is reserved for redeployment. Actual course length may be adjusted to account for other TLP requirements and/or Spanish national or regional holidays that may disrupt course continuity.

The TLP RMC Flying Course fly-window is one wave in the afternoon. This allows an additional 'shadow wave' in the morning or at night if appropriate bilateral agreements with Spain are coordinated. The maximum number of participants for a flying course is as follows: eight jets (four pairs) with their respective aircrews, Slot allocation will be coordinated during the annual Scheduling Conference for the following calendar year. In case of a high demand for the course the limit established is two persons per nation and the TLP member nations will have priority.

Other details of interest for non-TLP MOU nations or individuals, please identify the date of the next TLP Scheduling Conference, referring to TLP calendar to send a representative to participate in the planning process. Cost of an RMC slot will be the same as COMAO Flying Course.

INTEL Support to COMAO Flying Course

During the TLP's COMAO Flying Course the participants are faced by a large number of different threats and tactics in realistic and challenging missions. This will be done in a building-block approach to progress the crews through a total of twelve missions.

The Intel participants in the flying course will provide intelligence support to the course by preparing mission support products, briefing and debriefing the fully integrated multi-national crews. Focus will be on analysis of advanced intelligence topics featuring threats, tactics and targets. Specific attention will be paid to leadership, briefing and communication skills. While the main focus will be on Intel support to fixed-wing fighter aircraft in COMAO the course also provide for an opportunity to get acquainted with intelligence support to other elements. The participants will need to show they can effectively support a COMAO in order to graduate from the Flying Course.

The academic part of the Flying Course will comprise a selection from the following table:

Lesson Number	Description
INT-I	Course Introduction
INT-13	Intel Support to COMAO
INT EX-01	Falcon View Exercise
INT EX-10	Knowledge Test
INT EX-11 INTREP	(Intelligence Report) Exercise
COMAO 02/03	ISR Integration & RTMS (*)

(*) Intelligence, Search and Rescue & Radar Target Measurement Systems (ISR & RTSM)

A pair of Luftwaffe AN/ALQ 184 pods. The ALQ-184 is a self-protect electronic countermeasures (ECM) electronic warfare (EW) pod used on many air forces' tactical aircraft. Its computer-controlled multibeam receivers and mini-TWT amplifiers operate in both receive and transmit modes to selectively direct high power jamming against multiple emitters. The system provides instantaneous RF signal processing that is wide open in angle and frequency. Features such as a high sensitivity multibeam receiver, continuous wave, pulse and pulse Doppler allow a 100 per cent probability of threat detection. (*Salvador Mafé*)

The course begins with a series of lectures introducing participants to Intel support to COMAO. These lectures are followed by threat systems and tactics analysis seminars aimed at providing participants with a basic refresher on factors that impact COMAO and planning. After two days of academics, the course will be composed of a variety of missions offering participants the opportunity to support the aircrew.

The nominal course duration is three weeks (nineteen days). The TLP's COMAO Flying Course begins on Monday of the first scheduled course week. The first week includes all necessary academic lectures and the three synthetic missions, followed by two weeks filled with nine consecutive live-fly missions. The second Saturday of the course is a working day. Actual course length may be adjusted to account for concurrent flying/academic courses and/or Spanish national or regional holidays, instructor availability and other TLP requirements that may impact course continuity.

The NATO rank limitation to participate is OR-3 through OF-2 (Private First Class through Major). All course participants need to bring a copy of their NATO SECRET security clearance. English language proficiency SLP 3322 (Level 3) (i.a.w. STANAG 6001) is mandatory in order to fully understand the lectures and to productively participate in the exercises.

Rear view of a BOZ 107 EC pod (left) and a pair of AN/ALQ 184 jamming pods ready to be used on the Jabo 33 Tornado seen in the background. BOZ EC is a highly effective, combat-proven countermeasures pod for high performance aircraft. BOZ EC has extended pre-emptive and reactive self-protection capabilities through missile warning and flare-cocktail dispensing. The Enhanced Capability is available as an upgrade to the original BOZ pod that is operational on the Tornado Aircraft in all user nations. Using the battle-proven BOZ EC pod provides for lean aircraft integration with turnkey-ready self-protection. (*Rafael Treviño*)

As a matter of course, the TLP MOU establishes that the only official language of the programme is English and consequently, it is not contemplated to release any teaching or tutorial information in a different language. The participants must forward English SLP certificates to the TLP admin. section at least one week in advance. Participants should also have graduated from formal national intelligence training and should possess a basic understanding of threat aircraft and armament, SBAD systems, electronic warfare, and also demonstrate knowledge of NATO air operational doctrine (HQ AC RAMSTEIN 80-6 manual).

C2/ISR Participants

Each course includes GCI Controllers, AWACS Controllers, and ISR Operators. They are full course participants and have to liaise with external agencies and to brief/debrief aircrew participants during the course. These personnel should also be prepared to give presentations covering their own areas of expertise.

The overall objectives for participants are to improve individual support to COMAO, learn to work as a cohesive team in an international environment, develop basic leadership skills within an international environment, and gain appreciation and understanding of other COMAO assets.

Up to six C2/ISR participants are expected. They should have already received basic training and one–two years of experience supporting flying operations. Additionally, all C2 controllers are expected to have 'live' controlled missions with a minimum of six aircraft, should have experience in joint and/or combined operations, in TEAM-controlling mission sets, e.g. A/A, A/G, AAR in one mission profile, or are already experienced in ACMI campaign or COMAO controlling.

Since flying courses are conducted in English and participants are expected to brief in English, we strongly urge participant nations to submit only sufficiently qualified personnel with an English proficiency level SLP 3332 according to STANAG 6001.

Reports and Critiques

TLP depends on the feedback received from participants to improve the syllabus and general structure of the course. Consequently the TLP Staff encourages and asks the participants to complete critique sheets after each day of academic training, giving the opportunity to comment on every flying mission. At the end of the course, the Class Senior will be asked to prepare a more formal critique, which should represent the views of all the participants and should cover all aspects of the course.

Once the course has been completed, Detachment Commanders are asked to prepare a written 'Course Report' summarizing the lessons learned and identifying areas for improvement. This report should be forwarded to TLP for the attention of the Chief Flying Branch, not later than four weeks after the end of the course. In the case that those reports contain items of national sensitivity or bear a national classification, they should be sent to the appropriate Senior National Representative or Liaison Officer.

Conclusions

In Florennes the TLP had six four-week courses per year, including 19 working days per course, 50 hours of seminars, 45 hours of flight briefings and debriefings, and 15 complete missions, admitting 24 slots (aircraft) per course and a maximum of 140 slots per year, including guests.

When it moved to Spain there were also planned six courses per year, as deducted of the numeration assigned to the courses at least until 2014, that I have been able to find, six courses were held per year. They were then reduced to four four-week courses.

In fact there has been no update on that. The MOU allows up to the aforementioned maximum of six, courses although problems of scheduling conflicts with other national and international exercises, which prevents being able to take more than the four courses a year that, at best, have been done in the best of cases.

Thus and due to various external circumstances, never have six courses been held in Spain. Only three times (the last in 2019) have there been four. The normal situation has been three courses per year. The main reason for doing four instead of six can be attributed to the great difference in the number of missions that were cancelled due to weather in Florennes compared to Albacete. The second reason has to do with the number of slots that each country has. Currently, this number of slots is eighty-four which, added to the 'guests', means organizing about four courses, with an average participation of twenty-two to twenty-four planes participating as Blue Air. For a detailed list of the courses celebrated/cancelled in Spain, see the table included.

COMAO and the role of the Mission Commander. Some considerations.

In this chapter we have reviewed how TLP trains pilots to graduate as COMAO's Mission Commanders (MC). Now we want to describe how these graduate pilots develop their skills and put in practice the lessons learned in real terms during their service time.

To explain how this training in proficiency is carried out, it is interesting to use the official documentation as a source of information.

NATO's document entitled *Allied Joint Doctrine for Air and Space Operations. Ed. B, Version 1, April 2016* provides some useful definitions and insights on how and when to use air power:

A BOZ 107 EC pod seen installed on an Italian Tornado of the Diaboli Rossi Stormo. (*Salvador Mafé*)

Given the complexity of the modern world, NATO seeks to achieve its objectives via a comprehensive approach, that requires effective coordination and cooperation among national governmental departments and agencies, non-governmental organizations (NGOs), international organizations (IOs) and the private sector.

This, NATO's capstone publication for allied joint doctrine, states that NATO forces must expect to perform a wide range of potentially simultaneous activities across a spectrum of conflict, from combat action to humanitarian aid, within short time-frames. This spectrum of conflict is the backdrop against which all joint air and space operations are conducted, the principal discriminators being the level of violence and complexity of actors engaged in the conflict. Air and space operations can contribute to all three NATO military missions, which are:

1. Article 5 collective defence,
2. Non-article 5 crisis response operations (NA5CRO), and
3. Consultation and cooperation.

Up to here is explained in the main text when to use aerial power and continues explaining why air and space power are the preferred tools to be employed in certain situations of international tension.

An AGM 88 HARM missile installed on an Italian Tornado. The AGM-88 HARM (High-speed Anti-Radiation Missile) is a tactical, air-to-surface anti-radiation missile, designed to home in on electronic transmissions coming from surface-to-air radar systems. (*Salvador Mafé*)

Moreover, the unique attributes of air and space power offer politicians and commanders the means to create a wide range of effects including contributing to engagement, deterrence and coercion activity at the tactical, operational and strategic levels; often within time-scales that other elements of the military instrument cannot match.

The employment of air power can be defined in terms of roles, missions and sorties. This introduces four broad, fundamental and enduring operational roles of air power that are used to achieve strategic, operational and tactical level objectives: counter-air, attack, air mobility, and contribution to intelligence, surveillance, and reconnaissance.

These roles are not unique to the air component, and other components do perform them or similar activities to varying degrees, but because of its unique attributes: speed, reach and height, air power has become the preferred instrument for politicians and military commanders to achieve strategic and operational and objectives across a wide spectrum of conflicts ranging from the delivery of humanitarian aid to combat actions.

This, understandably, identifies the need to employ combined operations including several specialized branches of the armed forces to ensure the success of the mission.

The use of air power has led to the term 'aerial warfare', which NATO defines as 'the use of military aircraft and other flying machines in warfare, which includes a wide range of aircraft, helicopters, missiles, UAVs, designed to establish the control of the airspace, attack targets, maintain air mobility, and to conduct intelligence gathering, surveillance and reconnaissance activities'.

This definition clearly suggests that air warfare, individually considered, is a complex activity in itself that becomes more complicated when performed by several actors belonging to different countries, with different cultures and using similar or different assets. Another peculiarity of aerial warfare is that it is in permanent evolution because of the constant changes of the technologies involved and because the bad guys have habit of opposing and disrupting such good guys' activities.

Now the general criteria for the use of air power have been defined, we will go on to review the details of how COMAOs are developed, specifically from the point of view of the Mission Commander.

The role of the Mission Commander (MC)
As has already been said, TLP courses were initiated just to train air crews to develop their skills to lead and participate in these combined air operations and to such purpose were created the COMAO courses, that later were evolved in three complementing learning branches, the Flying Branch, the Academic Branch and the Concept and Doctrine Branch.

Another interesting document we have used and that goes into detail and gives insights about the tasks of the MC when preparing and launching a COMAO is the one entitled *Interaction in Aerial Warfare: The Role of the Mission Commander in Composite Air Operations (COMAO)* by Pål Kristian Fredriksen of the Royal Norwegian Air Force Academy. This

A Learjet 35A with a different jamming configuration with a AN/ALQ 119 pod under the right wing and another sensor pod under the left wing. (*Salvador Mafé*)

may allow the reader to compare how COMAO missions are planned and developed in reality with the teaching process used in the TLP courses, which is practically identical.

Whilst the Alliance can use a variety of military and non-military tools to change the behaviour of decision-makers, states and non-state organizations, the particular attributes of air power offer specific, flexible and responsive ways to create and exert influence, ranging from direct physical attacks to more nuanced, psychological effects. The ability of air power to create influence leads to another definition of air power as 'the ability to use air capabilities to influence the behaviour of actors and the course of events'. Within NATO's environment, these air campaigns are conducted by means of a series of parallel and sequential COMAO, which has become the term used when dissimilar types of aircraft and other naval and ground assets are used, interacting in coordinated actions, to achieve defined military or humanitarian objectives within a given time and a geographical area.

This type of operation frequently involve numerous international formations, numbering between 20 to 100 aircraft. In order to achieve the desired affect and success through the interaction of all the aircraft involved in COMAO, a key leadership principle, also used by NATO is 'a centralized control and a decentralized execution'.

NATO states that the centralized control of a mission:

places the responsibility and authority for planning, directing and coordinating air capabilities with a single commander and his staff. It maximizes operational effectiveness and avoids duplication of effort by allowing commanders to prioritize, synchronize, integrate and deconflict the actions of assigned, attached and supporting capabilities in time, space and purpose to achieve assigned objectives as rapidly and as effectively as possible.

Similarly, decentralized execution is defined as

the delegation of execution authority to responsible and capable subordinate commanders to make on-scene decisions that exploit opportunities in complex, rapidly changing or fluid situations. It provides for maximum responsiveness to cope with the uncertainty, disorder and fluidity of operations and makes it possible to generate the tempo of operations.

The centralized authority is usually located at a Combined Air Operation Centre (CAOC), that in the case of Spain falls within the Combined Air Operations Centre Torrejón, a frequent collaborator with the TLP courses, which is manned with a staff from seventeen NATO nations, currently filling 185 peacetime positions, which will increase to 190 to support an adapted structure. The post of the Commander is filled by a Lieutenant-General (OF-8) of the Spanish Air Force. For exercises and crisis response the unit maintains the ability to deploy its staff to contribute to NATO's Joint Force Air Component

As mentioned, decentralized execution involves delegating the execution authority to sub-commanders, who are the ones who should make decisions on the spot to exploit opportunities in complex and rapidly changing situations. The person on whom this delegated leadership role falls is defined as the Mission Commander (MC).

When a COMAO is launched, the essential tasks are given to the MC by means of an Air Tasking Order (ATO) that contains the objectives, a relation of the participating forces, target, time frame, Rules of Engagement (ROE) and deconfliction parameters. Although the ATO contains a lot of information, it only serves as a broad set of parameters for the execution of the COMAO.

It is then when, by means of the planning and coordination with all the participating forces, the MC must develop an air operation plan that enhances interaction and ensures effectiveness as well as minimization of threats to the COMAO.

Obviously, being the MC is an extraordinary leadership challenge. The role implies in addition to the overall responsibility of the COMAO, the coordination for success of a large number of participants with different aeronautical military cultures and expertise, different or similar aircraft models with different capabilities, and solving the specific tasks as a flying crew member within the COMAO. It is then when courses such as those given in the TLP, for the training of leaders for this type of missions, make sense.

According to Fredriksen, the key leadership qualities needed are the ability to:

• Create an effective interaction with professionals across organizational boundaries.
• Create and maintain interaction with co-located and geographically distributed forces.

A Spanish Air Force 221 Escuadrón P-3M Orion, during a 2018 TLP in which it acted as an ISTAR platform. Spain's veteran Orions will be replaced from 2028/29 by six Airbus C295ASW Persuaders. (*R. Treviño*)

- Maintain high situational awareness (SA) in dynamic and rapidly changing situations.
- Make sound decisions under time pressure, with limited information and means of communication.
- Cope with stress.

Regarding the organizational structure of COMAOs, it is described as a multi-team system (MTS) that is defined as two or more teams that interact directly and independently in response to certain contingencies to achieve common objectives.

The COMAO structure normally comprises four levels:

- The Centralized Control Level or Combined Air Forces Operations Centre (CAOC).
- The Decentralized Execution Level or Mission Commander (MC).
- The Sub-commanding levels, that include: Offensive Counter Aid Commander, the Strike Package Commander, Suppression of Air Enemy Defences Commander, the Surveillance Commander and the Air Refuelling Commander.
- The Team Level that includes the forces assigned to each one of the above sub-commanders.

This structure outlines the participation of several specialized teams with and the individual roles assigned to them.

Putting the pieces together

The experiences gained in decades of air warfare clearly indicate that to develop an interaction between army formations and nationalities, it is training. In the common parlance among pilot communities, this is referred to as 'establishing mutual support.'

Since WWII it has been established that mutual support between aircraft acts as a force multiplier. A formation of two fighters can outperform two fighters employed individually. This principle is today used operationally by the multirole 4th and 5th Generation aircraft.

At scholar level, we can find several definitions of the concept of 'interaction', but regarding the practice of an effective interaction during a COMAO, under threats and in a war campaign, is regarded as a skill that must be mastered.

Fredriksen emphasizes the importance of training. He states that one well-known training principle for effectiveness is: 'You train as you fight', implying that the training must be in accordance, or as similar as possible, as you will do in actual combat. This, that is viewed as an obvious lesson today, was not so obvious decades ago, as the Vietnam War demonstrated. Assuming this idea, if NATO practises COMAO in peacetime, it must be in the most realistic manner.

Prior to this idea, the USAF, as mighty as it was, experienced many restrictions in training, and consequently, the crews were not prepared to face the threats they encountered in real war, resulting in heavy losses of men and material in Vietnam. Once the bitter reality was accepted, the Red Flag exercises were established to generate better-prepared air crews for war.

USAF air crews started to train systematically during peacetime, employing the COMAO principles, that are being refined over the years. Today, Red Flag provides a realistic training in combined air, ground, space and electronic threats environments, creating a learning environment were ideas can be exchanged. Due to the success Red Flag is today one of many exercises where NATO aircrews interact in COMAO training. The sole purpose is to reach a level of proficiency to support the demands of modern aerial warfare.

As mentioned in the introduction to this book, the differences between TLP and Red Flag is that TLP creates graduated MCs, who later must develop their skills in exercises such as Red Flag.

A second important factor of COMAO training is that it needs to be conducted with a progression in challenges, which is a trend followed by the TLP Flight Courses. NATO is today considered as the world's dominant air power both in terms of numbers and technology, but a risk in a realistic training scenario is to face an opponent who does not offers a challenge to your skills.

For that reason the COMAO exercises, that normally last for ten days, are designed with a progression in challenge, normally starting out with realistic best-case and expected scenarios based on likely war scenarios of today's world, progressing to worst-case scenarios and occurrence of unexpected events. In this way, aircrews are exposed to different interaction problems in controlled scenarios allowing them to learn from different situations.

A third factor that affects the training efficiency is the willingness of all participants to share their own mistakes and give the others a chance to learn from them. As it is said, people learn from their own mistakes … but smart people learn from others' mistakes. Therefore, joint exercises provide NATO forces with a unique opportunity for collective

Transport aircraft, like this Italian C-27J Spartan, besides acting as logistics platforms, also act as 'slow movers' during the flying courses. (*Salvador Mafé*)

learning and thus the joint practice of skills required for effective interaction in combat leads to the development of standardized concepts of operation, tactics and standard operating procedures (SOP).

In most COMAO exercises, the participant forces are brought together at a common airbase. They meet face to face for planning and learning processes and continue interacting in social programs in the evening. All these activities are designed to develop mutual trust and respective knowledge about differences in norms and culture.

COMAO's practical process

To succeed, every COMAO follows a standardized working process of four phases, led by the MC:

1. A planning phase.
2. A briefing phase.
3. An execution phase.
4. A debriefing phase.

The cycle last about twelve hours; four hours dedicated to planning, two hours to briefing, four hours performing and two hours debriefing. We can see that planning is the phase that absorbs more time.

This process not only applies to the conduction of the overall COMAO. It also applies to all sub-levels in the hierarchical structure of the COMAO. In parallel to the COMAO learning process, all air crews need to participate in the learning process on the sub-commanding levels, the information level and on an individual level.

Let's review the particularities of the four COMAO phases.

Planning

According to an anonymous MC: 'The planning phase is the most challenging process to lead. First of all, you need to come up with a good plan. Then you have to make sure that everybody shares a common understanding of the plan. If not, there will be misunderstanding and chaos.'

The planning process serves two main purposes:

1: To create a plan that will solve a specific task and meet established safety requirements.

For this purpose, the MC normally uses a checklist that serves as a guide through the stages and issues that need to be resolved. Although there are standardized checklists, many MCs prefer to use personalized checklists that are tailored according to their personal experiences and planning knowledge.

Before the actual planning starts, the process begins with a brain storming session that is often referred as 'the 4 Ts', that stand for 'Task, Target, Threats and Tactics'. This is coincides with the statements of Lt. General (OF-8) Ignacio Bengoechea on the teaching

Aeronautica Militare 14ª Stormo Gulfstream CAEW, during TLP 2019-1. (*Salvador Mafé*)

method used by the TLP, who has pointed out 'that during decades has revealed as a highly effective pattern for tactical mission planning'.

The following table, based on the syllabus in the Tactical Leadership Program COMAO Course, outlines the list of question that the airmen try to respond during the brainstorming session.

TASK	Analysing the task given in the ATO: What is the commander's intent? What are we supposed to achieve? What is a satisfactory end-state? What are the resources? What are the limitations?
TARGET	What are the goals? Which targets are to be attacked? At what time? What kind of damage level is required?
THREATS	What may stop us from achieving the goal? What can intelligence tell us about the enemy? Weather, clouds, terrain, time of day?
TACTICS	Analysing task, target and threats: What is a suitable plan for this COMAO?

2. The second purpose of the planning phase is to disseminate a collective situational awareness (SA).

After having decided upon the general plan of action, the actual planning phase of the process or detailed planning, coordination and decision-making begins that must be resolved before the COMAO is launched in a safe manner.

Representatives from all participating formations participate in this planning phase. This practice has several advantages:

- The MC can monitor the progress of the planning process and interact with sub-commanders to solve problems immediately when necessary.
- The MC can call for a status meeting, that usually last only 10 minutes, to get and give all participants an overall status of the process.
- All formations flying in the COMAO have one representative who has a SA over the process, and thus can relay information to planning processes that are taking place at formation and individual level.

All this contributes to a collective SA, as almost 20 per cent of the aircrews flying the COMAO are directly involved in the creation of the action plan, and know their own specific task and what role it will play in solving the overall objectives of the COMAO.

Contingency Planning

According to definition of the Cambridge Dictionary, a contingency is 'something that might possibly happen in the future, usually causing problems or making further arrangement necessary.' or that of the Oxford Dictionary: 'a future event or circumstance which is possible but cannot be predicted with certainty.'

All plans are made with the assumption that future events will unfold according to an expected way, but this type of assumption is subject to many factors that can make our plans vary substantially and according to Murphy's law, 'if something can go wrong, it will do it at the worst moment', so it is smart to make plans to cover possible contingencies that may occur.

Basically, planning for contingencies is a risk-assessment and risk-management process, and the Royal Norwegian Air Force (RNOAF) incorporates an Operational Risk Management (ORM) as a standard procedure. Due to the pressure of time in the planning phase, a mental ORM should be performed. This means that the ORM process is carried out verbally as opposed to a more time-consuming written process. Subject to so many different types of hazards, this may seem inadequate, but separate contingency-planning processes are completed on all hierarchical levels in the COMAO organization, covering actually covers a wide aspect of potential dangers.

The contingency planning process usually reflects changes in four assumptions:
The enemy's suspected course of action,
The environment,
The technical equipment and …A reduction in capabilities (aircraft performing specific tasks)

Changes in any of these factors are compared with what the ATO depicts as an Acceptable Risk Level (ARL) for the COMAO. The ARL is a guideline for how many people and aircraft the commander is willing to lose to achieve the goals of the mission. The MC must use his <u>deduction</u> abilities to reflect the scenarios that may be unique to the specific mission, and his <u>experience</u> when reflecting the different scenarios that are known to happen in COMAO

The result of this process ends up with a 'picture' of changes that might lead to the cancellation of the entire COMAO (known as a 'NO GO' situation) or for changes in the assumptions that will require adjustments to the main plan.

A complete planning process will therefore result in a main plan, the establishment of NO GO criteria and a number of alternative plans that will take effect when unexpected events occur. As a principle, all alternative plans are kept as close as possible to the main plan. All planning information is written down on a coordination card that all participants receive in the MASS BRIEFING.

When leading the planning process, the MC needs to have enough experience and knowledge of all capabilities in the COMAO to create an initial plan that makes use of all the resources at hand. The MC must be able to engage in fruitful discussions with sub-commanders and formation leaders and make decisions that take into account individual needs without hampering effective interaction in the overall COMAO plan. Keeping oversight of the process, delegating and engaging in problem solving are important qualities. As he/she normally works under time pressure, the MC needs to demand progress in the work, balancing communications to respect cultural diversity.

Pre-Mission Briefing
The importance of performing a good Pre-Mission briefing is explained by the statement of a MC belonging to the RNOAF: 'What separates the excellent MCs from the others is their ability to convey the plan in the MASS BRIEFING in such a way that everybody understands the big picture and how their task is important in the plan.'

The briefing, previous to the launch of the COMAO mission, is often called the MASS BRIEFING and it is considered as the most important leadership process in creating a collective SA. All participants in the COMAO attend the MASS BRIEFING, as it is considered to be too dangerous to have participants who are not completely informed about the entire COMAO plan. The content of the brief is a repetition of the '4 Ts', that balances the level of detail to what is relevant for all participants. The details that are only relevant at the sub-commanders or formation level are covered in a separate briefing held after the MASS BRIEFING. At the end of the briefing, all participants should know what the plan is and why, what are their individual tasks in the main plan, as well as the different contingency plans.

The briefing process follows certain norms. It always starts punctually with a roll call of all formation members. The briefing is a one-way communication process lead by the MC, and is supported by sub-commanders and other personnel who have delegated responsibilities in the COMAO planning phase. In order to ensure efficiency, questions are always addressed at the end and they are limited to clarifying or confirming information.

At this point, there are two alternatives; either the plan is safe and sound or the COMAO must be cancelled. At this stage of the process there is not the time to make major changes.

The MASS BRIEFING also serves to test the MC's communications skills. The plan needs to be visualized for the participants. They must understand every time-critical interaction that happens in the COMAO, potentially dangerous situations that can occur with non-compliance, and which events that could trigger changes in the plan.

The Die is Cast

Again according to an anonymous mission commander: 'The MC needs to have enough brain bytes available to maintain SA on the COMAO, and not only the action that is going on within his own formation. I have seen many times that trigger events occur that should alter the main plan, but the MC for some reason doesn't act on it.'

In the execution phase, the COMAO faces reality, or in other words, it is when the theory is tested against practice. The main focus of the MC is to maintain a high SA and to monitor the COMAO. The UHF radio is the means of communication between the different formations in the COMAO. Since radio communication is limited to one person speaking at a time, it is difficult for the MC to give instructions to the other elements during flight. It requires significant communication discipline and solid communication plans that establishes how the traffic of information is prioritized on the common UHF frequency. Link-16 is another form of communication between formations. Adherence to the communication plan is the most important factor to maintain a high collective SA.

If the assumptions for the plan are correct, the COMAO will be executed in an orderly manner with effective communications, fostering a collective SA in the COMAO that will be high, resulting in actions being performed without the need for further coordination or communication.

But when unexpected events happen, called 'trigger' events, it is of utmost importance that this is recognized by the MC and that he/she reacts to it in accordance with the contingency plan. If this is the case, an unexpected event may not create a problem for the COMAO. If not, a dangerous situation might develop, either because formations are flying in accordance with a plan that is not based on the right assumptions, or because formations are executing different plans.

In both cases, the collective SA suffers, and results drastically reduced and actual communication increased making it even harder for the MC to re-establish control and give instructions. Degraded SA often leads to formations prioritizing safety actions, rather than executing the planned task.

A typical COMAO includes the following Command and Sub Command elements:

1. A Combined Air Operation Centre (CAOC).
2. A Mission Commander (MC).
3. An Offensive Counter Air Commander with four F-22s, eight F-15Cs and eight F-16 CJs.
4. A Strike Package Commander with four GR4s, eight F-16CJs, four F-35s and four M-2000s.
5. A Suppression of Enemy Air Defence Commander with sixteen F-16CJs.
6. Surveillance Commander with two E3A AWACS.
7. Air Refuelling Commander with four KC 135s.

(Note: The number and models of aircraft assigned to each commander are only indicative as examples. A fighting team in air combat is called a formation and normally consists of four aircraft.)

Improvisation

Since the COMAO planning covers a lot of contingencies, the occurrence of unexpected events that the MC is not prepared for is rare, but it happens, and those pilots that have played the role of MC can tell you about it. Consequently is wise to be prepared for such things.

A COMAO plan almost always requires small adjustments during the performance phase and these adjustments or improvisations follow specific patterns. The communications needed to initiate improvised actions cannot be open for discussion or exchange of vast amounts of information due to the means of communication and circumstances. Thus these instructions are transmitted as orders to be recognized and confirmed. The changes implemented for the improvised actions are limited to as few as possible and decision-making is delegated to the most suitable level of authority in the hierarchical structure of the COMAO. This action limits the problem-solving process to the formation affected by it, and leaves it up to the specialists to make the right decision.

Decisions made during the improvisation process are a balance between obtaining goals and maintaining safety, which is always the predominant criteria.

Post-mission debriefing

The purpose of this phase is to create learning. As in previous steps in the COMAO learning process, the debriefing is conducted at all hierarchical levels. The MASS DEBRIEF focuses on the overall execution of the COMAO. The goal is to identify learning points that are relevant for all participants. The later formation debriefings will cover more specific learnings points relevant for the formation or individual pilots. In total the debriefing process will cover a spectrum of operational and tactical learning points, down to individual pilot switch actions and manoeuvrers in specific situations.

The air crews use two terms in the learning process: 'lessons identified' and 'lessons learned'. The goal of the debriefing is to identify important lessons that the participants can add to their knowledge for future COMAO operations.

The 'lessons identified' are not considered as 'learned' until the application of action has changed. As in most cultures, a debriefing is mainly concerned with 'what went wrong' and subsequently adopt the pertinent measures to correct these errors. Such a debriefing seldom addresses the aspects that have worked well as time to devote to possible learning points is limited in the debriefings.

A debriefing process mainly addresses four questions:

1. Where there any safety issues?
2. What happened?
3. What went wrong? Why?
4. How do we change next time?

As mentioned previously, safety is paramount in COMAO exercises. What cannot be performed safely in a training environment, will become hazardous when performed in the fog of war.

During the debriefing anybody can address issues concerning any aspects of the COMAO. Bringing up safety issues in the beginning of the debriefing has two important functions:

1. Point out important learning points so they can be corrected.
2. Situations that affect safety usually generate feelings such as fear and anger and both have a negative impact on analytical learning processes.

The reconstruction of what happened is really the key to create valid learning.

During peacetime in a COMAO scenario, in which some 100 aircraft are performing different tasks in a dynamic air combat environment, none of the participants has a complete SA of what is happening. The fundamental difference is that in times of war this type of situation is more susceptible to confusion, as real weapons are launched, targets are destroyed and planes are shot down. Instead, in a COMAO exercise weapons and missile launches are simulated, but even so, these types of actions need to be assessed in real time in the air, they need to be validated on the ground after the flight to ensure that the assessment is correct.

For this purpose different helping tools, like radar picture recorders are utilized to reconstruct the COMAO execution and replay it chronologically for the benefit of the participants during the debriefing. Simulated munition and missile drops are called out at the correct time, with validation by the pilots performing the action. At the end of this run though, the MC and the COMAO participants have a picture of how the plan was actually executed in the air by the COMAO, including which targets were destroyed, how many aircraft were shot down and their own losses. Then, the information can be compared to the original plan of the mission, and highlight what could have been done differently to increase performance.

Leading by trust

At all levels in any organization, leadership is appraised as an important factor in task performance. However in COMAO, leadership seems to be of utmost importance. The main reason for this is the constant time pressure that comes with the task and the small margin for error.

Time is often described as your worst enemy, especially in the planning phase, as the MC needs to keep pushing for results to meet deadlines given in the ATO. Trust is a factor that correlates with interaction and performance, but a high-risk and high-stress environment like COMAO gives very little time to build trust.

The initial phase of working together in the COMAO is therefore crucial for establishing trust. During the initial planning meeting, the MC needs to give an impression of control over the situation. This is conveyed by demonstrating self-confidence, and by providing an initial idea of how the task and the process can be solved, as well as through his ability to delegate tasks. Furthermore, the MC needs to be open minded to other solutions suggested by participants, challenge new ideas and only accept them if it contribute to a better plan for the overall COMAO.

Language skills seems to play a vital role in establishing 'swift trust'. The MC needs to be confident in speaking English, which is one of the reasons why for participants in the TLP courses, an English-language proficiency SLP 3322 (Level 3) (i.a.w. STANAG 6001) is mandatory in order to fully understand the lectures and to participate productively in the exercises.

The MC also should have a good grasp of the basic professional terms used by the different capabilities in the COMAO, and understand typical problems that may contribute to degrade their performance.

In the planning phase, the MC needs to keep the pressure up in order to achieve results. Showing signs of hesitation will only cause frustration and reduce trust. Therefore, tasks ate often delegated to nationalities and formations that have shown solid performance in the past. This type of MC knowledge is only gained through experience and participation in the COMAOs. Hence, the MC is always a very experienced and highly-qualified pilot.

And finally, to highlight the importance of trusting your MC during a COMAO, we bring the statements of an anonymous MC: 'In some cases, my confidence in the MC and the plan have been so low that the mindset leading my own formation has been to avoid collision with other formations and get us all back safely on the ground. These missions have no tactical value, except learning how not to do it.'

Chapter 8

TLP Academic and Doctrine Branch Courses

The TLP has three independent branches: the Flying Branch, the Academic and Doctrine Branch, and the Support Branch.

The Academic and Doctrine Branch is the workplace of thirteen instructors from nine NATO nations. Of the thirteen, seven are aircraft pilots, both fixed-wing and rotary-wing. These seven instructors have a total of more than 20,000 flight hours between them. The other six instructors have extensive experience in intelligence and electronic warfare. They amass a total of 95 years of experience and have worked in various positions within their air forces at the squad, group, and wing levels. All instructors have also supported numerous real operations in Libya, Kosovo, Serbia, Bosnia, Lebanon, Iraq, Afghanistan, Syria, etc. This group of highly-trained veterans provide TLP course participants with high-quality instruction.

Two RAF Typhoons photographed during TLP 2015-3. (*Tono Fernández*)

A pair of 'Tonkas' landing at Los Llanos, TLP 2013-1. (*Tono Fernández*)

Sunset at Los Llanos. (*Tono Fernández*)

The main function of the Academic and Doctrine Branch is to develop a series of specialized courses throughout the annual calendar. These courses are offered up to seventeen times throughout the year. No aircraft are used in those courses. Only when it is necessary, as in the COMAO course, is the synthetic simulation system used.

Academic courses available in 2020 were:

• SUPPORT COURSE (eight days)
• COMAO Synthetic Course (two weeks)
• CSAR/RMC Academic Course (one week)
• INTEL COURSE (two weeks)
• EW COURSE (one week)

Additionally the Net Enabled Warfare (NEW) course was designed for all those aviators who use the data links in their work. This includes pilots, ground-based radar controllers, and command and control (C2) centres.

The Electronic Warfare (EW) course is a week long and is taught by an expert in Air Battle Management (ABM) of the TLP. It is aimed at electronic warfare specialists. The course is addressed towards squadron-level officers newly assigned to electronic warfare, although it is open to anyone wishing to increase their tactical skills.

But the courses evolve with time and as an example the above-mentioned NEW course that dealt mainly with the subject of data links (Link-16) as mentioned, was held for the

Typhoon FGR4. Note the inert/training AIM-132 ASRAAM. (*Tono Fernández*)

The last time that RAF Tornados were deployed to Albacete was on TLP 2013-4, when five GR4/GR4As participated, most in 31 Sqn markings. (*Tono Fernandez*)

last time in 2014. Later there was an EW course, which dealt with both the principles and basic aspects of electronic warfare, as well as related systems and their tactical use. This course has also not been carried out for several years.

The TLP EW course is primarily aimed at junior fast jet aircrew but includes all potential junior personnel including tactical air transport, rotary wing, intelligence, C2, and squadron mission planning personnel. The lectures and exercises are designed for the less experienced tactical operators or these individuals with no-to-limited EW knowledge and experience.

This course is managed by the EW Course Director and will be delivered to both TLP MOU and non-MOU nation personnel, who have at least a NATO SECRET security clearance. The course aims to introduce participants to EW and EW support functions and provide a broad awareness of them. The course will run with a minimum of twelve participants of any role/speciality.

The course normally starts on Monday of the scheduled course week. Nominal duration is five days. An academic day is defined as six–seven hours of lectures/exercises per day. Time is allocated, but not specifically listed, for miscellaneous events such as course dinner, breaks, etc. See below for example course contents.

- EW Basics
- Basic Radar Principles
- Infrared Principles
- Indirect and Direct Threat
- Radar Jamming Fundamentals
- Direct Energy (LASER)
- Counter Radar (Stealth)
- RWR (Radar Warning Receiver)
- Threat Analysis
- IADS (Integrated Air Defence Systems)
- SBAD (Surface Based Air Defences)
- Air Threat
- ISR support to EW
- Space EW
- EW in the fight

The INTEL course aims to enhance the participants' skills required to provide intelligence support to COMAO. In order to achieve this objective, the course focuses on analytic skills and advanced intelligence topics featuring threat, tactics, and target analysis. Additionally, participants have an opportunity to apply what they learn in a realistic training environment. Specific attention is be paid to briefing skills and communications techniques. The course is mainly focused on Intel support to fixed-wing fighter aircraft in COMAO. The participants will need to pass an examination (or re-examination) with a 70 per cent mark in order to graduate from the course.

31 Squadron golden star. (*Tono Fernandez*)

The course begins with a series of lectures introducing participants to strategic-level analysis and ISR systems and methods. These lectures are followed by threat systems and tactics analysis seminars aimed at providing participants with a basic refresher on factors that impact COMAO and planning. The last phase of the course will be entirely composed of exercises offering participants an opportunity to use their newly acquired knowledge.

The participants should bring running gear to the course for two team-building exercises. The course takes nine full days (the course starts on Monday morning at 08:30 and finishes on Thursday the next week at 21:00). The course is offered two to four times per year depending on the demand.

Up to twenty-four participants are expected. The target audience for this course is junior INTEL personnel with one–two years working experience and posted at a tactical-level fixed-wing unit providing Intel support. Personnel who do not meet the course prerequisites need to request well in advance through the usual registration process, because a waiver needs to be approved under the guidance of the TLP INTEL staff and TLP Chief of Academic Branch. At the end of the process, TLP Admin. confirms your participation.

The NATO rank limitation to attend this course is OR-3 through OF-2. All course participants need to bring a copy of their NATO SECRET security clearance. English language proficiency: SLP 3322 (i.a.w. STANAG 6001) is mandatory in order to fully understand the lectures and to productively participate in the exercises. Please forward your English SLP certificate to at least one week in advance. Participants should have graduated from formal national intelligence training and should possess a basic understanding of threat aircraft and armament, Surface Based Air Defences (SBAD) systems, electronic warfare, and also demonstrate knowledge of NATO air operational doctrine (HQ AC RAMSTEIN 80-6 manual)

This intensive course will comprise a selection from the following table:

	LESSON NUMBER	DESCRIPTION
1	TLP-I	Introduction to TLP
2	TLP-A	Administration/In-processing
3	INT-01	Course intro
4	INT-02	Intel process
5	INT-03	Critical thinking
6	INT-04	Briefing skills
7	INT-05	ISR
8	INT-06	IADS analysis and assessment
9	INT-07	SBAD threat analysis
10	INT-08	Air threat analysis
11	INT-09	Air to air tactics
12	INT-10	Air to air missiles
13	INT-11	ETAT current developments
14	INT-12	OSINT (Open Sources Intelligence)
15	INT-14 (*)	Intel support to COMAO
16	INT-15	Intel support to operations
17	INT-16	Target analysis
18	INT-17	COMAO EX intro
19	INT-18	Course evaluation
20	INT EX-00	Team building exercise (running gear required)
21	INT EX-01	Falcon view exercise
22	INT EX-02	IADS analysis exercise
23	INT EX-03	SBAD analysis exercise
24	INT EX-04	Air to air analysis exercise
25	INT EX-05	Assessment exercise
26	INT EX-06	OSINT exercise
27	INT EX-07	Target analysis exercise
28	INT EX-08	COMAO exercise 1
29	INT EX-09	COMAO exercise 2

TLP Staff
(*) Note that there is not an INT-13 lesson number. Coincidence or superstition?

The Air Land Integration (ALI) academic course, was usually imparted by a pilot from the Air/Ground section. It aims to provide the fundamental teachings on how to integrate

Tornado GR4 of 617 Sqn 'Dambusters', shortly before it converted to the F-35B Lightning II. (*Tono Fernández*)

Magnificent image of a Typhoon FGR4. (*Tono Fernández*)

the air component with the ground component in order to provide maximum support to the mission, but since 2014 has been discontinued.

This course was oriented to everything related to missions to support the land component. Currently, the academic courses offered for 2021 are: COMAO (three of two weeks), Intel (two of two weeks), Support (two of two weeks) and CSAR/RMC (two of one week).

The second part of the Academic Branch is precisely that of Doctrine. One of the roles of the staff of the Academic Branch is to update, according to the lessons learned, the NATO 80-6 publication titled 'Allied Joint Doctrine for the Conduct of Operations AJP-3' and subsequently send it to the Ramstein Headquarters for edition, publication and distribution to all NATO nations.

Also, the Academic Branch provides an instruction training annually for all TLP personnel. This annual training consists of a seminar in which the analysis of the technical and educational procedures of the instructors is reviewed.

Although the TLP is subdivided into three branches, there is enormous transversal support between them. The instructors in one branch give their support to the other in order to carry out their mission. The Academic Branch complements the Flight Branch and vice versa. The instructors of the TLP are not limited, therefore, to their respective branches of responsibility. A wide variety of positions are used in order to provide participants with the highest-quality learning possible.

RAF Typhoon T3. (*Tono Fernández*)

Chapter 9

Supporting the TLP

As a teaching institution, all the TLP's resources are dedicated to that purpose It also has some ground support assets, but does not have any aircraft assigned. Like ordinary students when they go to school must take their notebooks and textbooks, the TLP students must bring their own planes and specific support assets.

Therefore, to develop the intense flight activities, which sometimes equate to a full wing flying daily, the TLP needs the support of other organizations to accomplish its mission successfully. We classify those support elements into three types:

1. General Support Assets.
2. Direct Maintenance Personnel (Day to Day of Maintenance Personnel).
3. External Organizations Support.

General Support Assets

Everything about military fast jets is wonderful; streamlined shapes, powerful engines, innovative sensors, mighty weapons and bold pilots ... but all this cannot function without the silent, dedicated and often forgotten and unsung work of the maintenance/support personnel.

The TLP courses are no exception, and to keep the large number of participating aircraft airworthy during the intense weeks of the course (four weeks in the past) is no mean task.

Technical Support Detachments and aircraft arrivals

The technicians that support the aircraft detached to the TLP are a fundamental component of the success of the course and consequently must be ready. They can arrive at the base via a variety of means, but the requirement is that the Technical Support Detachments are expected to arrive in good time to receive their aircraft and prepare them for the first TLP mission. Arrivals outside duty hours must be coordinated with TLP Administration. Technical Support Detachments are authorized to change only once during the weeks that lasts the course. Any changeover must be completed within one day, as there is no spare accommodation at Albacete.

Some squadrons, especially those of the more wealthy countries, usually send one or two spare aircraft to cover any unserviceability, but we have seen three consecutive aircraft of the same squadron abort their intended participation in a course's air exercise. These aircraft must be airworthy for the next day and this could imply for the maintenance/support personnel long working hours at night.

A group of technicians with two APUs and a tractor, waiting for any problem that may impede the normal operations of the aircraft. (*Salvador Mafé*)

The courses are expensive ones. The displacement of aircraft, personnel and equipment to Los Llanos Airbase, sometimes from distant countries, therefore must take full advantage of every dollar or euro expended in the participation. An aircraft grounded or unserviceable means a pilot that cannot completely fulfil the syllabus of the course and this is wasted money, which is not good news in times when military budgets are being trimmed.

All this is known and consequently, the TLP organization tries to manage the support operations in the best possible way in order to optimize aircraft participation and maximise efficiency. It must be understood that during the three weeks, personnel of different nations live and work together, with idiosyncrasies, operational methods and different aircraft types that must be put together.

For this purpose the TLP releases a document entitled *Engineering Joining Instructions* (EJI), available in advance to all the participants, in which are collected a series of rules to make life easier for the participants and the organization itself, that in case of difficulties, becomes the 'wailing wall' of the affected unit.

In normal conditions, the period between two consecutive courses is dedicated to the planning of the next one. The particular requirements of the participants are received and if possible catered for and the arrival dates of the participants arranged.

As a general rule, all the aircraft arrivals, departures and exchanges must be coordinated with TLP Operations Department for Prior Permission Request (PPR) clearance to fit into the Spanish Air Force flying window which is 07:30–14:30 Monday to Friday.

It must taken into account that the runways of Los Llanos AB are shared by the fighter aircraft of Ala 14, the *Maestranza de Albacete* (MAESAL) for test flying, and also by the civilian aircraft that operate from Albacete's airport.

When possible, the operations that evolve before the TLP courses proper are initiated, try to respect the normal working timetables and schedules of the personnel so as not to overwork them, because when the courses are initiated, 'there is no timetable'. It is frequent that the debriefings after the last flying period of the day end after 22:00.

In every TLP course the first to arrive at the base are the support assets that every participating unit considers necessary in addition to those supplied by the organization. Depending the size and quantity of those assets, they can arrive loaded in cargo aircraft, or in military or hired civilian trucks. Often the maintenance support personnel also arrive with the cargo aircraft. Anyway, the maintenance personnel must arrive in good time to receive their participating aircraft.

With the prior permission of the host base, the cargo aircraft can arrive or depart outside of the normal timetable, but remain parked for unloading in the next day's working timetable. There is no unloading or loading at weekends

The trucks are a special case. The military trucks are allowed to stay at the base overnight or at weekends, while the civilian trucks are only allowed to enter the base from 08:00 to 17:00 Monday to Friday, and are not allowed to stay overnight or weekends. An unloading ramp with adjustable height is available but can only support one truck at a time and must be used on a shared basis by all the units.

Probably under the influence of the economic situation, during the last courses it has been noticed that the use of trucks to transport the support elements instead of transport aircraft is becoming more frequent. In fact, the week before the start of a course, the base is 'invaded' by trucks carrying all equipment, small tractors, containers, etc. Another detail is that the support equipment not listed in the EJI instructions, like ground wires or chocks, are not available and will not be provided.

To avoid problems, no one will be allowed to perform maintenance on participating aircraft except the personnel of its own unit, so consequently they must plan accordingly.

The last mission is normally flown on the Thursday of the third week (on the fourth week, before the course had been shortened in a week) and the participants can fly-out next Friday from 07:30 to 14:30, and the TLP's Maintenance Coordinator should be informed of the recovery details as soon as possible to prevent delays.

As a general rule the EJI states that 'Anything you brought with you must leave with you. Nothing is to remain at TLP between courses.' And this is true. During the courses the surroundings of the TLP's main hangar look like a gypsy technological camp, full of all kinds of elements; once the course is finished, days later it appears totally deserted.

Technical or Maintenance OIC/NOIC Briefings

Concerning Support Maintenance activities, there are several key figures. One is the Maintenance Coordinator (MC) whose responsibility is to assist the participants with their problems. Other are the Officer in Charge (OIC) or the Non-Commissioned Officer in Charge (NOIC) who, prior to the first flight of the day, attend an engineering brief with the TLP's Commandant, the TLP Chief Flying Branch (CFB) and the TLP's MC. Additionally, weekly maintenance briefings are held throughout the course.

Once the planes have taken off, a certain sense of tranquility takes over the ground crews. (*Rafael Treviño*)

The briefings' standard language is English, but some MCs can speak Spanish, French, Italian or German if clarification is needed. It is advisable that the personnel attending can understand what it is said.

It is stressed that attendance for all personnel involved in those briefings is mandatory.

Maintaining and Supporting the Aircraft

While deployed to TLP, all units will operate according to their own Squadron Engineering Orders. In some cases TLP's own regulations may add to but will be allowed to separate from the deployed units' requirements and just in case of conflict, the TLP's MC must be informed of them to work out a solution.

As has been said, the MC is the focal point for all engineering activities and all the requests for assistance are directed through them and not directly with the Host Base. The working hours during the courses for day flying are from 08:00 to 23:00.

While the aircraft are deployed for the course, they are parked in the open in front of the TLP hangar. The parking ramp can accommodate up to thirty-one fighters or aircraft of similar size. Larger aircraft such as AWACS or transports are normally also parked in the open, using the ramp assigned to the Ala 14 fighters which is larger. The squadron can put its aircraft inside the unit hangars, saving space outside for the benefit of the TLP.

Helicopters or aircraft as the MV-22 Osprey, because of their peculiar and potent downwash, are also parked in separate areas from the fighters. Every parking spot has individual ground hearth points to discharge static electrical loads and the TLP recommends the use of leads at least 15m long.

Normally the line service of the aircraft is performed in the open but those maintenance operations that require removal of panels or night working hours are performed inside the TLP hangar to protect the maintenance personnel from the environment. It is noteworthy that in wintertime, Albacete is one of the coldest places in 'sunny' Spain, usually recording freezing temperatures.

Depending of the type and size, the hangar has space for up to six aircraft for sheltered maintenance at the same time and there are no hardened shelters available for individual use. The ones existing are for the use of Ala 14 aircraft.

There are electrical power supplies of the most common AC voltages and amperages in use in military aviation, with four distribution units with standard European sockets. Also available are compressed air with outlets rated at 8K pressure levels at various places within the hangar.

Equipment Storage Facilities and Procedures

The maintenance assets, equipment and facilities assigned to the TLP courses as well as the financing, are not provided by the Spanish Air Force, but are those agreed by the founder members.

Each squadron are allocate a storage area within the hangar of +/-50m² that can be used for those materials of a delicate nature that cannot be left outside. Usual items that can be seen stored inside the hangar are big packs of spare aircraft wheels and tyres.

The larger assets as Ground Support Equipment (GSE) and Associated Ground Equipment (AGE), because of their usual cumbersome nature, are to be stored outside. Similarly, each unit has an assigned external storage area. There is also one room available for tool kits, spare engines, parachute repacking, etc. to be used in a shared basis. The TLP organization recommends to the participants bring the minimum required to support the aircraft because those items that cannot fit in the assigned storage inside the hangar must be put outside due to limited space.

Aircraft maintenance also requires some dedicated time for office work and thus each squadron has a detachment room in the hangar that is equipped with tables, chairs and telephone and internet connections.

The participating units must assume that there is no equipment available other than the following that provided by the TLP:

1 x nitrogen trolley with maximum pressure of 2,800 PSI.
2 x aircraft tow tractors that can be used to tow support equipment.
4 x aircraft universal towing arms compatible with F-15 and F-16 fighters.
2 x aircraft generators.
1 x 8-ton capable forklift.
1 x chaff & flare vehicle that is a general purpose box van.

Those items are to be used on a shared basis and the units must bring their own trained operators. The TLP does not have de-icing facilities, so units must bring their own, if desired.

While the planes are flying, many ground crews take the opportunity to take a relaxing sunbath. This is one of the reasons why the TLP came to Spain; the good weather allows a high number of flight hours and rare cancellations. Notice that the hammock has become part of the 'Ground Support Equipment'. (*Rafael Treviño*)

Maintenance Vehicles Management

Only flight-line vehicles are allowed on the aircraft parking ramp. Only one vehicle per unit will be allowed on the parking ramp and only military vehicles are allowed to circulate in the maintenance area. When driving on the flight line, the driver's side must be kept closer to the aircraft with vehicle lights and four-way flash/hazards switched on.

The right of way will be yielded in the following order:

1. Aircraft moving under own power.
2. Aircraft being towed.
3. Emergency vehicles.
4. Maintenance vehicles.

Vehicles are to stay on paved areas at all times to prevent moving objects from unpaved or dirty areas to the runways and parking areas and thus avoid foreign objects damage (FOD) to aircraft. No driving on the taxiways or runway will be permitted unless escorted by TLP or host base staff.

No vehicles are allowed to be driven on the parking area during launch or recovery operations and no bicycles are allowed on the aircraft parking ramp.

Refuelling and Refilling Procedures

The refuelling operations of so many aircraft have the risk of becoming a bottleneck. Consequently they should be carefully planned and are arranged by the MC. This is especially important as the bowsers or fuel pumping equipment is limited and only one bulk fuel point is available, so the refuelling of aircraft can be a lengthy process and planning and patience are required. In case of need, the fuelling trucks assigned to Ala 14 can help. Like in US Navy aircraft carriers, inside the MC's office, there is a board on which is indicated the position in the parking area of every participating aircraft indicating unit, model, etc. As a safety rule, the refuelling of aircraft with engines running (hot refuelling) is not allowed in the parking area.

The refuelling of all the diesel-operated GSE/AGE must done at the fuel pumps as there are no diesel fuel bowsers. On the host base there is only aircraft JP-8 (coded as F34 by NATO) and Jet A-1 coded as F35 by NATO) plus diesel fuel available but no petrol, and only military vehicles are allowed to refuel on the base. Normally, the refuelling operations begins at the end of the last flights of the day, just to have the aircraft ready for the next day.

To refill the aircraft's crew breathing equipment there is a 5,000-litre liquid oxygen (LOX) tower plus a portable 50-gallon LOX tank. The LOX replenishments are to be carried out by the participants themselves. It is also possible to recharge with gaseous oxygen and the participants are allowed to bring their own bottles or trolleys if required.

All petroleum, oils and lubricants (POL) must be brought by the detachments in sufficient quantities to last the period. Where the units have a regular re-supply runs organized, the quantities should be restricted to the minimum and once the course is finished, all the POL products must be taken with the units when they leave the Host Base.

Fuel and oil spillages are considered a major issue. The units must bring their own trays and supplies of absorbent materials, rags and other means to treat minor spillages on the line or in the hangar while servicing aircraft. Albacete AB is credited under ISO 14001 (EU environmental protection law) therefore any oil or fuel spillages must be avoided or stopped and affected areas treated intermediately.

Very important for the diagnosis of impeding breakdowns, especially those of internal parts like engines' gearboxes, gear wheels or bearings, is the analysis of lubricating oil samples. When one of these parts starts to break down, it normally generates small metal particles that circulate in the lubrication oil circuit and are retained by the devices, usually called 'chip detectors' placed in strategic points of the oil circuit, or oil filters. Those have a magnet that retains the metal particles and at the same time closes an electric circuit that gives a luminous warning signal on the pilot's cabin panel.

Once these chip detectors are removed, the colour of the particles is informative. If they are silver in colour the part breaking is made of steel, which indicates that the part being degraded is a gear or the ball or races of a bearing. If yellowish in colour then they would be from a bronze bearing. The spectrometric analysis of the oil can provide additional information as it usually provides the type of alloy of the particles and, once this is known, the technicians can almost trace where is the part that is about to fail.

The TLP does not have the equipment to accomplish Spectrometric Oils Analysis Program (SOAP) nor Joint Oil Analysis Program (JOAP) to test these oil samples, but can provide a room/workshop in the hangar complex to be set up as a laboratory to be used by

Sometimes the work of the maintenance staff is not directly related to the aircraft. In this case, they are removing the cover plate from a trap near the taxiway raised up by the strong down-wash of an MV-22. (*Rafael Treviño*)

all the nations. In such cases the TLP can assist the participants to send and recover the oil samples to the Instituto Nacional de Técnica Aerospacial (INTA) in Torrejón (Madrid).

Armament

As a safety measure, usually the use of live armament is not allowed during the course. The chaff and flares are removed when the aircraft are parked on the ramp and stored in the HB's explosives bunker.

All the squadrons that employ a standard procedure to stow safety pins within the aircraft before flight, should bring a spare set of armament safety pins for emergency purposes. Armament pins must be installed at all times while the aircraft is on the parking ramp, and only are to be removed at the Approved End of the Runway (EOR) check area. After each mission these will be removed and stored in the bunker. Once the course is finished the unused chaff/flares must be taken back with the units as it is not allowed to leave supplies of chaff/flares between courses.

TLP Engineering Regulations

The following maintenance activities are subject to TLP Engineering Regulations and must be processed through Maintenance Control:

- Engine runs.
- Hangar space for servicing.

- Movements of aircraft.
- Assistance from other nations.
- Refuelling and de-fuelling of aircraft.

The engine runs are subjects to certain procedures. Prior to any engine run, permission must be obtained from the MCs. The station engineering orders require that TLP informs air traffic control and the fire department prior to any aircraft start. The maximum engine run rate on the TLP parking is Ground Idle. As commented previously, aircraft refuelling is not allowed while engines are running. In the case that maintenance personnel deems that high-power engine runs are necessary, then those must be coordinated with the MCs and the aircraft must be moved out to the designated engine-runs pad area.

There is no engine run tie-down capability on the base. The engine run pad only has anchored chocks. For aircraft that would require tie-down, this can be coordinated with the base to have a pilot of the involved unit seated in the cockpit. Engine runs are only allowed between sunrise and sunset.

Computer and Information Systems

Access to computers and the internet are essential, especially when many aircraft systems are computer-centric. The TLP maintenance hangar provides the following facilities in each assigned office:

- One telephone.
- One computer internet connection point.
- A second internet connection point available upon request.

Also there is a fax machine in the MC's office for shared use. The internet connection is to be used under the following conditions. The internet service at TLP HQ and the hangar is for official use only and can be monitored. If the system is found being used for unofficial purposes the service would be switched off at the offending office.

Units are not allowed install or use communications systems such as computers, radio equipment, faxes, satellite or aerials, without prior coordination with the TLP Information and Technology Department (IT). Wireless communications are not authorized. Request for use or installation of special communication systems must be submitted at least two weeks in advance of the start of the course. These are to be addressed according to NATO 14 Point Format Forms and submitted to TLP IT Section at least six weeks prior to the start of the flying course. The 14 Point Format Forms can be found on the TLP website under the label 'Joining Engineering'. The TLP IT remains available for further information, assistance or other requests.

Flight Line Communications

All participants are to confirm their maintenance radio requirements prior to the start of the Flying Course. The TLP MCs and the TLP IT Department will then advise on how each detachment's requirements can be best supported. The unauthorized use of aerials, antennas and frequencies is against the law and is not permitted without prior coordination and pre-approval. One radio will be issued to each participating unit to allow contact with the MCs or the MCs with the unit during operations.

The number of aircraft is variable and accordingly the personnel that arrives with them, thus if any participating unit that would like to bring their own or additional land mobile radios (LMR), the TLP organization can provide the approved frequencies by the host nation for the TLP. It will be required to set these frequencies on the radios prior to arrival.

J-TIDS, Mode 4, Have Quick

The Joint Tactical Information Distribution System is an L-band Distributed Time Division Multiple Access (DTDMA) network radio system used by the United States armed forces and their allies to support data communications needs, principally in the air

Now, both men and women support the TLP aircraft. Two French ground technicians walking toward their aircraft. (*Salvador Mafé*)

and missile defence community. It produces a spread-spectrum signal using frequency-shift keying (FSK) and phase-shift keying (PSK) to spread the radiated power over a wider spectrum (range of frequencies) than normal radio transmissions.

Have Quick is the codename of an American frequency-hopping system introduced in 1980. Have Quick was developed because in the 1970s it became clear that aircraft communications could be intercepted or jammed easily and very inexpensively. Frequency-hopping is not encryption, but rather increases security by rapidly jumping from frequency to frequency. It uses Time of Day (TOD) and Word of Day (WOD) to coordinate with other friendly frequency-hopping communication systems. Because of this, it functions properly in active electronic warfare environments, avoiding jamming interference or interception of the signal. All units are to bring the correct equipment and qualified personnel to load these systems. Frequencies and codes will be provided to the pilots by the TLP Flying Branch.

ACMI Data

The TLP no longer owns an Air Combat Manoeuvring Instrumentation (ACMI) system. Instead the TLP now uses the 'TLP Debriefing System', which uses a combination of Link-16, GPS trackers and Exercise Analysis Group (EAG) files which can be used in conjunction with each other or independently. The TLP OPS section is available for further clarification.

Emergencies Management

An aircraft returning to base with an emergency will be initially dealt with by the HB. The MCs will then coordinate the aircraft recovery with the appropriate squadron. Whilst the aircraft are airborne, recovery teams for each squadron must be immediately available within the hangar area. All the ground personnel who are in aircraft manoeuvring and maintenance areas must worn reflective vests or belts at all times.

The following incidents are to be brought to the MC's attention immediately:

- Injury to personnel.
- Fire.
- Hydrazine problems.
- Hot brakes.
- Losses from aircraft in flight.
- Fuel/oil leakages or spillages
- Chaff spillage.
- Any identified hazards.

TLP's Initial Investment for Support Equipment

Since its move from Florennes to Spain, the support assets available for TLP operations have been increased, including the availability of refuelling trucks that was a problem at Florennes.

The available assets are as follows, including the quantities percentage financed by TLP and the Host Nation.

Items	Quantity	Per cent TLP	Per cent host nation
APUs	2	30	70
Hangar Sweeper	1	30	70
Elevator	1	30	70
Pallet Holders	4	30	70
Generator Sets	2	30	70
A/C Tow Tractors	3	30	70
A/C Towing Bars	4	30	70
Loads Transfers	1	30	70
H.W. Fuel Bowsers	2	30	70
Fire Extinguishers	16	30	70
Land Mobile Radios	16	30	70
Radio Transmitter	1	30	70
Approach System	1	30	70
Emergency Power Supply	1	40	60
Vehicles (1 Bus, 3 Micros)	4	50	50
Vehicle (Chaff, Flares)	1	50	50
Network Operating Systems		100	0
Telephonic System		100	0

TLP's MOU.

Before the start of the mission, the ground crews (with fingers crossed that no problem prevents their plane from taking off), eagerly await the permission to take off. (*Salvador Mafé*)

Those valued assets sometimes disputed by other flying operational units are clearly marked as 'TLP Property', 'to avoid confusions', but in spite of that, situations occur beyond the control of the organization.

Anecdotes around the aircraft tow tractors seem to be abundant. We are told of the case of a brand-new tow tractor, which after a few days was picked up by a C-295, with orders to take it to Senegal to support the Ejército del Aire aircraft deployed there. When it was returned months later, the state of the tractor left a lot to be desired relative to its original condition.

While all the auxiliary ground equipment (AGE) elements of the TLP are available to all participants, it is expected that it will be used in solidarity, but in the case of the tow bars and tractors, there are members of some air forces that manage to hide them, 'openly' to have first use of them.

Another funny anecdote refers to the start-up of one of the aircraft tractors. These are started by turning a key clockwise, just like in all cars. One day it was detected that someone had tried to start the tractor by turning it counterclockwise, with such force that he had bent the key. The key was straightened and returned to service, but the incident was repeated a couple more times, until the key was finally found broken and part of it inside blocking the lock, and rendering the tractor useless until, after a complicated repair, the lock was changed. It was never discovered who was responsible.

Upgrading TLP's Facilities for 5th-Generation Aircraft

The advent of 5th-Generation aircraft will undoubtedly change air warfare during the coming years. But meanwhile there will be a period in which 4th- and 5th-Generation aircraft must coexist and work together. Therefore, according to Colonel Andrés Maldonado, the current commanding officer of the TLP, 'The maximum priority of the TLP is to integrate, or better said, lead the integration of the 4th Generation with the 5th. The main reason is because in a very short time or even right now, six of the ten nations that forms the TLP are bound to be users of 5th-Generation aircraft.' That's true; Belgium, Denmark, Italy, UK, and the USA are already are using the F-35 and declaring its IOC status, and for example the Netherlands will become a user of F-35s only.

Some other nations very active in the TLP FCs, are also bound to use the aircraft. Poland has already agreed the purchase of thirty F-35s.

Greece is showing interest in the model as well as Spain, that finally will be forced to buy F-35s or renounce its stronger force-projection element, now formed by its Harrier force. Regrettably Turkey, while still a NATO member, has been expelled of the F-35 programme.

These plans are not new. The previous Commanding Officer, Colonel Luis Villar, already mentioned in 2017 that the TLP was aiming and looking for ways to manage that integration. Now these plans are plainly confirmed by Colonel Maldonado saying that: 'For the TLP Program it is vital or even existential, being able to integrate those aircraft in our courses, becoming a maximum priority.'

To fulfil these expectations, Albacete's airbase started in 2018 to improve its facilities to support the newcomers. Five strategies to this respect were designed, of which we will comment here on only those referring to support the aircraft.

The upgrade works were initiated in July 2018 with the cooperation of the USAF, whose experts carried out a security survey of the base. That's to say; inspected all the base to identify all the logistic needs and aeronautical safety requirements that might prevent the deployment of the F-35.

A second survey took place in November, led by Major Schmidt. They were studying the safety distances needed for parking the aircraft and the communications needs. A report was written based on all their findings and with that information the base started to work to comply with the requirements.

Later, in February 2019, there was a third, more important visit, this time formed by twenty people from Safety, that analysed all the capabilities of the base in relation to safety distances, communications and even the checking the pavement of the runway. Apparently, safety distances were an important issue as it was mentioned several times by Colonel Maldonado. Possibly the Americans used to their super-bases feel a bit uncomfortable with the size of European bases.

In March 2019 the final report was received. It was a very comprehensive and complete site survey with the conclusions that Albacete's AB would be capable for the deployment of twelve F-35s, supported with a Deployable Debriefing Facility (DDF). DDF is like a container connected via optical fibre to an internet web that allows connection with the ALIS Logistic System in the USA that is also of a very advanced generation.

The DDF containers are frequently seen in Albacete, brought by some of the participants in the FC. The case of the F-35 is special because of its dependency of the ALIS system. As is known, the ALIS has proven a failure and has been disregarded and replaced by a new system called ODIN, that would work using the same cloud-based optical fibre web.

One of the infrastructure examples we have accomplished has been the extension of the optical fibre net from TLP's Headquarters that we have extended around the platform were usually are parked the participants, up to an adjacent platform hat complies with the safety distances requested and the connections needed and that will be dedicated to the F-35s. This has required the installation of more than 2km of optical fibre lines, that will be duly finished in 2021.

Also there will be provisions to extend the optical fibre to other platforms or positions that comply with the safety distances in order to provide the service, just in case there is more than a squadron of F-35 deployed. The infrastructures go in that direction.

Additionally security cameras have been installed and by now, there is nothing important pending, and it can be said the base is prepared to receive the F-35s. The runway pavement is also being repaired and fitted with arresting wires.

These improvements are financed by TLP, which demonstrates the strong predicament of Spain and the Ejército del Aire (EdA) with the TLP.

Interview with D. Joaquín Criado Armengod.

Chief TLP Maintenance Coordinator, Suboficial Mayor (OR-9)

TLP's 2019-2 Flight Course took place at Albacete Airbase between 27 May and 14 June 2019 During those days, more than 350 people participated and 16 pilots, two Intelligence Analysts and six Air Controllers graduated. The important milestone was the participation for the first time of a pair or USAF F-35 as a first interaction with TLP to check how the base is prepared to operate in the future with 5th-Generation fighters and contribute to their integration with those of the 4th Generation.

During that course the authors were authorized to interview D. Joaquín Criado Armengod, Suboficial Mayor (OR-9) and current Spanish Maintenance Coordinator of TLP's National Component. These are the interesting results of the interview:

Question: With so much variety of planes out there, how do you organize yourself so that everything works?

Answer: In Maintenance we are four Maintenance Coordinators, one English, one French, one American and myself.

Q: Are these positions permanent?

A: The position is permanent, people change over time. The Americans rotate every two years, the French every three or four years, the English more or less the same. Normally the permanent position is Spanish.

Between the four of us, we take care of the squadrons that come here, of receiving them, both the transport planes and the trucks, because most of the detachments send the material by truck, not by plane; except perhaps those who come from far away, like the Turks, who always come by plane. Poles half and half.

Q: What aircraft do they use, C-130s …?

A: Yes, they bring Hercules C-130, C-295, transport planes …everything.

And …as I said, we organize them regarding maintenance.

We assign them the rooms that we have available in the hangar so that the staff can be there while they are not working.

We also assign them spaces inside the hangar so that they can place the materials that cannot be left in the open, anyway much of the material stays outside the hangar because inside the hangar space is limited, since it is more designed for maintenance, but it serves both functions.

When they arrive, shortly after arriving, the Maintenance Managers are summoned, precisely in this room, and they are given a briefing in which they are explained all the

A French Mirage 2000D begins to roll slowly towards the taxiway to head to the take-off point. (*Salvador Mafé*)

procedures that they have to follow here and all the procedures that they have to follow here, or what and has to do in terms of occupational hazards. Procedures on the ramp, during aircraft entry and exit, everything related to maintenance.

Q: Security too, I imagine?

A: Yes, security too, but in this case they come from the Base and they give them a brief briefing, since security is their responsibility, we don't intervene there.

Q: What qualifications does the TLP Maintenance Manager have, is this case you? But let's imagine that the same as your predecessors or your successors.
   Do you have any technical training or maintenance experience?

A: Well, I have been an aircraft mechanic since 1985. I have worked on Ala 14 with the F-1, I have worked for a long time also with the Caribou, a transport plane and also with the C-212, but the biggest part of the time with the F-1.
   In 2008, I applied for the vacancy here and went from the Wing to TLP.

Q: How appointed a Spanish Maintenance Coordinator for the TLP? Are volunteers requested?, or does the command designate a person based on their qualifications? How is that process?

A: The position is a vacancy of free designation, that is, it can be requested by anyone who meets the requirements, then the MAPER (Personnel Command) decides who is the most suitable person for the position and that is the one that is assigned. Here he remains here, at first, without limitation of permanence in the position.

You have to meet the requirements that are requested, which are, in addition to being an aircraft mechanic, and mainly in this specific position, have, at least, the English language, an acceptable level of English, and if you have another language, better, since here you have to deal with people of many nationalities.

Q: Do I think the maintenance and support staff are the first to come to the TLP courses? It's not like that?

A: Yes, of course, one of the requirements for the fighters to come, is that the maintenance personnel are already here to receive them … and yes, that is done like this, because otherwise it would be a chaos. That is written in the Joining Instructions that are sent to the squadrons before they come.

Q: When a 'rare' or infrequent aircraft model, for example a Mig-29, gets stuck here at the end of the course due to a breakdown, how do you solve this problem?

A: Well, it is solved by the personnel of the respective squadron. We do not touch the planes of the squadrons, nor each other. In principle, each one takes care of their aircraft.

So when deploying any type of aircraft, each squadron comes with its Maintenance staff. Each nation decides how many people should come. The Germans, for example, send a lot of personnel and a lot of material, the Americans quite a lot of personnel, in short, each nation decides how many people it must deploy to attend to its planes.

But that case you mention, has not yet occurred, but just in case, the necessary maintenance personnel would stay here until they receive the necessary material to recover the plane.

Q: What happens when in TLP medium, that is, for example, during the second week of the course, a model aircraft that cannot be supported with spare parts from here stays on the ground. When the course ends, the operational aircraft leave and that one has to stay here until it can be repaired or put into flight?

A: The case that you mention has not yet occurred, but the normal thing is that the maintenance personnel that is necessary to recover that plane remains here, the one that does not, for example the administration people, leaves. The people who have to recover that plane stay here until their nation sends them the material they need, either by plane or by trucks, and sometimes even through transport agencies such as DHL, SEUR or another similar.

When they receive the material they need to recover the plane, they repair it, the plane leaves and then the personnel. We are always the last to leave … and the first to enter.

Q: The Engineering Joining Instructions talks about the process of refuelling for aircraft, which, given the large number of participants, seems to me to be a complicated process, and since it is generally a relatively slow operation, I think it can be a problem. How do you have it organized? I believe there is only one tanker available.

A: No. Not just one, the Base can at times provide up to five cisterns at the same time. Depends on the circumstances. We have to coordinate it with the base, which is another of our functions …

Q: With the base? Are you referring to Ala 14?

A: Yes, we call it the Host Base for short, and they are the ones who fully support us, since we don't have refuelling vehicles, these are theirs.

Q: Are there no underground reservoirs?

A: Yes, but they belong to the Base. But for example, the system they have in Améndola (Italy), in which, fuel reaches the shelters underground, through underground pipes. No, we do not have it here. Normally, the planes are parked on this platform or also on the other, if there is no space here, and in neither of the two there is that system. Everything is refuelled with cisterns …

Once the flight has finished, the pilot of a Polish F-16 makes his post-flight notes and the ground technicians begin to prepare the plane to refuel and spend the night. (*Salvador Mafé*)

When necessary, we call the base and arrange some timing, that is, we assign a few hours for refuelling. When the weather is not so hot, we make a percentage, refuel some planes in the afternoon, and the rest in the morning.

Q: Early in the morning?

A: Yes, normally we refuel half in the afternoon and half in the morning, the cisterns arrive around 1100 in the morning. [Note: Normally flight operations start at 15:00.]
It is not necessary that they come earlier. But in this course they have come at 09:00 due to the event that has taken place at the base. [Note: F-35 presentation.]
In summer, the tanks come at 09:00, and all the planes are refuelled, because if they are refuelled in the afternoon, with the weather is hotter, when the morning comes, many aircraft have leaks and then you have to clean the spills because of environmental issues, and is an inconvenient and time wasting operation.

Q: What staff does the TLP have dedicated for maintenance and support tasks?

A: For Maintenance? Myself.

Q: So, you are 'alone against the world', right?

A: (Laughs) No, what happens is that the TLP is a multinational organization and each one work in certain areas. In Maintenance as I said before, we are four coordinators. In the National Component, there is only one; me.
Q: So, you don't touch aircraft?

A: No, we don't touch aircraft. Airplanes are owned by each nation and its personnel is the one who must touch them for whatever it is.

Q: Does this mean that your function is 'only' coordination and management?

A: Indeed. If you need to put fuel? We call the cistern at any time.
If you need to start up a fighter? We notify the control tower and give it permission, so that they do not interfere, because if someone wants to do it and there is a cistern nearby, it cannot be done, since you have to keep safety distances between an aircraft with engines running and a cistern, with which, you have to coordinate. It is necessary to coordinate that a plane does not starts up when there is a cistern nearby.
Anything they may need, we manage.
If they need a nitrogen bottle because the one they brought has been emptied, we coordinate to have it replaced.
Charging the oxygen converter? We also coordinate with the base's oxygen plant so that the staff can go here, to reinforce the schedules to refill the aircraft system.

A Polish technician performs a post-flight inspection of the rudder hinge of his F-16. (*Rafael Treviño*)

The exhaust nozzle receives attention before putting on the protection cover for the night. (*Salvador Mafé*)

Q: So all that depends on the Base? Do you refer to Ala 14?

A: Yes, Ala 14 is the one that provides the main support to everything, because in the TLP we have a certain amount of material that consists of two tractors, a claw, tow bars, and a couple of vans. One of them is for collective use, specifically prepared in case they have to transport flares or something like that to the hangar where this type of material is kept during the courses, although later it can also be used for other uses, for example; If they need to carry some heavy material to the plane, they are also allowed to use it, but it is in common use with which most of them bring vehicles, tractors, etc., otherwise it would not be possible. They brought in these on trucks and then unload at our loading and unloading dock for use.

Q: I thought that this type of material was not brought. That they only brought special spares, tools, or something specific to the plane, but that type of material was available here.

A: No, we have two tractors available for those who cannot or want to bring them. For example; The Italian helicopters that have participated in this course have not brought a tractor because they come for a few days and it is not worth deploying a tractor for that, therefore they use ours, but they use it in a shared way with other countries that do not have brought. There are many countries that bring it to them, they put it on a truck and they bring everything, tractors, hydraulic mules, electric generators, a bit of everything.

Q: This is my speculation, but, since it is a multinational program, wouldn't it be interesting to make an investment to reinforce these aspects and have them available here? I think it would be cheaper than not carrying them around every time they come to a course.

A: The investment would have to be very large. This course is quite weak, said in quotation marks, due to the number of aircraft and personnel attending, but there are courses in which more than 500 people have met in maintenance. If you go any further, in the past course, fourteen F-15s had been parked on the E3 ramp. There were only fourteen F-15s and the other ramp was also full of aircraft. So how many tractors would it take to serve so many people?

Q: And those who come more frequently, could not leave the material here from time to time?

A: When the TLP arrived here, the English, who were then the ones who had the upper hand, brought a lot of material, most of it for the Tornado and left it here, but then things slowed down, they participated little in the courses, and the material is still here, but it is here, most of it, waiting to be taken away. Some have discharged it [Note: refers to the RAF Tornadoes] and the material seems to follow the same fate, that is, they are going to cancel it, with which they will come to take it away.
   But the rest of the nations do not usually leave anything here. Some nation maybe yes, because they say let's see, if we are going to return next year, does it matter that we leave a tractor, a hydraulic mule or some external fuel tanks here, so that we don't have to take them away now and bring them back in a few weeks? and since there is room to spare, there is no problem.

Q: For example; Has that green shelter next to the hangar been brought by a country, or is it there permanently?

A: Yes, the Poles have brought it. It is a DDF (Deployable Debriefing Facility). It is a container adapted with instruments, so that the pilots do their national debriefing with the equipment they have installed.

Q: Should it be air-conditioned because if not, painted dark green and here in La Mancha, they should come out toasted? It's not like that?

Ground crews also make their entries in the plane's log books. (*Salvador Mafé*)

A: Yes, but it is actually damaged. It got here, it broke down, and we loaned them one of those little smaller ones. Everything can happen here; It may happen that the device arrives, that the air conditioning breaks down and we have to see how we fix it. You have to ask for support, both our maintenance personnel, as well as the maintenance personnel of the base, to see how you can give a hand and repair it. We can? Well, right? We cannot well, the problem is solved in another way. It is about facilitating their work as much as possible.

Q: And for all that support material that you have, there is a maintenance program for those items, for the Ground Support Equipment (GSE), because imagine that you have to tow that aircraft and the tractor does not starts?

A: Yes, indeed. The ones in charge of the maintenance of the ground equipment is the Host Base, again Ala 14, both of the GPUs (Ground Power Units), and of the tractors, the crane. The vanettes are the responsibility of the Base's Automobiles Section, and since this is practically what we have, there are no more.

Q: Does this maintenance have any kind of periodicity?

A: Yes, just like any other item on the base and like the planes, they have periodic inspections, so do the ground support elements.

Q: So when there is no TLP course in progress, do you stay 'unemployed'?

A: Well, in absolute unemployment, no. Concerning maintenance as there is no one to coordinate, we do nothing, but we manage another business. If we have another course ahead of us, as now for example, we are already receiving emails from the participants in the September course, who are already asking for doubts they have before its arrival and we have to be answering emails. Anyway, you have to program the next course.

Q: How do you start a course, two or three weeks in advance? that is, how far in advance do you have to start coordinating?

A: Normally those who are going to come as Maintenance Managers write emails to us. They ask questions, about items we have here, if they can bring this or that items. In short, about the doubts that arise.

Some ask about specific equipment, and we answer them if we have it or if we have some alternatives, or we tell them that at the Base we could get a similar one if necessary. These are the questions we normally get.

They also ask if we can do non-destructive testing. We comment on what the Maestranza can provide, upon request and coordination. This is required because normally, the Maestranaza is also overloaded with its MRO (Maintenance Repair and Overhaul) tasks.

Everything they thing would need, we tell them what there is, or that they have to bring it or not.

Many nations need special equipment, for example the Greeks and the Poles need a POL (Petroleum, Oils and Lubricants) equipment to test hydraulics and oils. There is no such thing in the Base and not even the Base does it here. Those tests are sent to the INTA in Madrid.

With which, we tell them that if they have to do the rehearsals here, they better bring the equipment.

Q: Is there a special procedure for handling the Hydrazine that use the F-16s, which is a very aggressive and corrosive product?

A: Yes, it is dangerous, what happens is that it comes very well sealed, if they bring a container, which in this case they have not brought, then we place it in a safe area behind the Headquarters, which is the place that has been established as the most suitable for storing such a drum. If they don't use it, and don't normally use it, since they bring it just in case they may need to use it, they take it, put it on another plane, and take it away.

They bring it just in case they have to use it, but so far, I have seen, they have never used it. It's just a matter of storage, just like for the chaff and flares.

French pilots leaving their aircraft after the flight. (*Salvador Mafé*)

The flares are used sometimes during the flying course, but when a plane comes and brings flares on, you have to take them off and store them in a suitable place that is near the powder magazine, there we have a small hangar prepared to store this type of material.

Q: Are real weapons used in these courses?

A: No, never.

Q: And what about that rumour that circulated about the Greek F-16 accident, that it was carrying live ammunition, live cannon ammunition?

A: I think it's a hoax. I can't be sure, because frankly, I haven't read the accident report. But I don't think so, because one of the things they are told is that they cannot bring, of course, live ammunition here, not even blank ammunition.

The first thing we tell them is that aircraft the most can carry is chaff; flares out, and of course live ammunition for what? if they don't need it.

Q: Returning to the topic we mentioned earlier about the periods between flight courses, that is the time you dedicate to prepare the next course, in addition to other tasks assigned to you, but I also suppose that when the flight course is being given it is the more demanding period for you and you have to dedicate more hours than normal. Is this excess of dedication compensated in some way?

A: Normally the Head of the Flying Branch, usually gives a few days off after the course to the personnel who have been involved, it is about three or four days off as compensation, because during the course, there are days that you arrive here at 08:00 in the morning and you leave at 20:00 in the evening or later and do more hours than normal.

When there is no course, we do the established schedule, which is from eight [08:00] to five [17:00], then to compensate for these excess hours, the boss usually gives a few days off.

Q: I mention this because when there is a course in progress, you have to spend a lot of time here during a month, almost living at the base …?

A: Yes but, since we four of us in maintenance, we stagger the schedule. One comes at eight, which is usually me, because in the mornings, if there is some type of work that involves the Base, as I am Spanish, the work is easier for me than for them.

Two others come at 10:00, and the last, the fourth, comes at 12.

Once the post-flight checks are finished, the technicians return to the hangar. Note the cart carried by the technician with a black case with special inspection equipment inside. (*Rafael Treviño*)

With which, I come at eight o'clock, and when the planes land and the refuelling and the other issues that may arise are more or less organized, I leave and the other three stay. A few hours later and once that the other issues have been clarified, two can leave and one remains to close the hangar when everyone leaves.

Q: So there are four of you, to somehow share the chore?

A: Yes, because we open at eight and sometimes close at ten [22:00] or eleven [23:00] at night, so we try to do it that way to make it a little more bearable. Anyway, nobody takes ten hours a day from us.

Q: Could you give us some biographical information so that when we write we will tell our readers who is providing us with this information?

A: Yes. I left in 1985 as an aircraft mechanic from the León's Specialists School with the rank of sergeant, and I was assigned here to Ala 14. My first destination was in Production Control, which is where the accounting of aircraft's flight hours of, and inspection entrances and exits … are carried out.

Q: Always in Ala 14?

A: Yes, always in Ala 14, I was here for a while and then I went to the Maintenance Squadron's Maintenance Secretariat, that was a slightly different job, more focused on personnel management than on aircraft. From there, I asked for a vacancy at the Defence Attaché in Morocco as an auxiliary to the Air Attaché, although it was more like Defence and Air Attaché, since we covered both functions. I was there for four years, and I returned here to Ala 14, where I was assigned to Programming, which is where the planes for missions are allocated and from there I requested a voluntary transfer for personal reasons to Maintenance, to the Second Maintenance Level, which is where I have been working most of the time directly on the plane and from there I went to the TLP.

Q: What year did you switch to TLP?

A: In 2008. It was when TLP was going to come from Florennes here, and vacancies were posted to fill the National Component.

Q: So you are in the TLP from the beginning?

A: Yes, since 2008, even before the facilities were finished. The flying operations began in 2009, but the staff was assigned before. We went to Florennes on some occasion to see how things were done there and to be able to take the idea and implement it and adapt it here in Albacete.

Q: We wanted to have interviewed Sergeant Major Zarantón, who has been performing similar duties to yours, but he refused, as you were now responsible and that you had also introduced some modifications or innovations in relation to what he was doing … Which have been those innovations?
[Note: Sergeant Major Antonio Zarantón has been the previous Maintenance Coordinator of the TLP's National Component, also a veteran of the courses since the first day of the transfer to Spain.]

A: Yes. Well, here each one is organized as best suits him, I don't know exactly to what he refers to, but the modifications have not been so many, they have been minimal.

Q: I suppose these modifications are dictated by day-to-day experience?

A: Yes indeed. If you see that something can be improved, then you try to improve it. If you see that something is not going well, then you have to find a way to make it go better. You have to have a bit of flexibility, you can't do things in a fixed way because, whether they are done well or done poorly.

Q: A question that happened to me before. I assume that these aircraft do have metal particle detectors or chip detectors in the oil circuitry, Is that so?

A: Yes, they do.

Q: When a warning light comes on, on an instrument panel oil system indicator for the presence of metallic particles, it is normal to do a PAESA (Program Electrolytic Analysis on Oils) analysis to see the concentration of these particles and its composition, can you do it here at the Base or do you have to send it to INTA?

A: No, these tests are the ones that I mentioned before that they cannot be done at the Base, or in Maestranza, nor of course in the TLP and they are the ones that must be sent to the INTA.
    Some squadrons bring the necessary equipment to do so. The Greeks usually bring it to you, the Poles sometimes also, because the F-16 is very prone to having PAESA checks made often.

Q: Does INTA respond fast enough so that a plane doesn't get grounded at a very inconvenient instance?

A Greek technician gives his pilot the signal to stop the plane at his parking spot. (*Salvador Mafé*)

A: The truth, the truth … I just remember … Look, precisely in this course, the Poles were a little overwhelmed because a particle indicator had turned on and they had not brought the equipment and the Greeks either. So, yesterday morning precisely, I was calling the INTA to ask where we should take the samples so that they could analyse them as quickly as possible and we would not be left stranded.

Fortunately later they came and told me that it was not necessary, that they had checked it and that it was not necessary.

In those cases, the first thing you do is get in touch with the INTA, with the person in question so that when the Pole arrives there at the site, that they tell him exactly with the GPS, there will be someone waiting to collect the sample, otherwise the result of the analysis can internalize.

Q: Yes, of course, everything is in a hurry here, those things are important. Anyway, I think there could be a PAESA team here. If there are portable equipments like the ones the Greeks and Poles bring here, there might be one here.

A: Yes, but that would imply that we would have to use it ourselves or explain to everyone how it works and let everyone touch it … [hesitates] Look, I'm going to show you something. [Note: The Sergeant Major takes a bunch of keys out of his pocket and shows them to us.]

Look … This is what they did yesterday with a tractor starting key. I will not say who, but some of them did, not once, but twice. I have two keys like that of the same element and all that twice. [Note: Shows us a fairly sturdy key from a tractor starter, not bent, but completely twisted, and continues …] If they can do this with a key, what won't they do to more delicate equipment?

Q: Yes, but it is assumed that the people who are related to the support of a fighter plane cannot be dummies, speaking plainly …but it seems that there are some of them.

A: Yes … Some … I refer to the facts.

Q: Yes, of course, if the key breaks and stays inside the drum, it is a problem. The machine stays stopped.

A: Yes, it stands still until we change the whole starting drum. Or rather, until the Automobiles Section of the Base changes it; the tractor would have to be taken there, or rather, they would have to come here, because we couldn't start it up and it cannot be towed easily; They would have to look for replacement parts and that is another story. The replacements for the equipment must be requested through the SEA (Economic Administrative Section) and it takes a little while, in short, things gets complicated, but fortunately, we have a third key that we have managed not to break. And yes, silly things like this make us waste a lot of time.

Q: With the incorporation of the F-35s, or when very new aircraft are incorporated, the maintenance coordinators receive some type of course, some explanation or briefing to learn how to deal with it?

A: We do not receive any type of course. All we do in the Joining Instructions is ask each nation to send us a form, which is included with the Joining Instructions, describing the critical areas of their planes, such as areas of composite materials, dangerous areas of the plane, places where are located the cockpit opening levers to release the pilot in case becomes trapped, in short, a series of data that appears on that sheet to pass it on to the base firefighters, who are the first to act in an emergency. That is the only thing we do. We know more or less above some characteristics of the plane, but simply to give information to the firefighters who would be the ones to act. But we don't have to touch the plane at all.
   If a plane breaks down, it stays here and the staff leaves, when a reasonable time passes, we sell it and that's all folks. [Laughs]

Q: Well I think that with all this we already have enough information. Do you have something that you would like to point out or something that has not been commented and you would like to explain?

A: Well, in principle I think almost everything has been said. Nowadays I would like to comment that I am very happy to be stationed here. It is a very interesting, intense, but very interesting experience, which makes you see the way of thinking and working of the military from other countries, you practice languages, you have contact with many other people who takes you out of the monotony that involves working in one place throughout life. And I like to interact with people.

You also have to have a bit of a 'left hand' to handle people as well as possible without having to clash, since here, sometimes people gets nervous.

But is getting along very well. I am also lucky to have some colleagues who are very nice and work very well.

Q: It's important to teaming to get along in an environment as intense as this. Are they (the other Maintenance Coordinators) posted here for a certain period of time, which is what your army asks of them? No?

A: Correct.

Q: How long are they destined at TLP? Some two years or more?

A: Well it depends. Americans usually turn every two or three years, at the top.
The British tend to be three or four years to the maximum.

Once the pilot opens the canopy, the technicians gather around the plane to receive instructions, if any. (*Salvador Mafé*)

The French also four, or at most, five years maximum.

I speak of these three because they are the ones with me. But there was a German pilot who was stationed here for five or six years, but that's rare, it's a punctual case.

The normal thing is three or four years.

Q: Turkey is not part of the European Union but they have taken part in some flying courses, are they members of the TLP?

A: No they are not members, but yes, they have come as guests. Just like the Swiss, like the Czechs, the Poles, who are countries that are often invited.

The members of the TLP are the countries whose flags are painted on the access door to the hangar and the Turkish one is not there.

Q: Finally, could you tell us any anecdote of the many that we imagine happen, an anecdote that you would like to highlight?

A: Yes, there are many. I remember when a Frenchman came to me once and asked if they could put a suckling pig in the base. I told him, but you mean a suckling pig? A live suckling pig? He replied, yes, we have a game that consists of spreading a suckling pig with pork butter, releasing it and then trying to catch it together, and whoever catches it, wins the game.

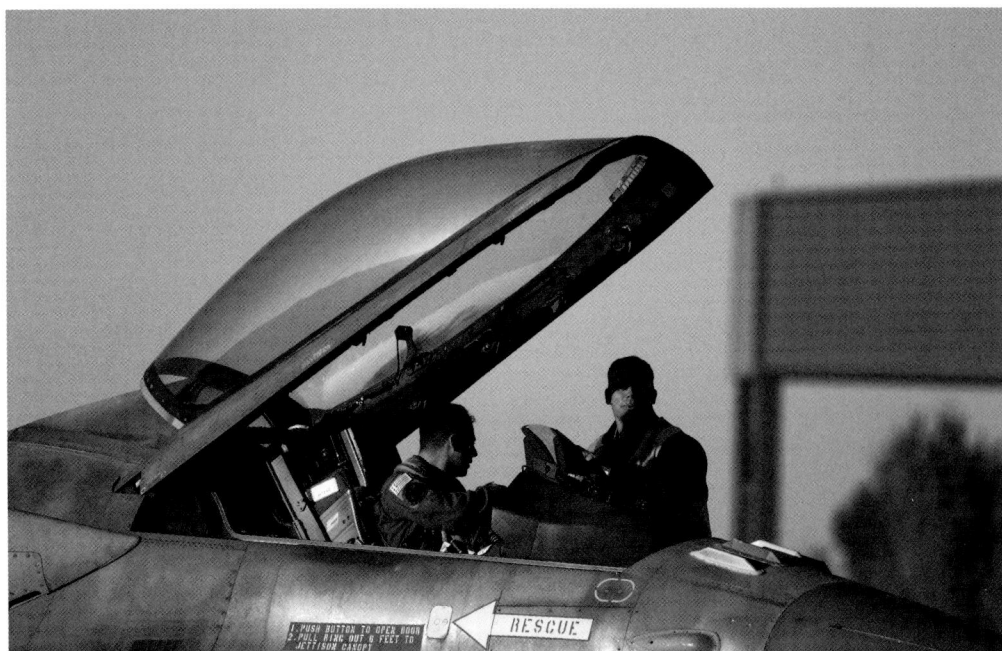

A ground technician helps his pilot unstrap himself from the plane. (*Salvador Mafé*)

But what are you telling me? I responded. You can do that at your base because you have confidence, but here, if I go to Veterinary Section and I ask them if we can put a live piglet in, they would look at me as if I came down from the moon. That is super-controlled here.

Apparently, that is a game, almost medieval, that they usually do. The truth is that I was surprised. And besides, since he asked me very seriously in English and with a French accent, I told to myself: Are this man asking me if he can put a suckling pig in here? I thought that I had not understood him well, but yes, yes, he was asking that.

There are things that surprise you, others that make you funny, others none. But hey, it was one more experience.

Day to Day for the TLP's Maintenance People

According to Warrant Officer (OR-9) Antonio B. Jiménez Zaranton, one of TLP`s MC veterans, the TLP is an atypical programme.

If is considered the usual constitution of the permanent military staff, we note a preponderance of officers in relation to non-commissioned officers.

Interestingly enough, in TLP, the maintenance staff is formed only of non-commissioned officers; namely a French adjutant, an American MS, an English sergeant and a Spanish second lieutenant. They form the team of Maintenance Coordinators (MC), and are the key elements and the obligatory referent of any activity of any type in the operational area. Their goal is that the Maintenance section assures excellence, in areas as organization, safety and operation, for all the squadrons.

In spite of that, all participating squadrons must try to be autonomous. This implies that when attending TLP courses, they must bring with them all the material and personnel they may deem necessary to carry out the missions assigned.

Additionally, 90 per cent of the participants as maintainers are technicians, so their natural workplace is the hangar. This fact, although a priori it could be considered to represent a potential problem of organization, has other positive aspects. The coming-together of technicians from different countries, who work with different aircraft, encourages the exchange of methods, procedures, and professional experiences for the common benefit. The human relationships that are established is another positive factor to consider.

To describe the day-to-day involvement of maintenance personnel, WO Jiménez Zarantón takes as an example Flight Course 2014-01, the one that has recorded the highest participation of aircraft and personnel in the history of the TLP, and that took place between 13 January and 6 February 2014.

During those four weeks the following aircraft were assembled there: Spanish Typhoons from Morón and Albacete, and EF-18s from Zaragoza and Torrejón, USAF F-15Es from Lakenheath, Dutch F-16s from Volkel and Leuwarden, French Alpha Jets from Dijon, Mirage F1s from Mont de Marsan, and M-2000s from Nancy, German Tornadoes from Büchel, Italian AMXs from Grosseto and Trapani and as guests, Portuguese F-16s from Monte Real. In total forty-two combat aircraft, including reserves. If you add the transient combat aircraft, about ten, the AWACS, and four helicopters – two French and two Italians – you can get an idea of the magnitude of that course.

One of the problems that MCs must face is the diversity of languages. Although 'officially', the working language is English, and although the MOU clearly states that 'The flying courses will be conducted entirely in English and all the participants should be sufficiently fluent in the English language', frequently squadrons participate with personnel whose majority do not speak English or do so poorly. This circumstance is prone to cause interference, delays, errors and affect the simultaneous activity of the squadrons, and even because of incidents or accidents. To avoid these situations, it is necessary that the MCs are able to make themselves understood and communicate the common operating rules and what is expected of each one, so it is very convenient for an MC to master two or more languages. Another potential source of problems is the different weapon systems with their different maintenance procedures and their incompatibilities.

One of the responsibilities of the MCs, as a standard working procedure before the first day of the course, is to prepare a Course Plan. This intends to have everything ready for the reception of the always numerous participants. This Plan takes into account all the mandatory requirements, including matters such as Safety, Environmental Protection and Labour Risks, which are not few. This plan establishes 'who, when, how and where' for all the tasks to be carried out during the deployment, operations and withdrawal phases.

In short, this plan determines the management of issues such as the parking of fighters, land transports, helicopters, AWACS and mobile units, the adequate spaces for loading,

A Spanish ground technician attends to the pilot's instructions after the flight. (*Salvador Mafé*)

unloading and storage of the material of each participant; the areas inside the hangar to store the material sensitive to humidity, temperature or bad weather; which rooms in the hangar are assigned for each squadron to place their necessary control equipment and communications with their home base; the shifts for the different services to be performed and even the refuelling sequences of the aircraft. Due to the amount of personnel, material and number of aircraft involved, this plan is essential.

According to WO Jiménez Zarantón's experience, it becomes essential to have this plan elaborated, because depending on who deploys, the needs can vary significantly, even if the same weapons systems are involved, so to make the arrangements, it is absolutely necessary to have a precise knowledge of the usual operating techniques of the attendant squadrons.

It is even necessary to have in mind possible unforeseen problems, such as the arrivals, because although in order to allow for planning the sequence of arrival of the fighters, land and air transports is communicated in advance to Albacete's airbase, it may be subject to unexpected variations.

Deployment

Deployment and withdrawal phases are the most demanding for Maintenance, because of the workload involved, the number of vehicles and material in movement and of personnel working simultaneously in a limited space. The MCs must 'deconflict', prioritize and in any case, prevent the activity of one squadron interfering with that of the rest. It is not an easy task.

Taking into account the geographical situation of Albacete (at one end of Europe), most of the deployments of equipment are done by road, essentially for economic reasons.

Referring to the 2014-01 academic course, although it officially started on 13 January, the previous week, on 7 January, just after the Feast of the Three Wise Men, the first fighters began to arrive; two USAF F-15s, three Hercules from the Netherlands, USA and Germany, and several heavy road transports that were already carrying part of the material and the necessary personnel to put it in use.

On the Friday of that week, the number of transports received increased. French, Italian and North American air transports deployed personnel and cargo, and six North American F-15s, two French F-1s and two Mirage 2000s, and four Italian Typhoons were already parked in the assigned slots.

On Monday the 13th, a striking increase in activity occurred: one Italian KC-767, three German and four Italian Tornadoes, two French A-Jets, one Dutch KDC-10, plus Italian and Portuguese Hercules and two Italian AMXs arrived.

At the same time, the flow of land transports did not stop and the planned storage areas were almost insufficient. For the German Tornadoes alone, the material deployed comprised twenty-two containers each 6.7m (22ft) long.

On Tuesday the 14th the reception of material and fighters continued; three Eurofighter Typhoons from Morón air base arrived, and finally marked the end of the deployment phase and the start of operations. Up to that point, sixty-seven land transports, eleven cargo planes and thirty-nine fighters had been received.

Operations

As standard procedure, the activities for the maintenance people begins on the first day of the course, with a meeting attended by all the technical officers of each detachment and the Colonel Chief of the TLP accompanied by the Chief of the Flying Branch and of course the MCs.

This is always a key meeting, since, after the colonel's words of welcome, the technical officers are informed by the MCs about the development and content of the maintenance course; what are their obligations, procedures to follow and how to solve the problems of execution and operation that may arise in the squadrons. These meetings take place weekly between the Technical Officers and the MCs for the duration of the course.

There is a peculiarity of this phase of the TLP. While normally in any other type of exercises, the maintenance personnel have a more demanding timetable and workload that the flight personnel, here the opposite occurs.

During the TLP only one daily COMAO mission is carried out during the afternoon, but also during the morning are flown one or two 'wave' missions of less aircraft, which does not suppose an excessive effort for maintenance personnel (if there are no breakdowns). Instead the pilots are subject to greater pressure and demands, with very prolonged timetables. The missions always have the same schedule and the same duration with very few variations, so once the material and the established communications have been distributed, the technical personnel do not have much difficulty adapting to the environment of the TLP.

Wednesday the 15th was the first day of flying, and as the first pilots appeared on their way to the personal equipment room, activity on lines E-2 and E-3 multiplied, with line mechanics and armourers in position, and the rest of the personnel in the vicinity in case their presence was required, the technical officers attentive to their respective squadrons and the MCs keeping everything in order and under control.

This is the moment to establish and verify communications between each squadron and MCs, between MCs and TLP Operations, and TLP SOF. The MCs distribute themselves, covering the entire area of activity around the aircraft. In this way, if any expected or non-expected situation occurs, their knowledge on who should be informed and the response are immediate. These networks are activated from before the engines start until the last plane returns from the mission and parks in its place.

Depending on the type of mission planned, the take-off sequence varies, but as we have mentioned previously, the aircrafts' mission type and where it occurs, does not make a difference for maintenance. The actuation of maintenance is the same and independent of the mission type.

The planes leave in pairs with two-minute intervals, although there can be some changes. Usually they accomplish the mission and generally, return with the same separation, although the order can change on the way back.

With so many participating aircraft, take-offs and landings last for at least an hour. Once the planes are parked, the refuelling is organized. When the number of planes is very great, as in this case, it is carried out in two phases: one after the mission and the other the following morning. In any case, each day a different squadron is the first to be served, to distribute the waits evenly. This was one of the biggest problems in maintenance when the TLP was at Florennes, as there were not enough cisterns available and refuelling took hours. Now this problem has disappeared, so in addition to the three problems that promoted the change to Albacete AB, refuelling procedures have also been improved.

Once the mission is finished, post-flight inspections and repairs of possible breakdowns are carried out, either on site or in the hangar, depending on environmental conditions or the resources necessary for the repairs. This is the daily routine.

On the 17th, a NATO AWACS based in Geilerkirchen deployed. The days passed and the end of the second week arrived, when the NATO A-Jets and the AWACS left.

The third week included night flights. Three EF-18s arrived from Torrejón and a French AWACS remained at the base until the end of the course. If the opening hours of the hangar with daytime missions are from 08:00 to 22:00 (if there is not a squadron that requests to stay working longer), during that week the opening hours are from 12:00 to 02:00 … in theory. WO Jiménez Zarantón says 'in theory', because throughout this course there were also morning missions directly coordinated between the different countries and Spain, which meant the hangar had to be open from 06:00. How do you do this with only four MCs? Simple; just wanting to get the job done, with professionalism and strenuous work day after day.

On Friday, after the mission, the EF-18s returned to Torrejón and were relieved by fighters from Zaragoza. It was during the fourth and last week of the course in which more personnel and material participated, when Personnel Recovery (PR) missions were flown. Everything went as planned.

Another of the TLP's peculiarities relates to emergencies; should any occur, there is an Operating Procedure (OP) established by the Base (and agreed with the TLP) by which the rescue services of the base participate in the rescue of the aircraft, reinforced with the necessary TLP personnel, according to the type emergency and the squadron to which the plane belongs. The establishment of this OP was a success, given the varied types of participating aircraft, the exhaustive knowledge of the Base Rescue Services was incomprehensible for the normal maintenance technicians, apart from the quantity and variety of specific rescue material and equipment necessary for each case. It was certainly a success. In fact, accidents are waiting to happen, and safety measures never are excessive.

During the 2014-01 academic year several emergencies were dealt with, all swiftly, professionally and successfully. The most serious incident was when a helicopter with thirteen people on board had a total failure of the hydraulic system.

Once the aircraft leave the parking area and before returning after the flight, the armourers activate or deactivate respectively the pyrotechnic materials such as flares, to avoid any risk of spontaneous firing. Armourers serving a Greek Mirage 2000 after a mission. Their job consists of deactivating the flares before entering the parking area. (*Salvador Mafé*)

But also some other minor accidents happened during this course. One of those occurred with an aircraft parked and properly grounded, when one of the mechanics, leaning on the windshield's arc, received a strong shock of static electricity. This suggests that although the static discharge wire was grounded, it was possibly broken internally, not performing its function of discharging static properly. Another accident was related to a line mechanic, used to working around the planes, who hit his head on the fin of a missile, receiving an injury requiring five stitches.

And so we come to 6 February with the last mission and the beginning of the withdrawal. At noon, all the technical officers were summoned to the closing meeting of the course. Attending are the Colonel Chief of the TLP and the Chief of the Flying Branch. This is the time when the TLP chief colonel thanks each squadron for their effort in achieving the objectives and for the technical officers to present their ideas directly to the 'Big Chief', bypassing the MCs.

Withdrawal

That same day, once the mission of the day was over and the planes returned to the base, eleven fighters returned to their home bases with the activity in maintenance *in crescendo*. Everything had to be organized and palletized.

Everyone wanted to be the first, everyone with established departure time and everyone wanting priority. It is understandable that after a month away from home, everyone was looking forward to going back.

On 7 February activity continued at an intense level. The usual thing was to have everything ready, so that, after the departure of their own fighters, they finished loading and thus returned home as soon as possible. Others, once everything was palletized, left, leaving their transport in charge of the logistics teams that would take care of it.

The same number of air and road transports were received again; this time to take away what they had brought. Now the staff was not coming, but departing, and leaving the operations area empty. The course as everything came to an end. In all, almost 1,200 people had participated with a peak of 580 operating at the same time.

To pass from some days of intense activity, with the runways and aprons full of people and planes to see in hours the same spaces practically empty and as if nothing had happened, leaves a strange bittersweet sensation floating in the air.

Conclusions

With his experience in mind, WO Jiménez Zarantón outlines the following:

- A common language for joint operations must be mandatory.
- Safety is never absolute, even if it seems like it.
- Personal Protective Equipment (PPE) is to be used 'always'.

Interview with Chief Warrant Officer (OR-9) Antonio B. Jiménez Zarantón

Antonio B. Jiménez Zarantón is a true TLP veteran, having been there from the very beginning. He has served under all the Spanish commandants and has broad, first-hand insight of the courses and therefore his opinions are very well founded.

After long years of service in the Spanish Air Force, he has recently retired with the rank of Lieutenant (OF-1) enjoying a well-deserved rest.

Q: How long have you been assigned to the TLP?

A: I have been assigned to the program since 07/01/2007.

Q: What functions have you performed? What are your current obligations?

A: When I went to Florennes, I was working as Maintenance Coordinator and later, in 2008, I was appointed as Maintenance Manager, a newly created position. With the relocation of the TLP in 2009, at the Albacete Airbase, my task consisted of defining a new maintenance system due to the particularities that the Airbase that currently hosts us has and making it work in a safe and operational way. With my promotion to Chief Warrant Officer, I left my duties in Maintenance to take on new responsibilities. Now I advise the TLP Commandant on various issues especially regarding personnel and I assist him in matters of protocol. I am an integral part of the Flight Safety and Ground Safety teams, I act as a liaison between the TLP and the Base in relation to maintenance, I am responsible for preserving, verifying and processing the security clearances of the TLP staff and I manage the Environmental Protection and Labor Risks systems of the TLP, in addition to those particular tasks that the TLP Commandant charges me with.

Q: During all this time, what aspects would you highlight about the evolution of the program. What aspects of progress would you indicate?

A: The current TLP is little like that of 12 years ago. For the participants, the use of new technologies makes everything more instructive and realistic, with which the training has improved a lot in quality. The courses are larger (in number of planes) and more ground and air support means are involved, so the mission can definitely be compared to a real mission. With regard to facilities, as they are all new, they have been designed using current techniques, for greater practicality, meeting all needs and requirements. In addition, with the relocation of the TLP to the Albacete Airbase and due to the good weather in this area, the number of mission aborts due to meteorological causes has practically been reduced to zero, which means that the expenses caused by the course are fully amortized.

Q: Always according to your experience: What is missing and what is to spare from the program?

A: In my opinion, the TLP, has nothing spare. On the contrary, during flight courses, when the schedule is extended from 08:00 to 22:00, a little more permanent staff would be very useful.

Q: What are the main difficulties of working with so many different types of aircraft and people?

A: Indeed, I think that is the greatest challenge of working in TLP and especially in Maintenance. Different weapon systems[2] with different procedures and requirements, personnel with not very good knowledge of the working language [English], all working at the same time …coordinating everything and everyone in a relatively small space, without affecting the activity of some to others and that the execution of each and every one of

---

2. Although this comment may suggest the use of real weapons in the TLP courses, it is not like that, but just a professional way of speaking. In general, a combat aircraft is a weapons system, even some prefer to call it a system of systems. For example, it has a fuel system, a hydraulic system, an electrical system, a communications system, a weapons system, etc. In the TLP courses, the warplanes only use electronic equipment that simulates real weapons, but only from the electronic point of view, providing the pilot with electronic signals similar to those produced by real weapons. The use of real weapons is expressly prohibited.

Armée de l'Air et Espace Alpha Jets are frequent participants at the TLP's Flying Courses as 'Red Air'. (*R. Treviño*)

the activities is maintained with safety standards with excellence a lot of work, effort and dedication is required.

TLP's External Support Organizations (Los Llanos-Albacete's Airbase)

For the successful development of the TLP missions, the support provided by the neighbouring Albacete Airbase and some sections of the Ala 14, as we will see, is essential.
As an Ala 14 colonel said:

> The TLP plays a very important role in the daily work of Albacete's Airbase and it is our duty to provide them with all the support they need, so that they can take the courses forward. We must also take into account that we are the showcase of the Unit before the international component, with all the implementations that this has, because what is at stakes is the prestige of the Unit and therefore that of the Ejército del Aire.

Supporting TLP (The Base)

One of the fundamental support elements that the TLP needs is the fuel for the aircraft. It must be taken into consideration that when the courses are in progress, there is an estimated average of 600-plus sorties during the four/three weeks the flight courses are running. This is addition to the normal fuel required by the fighters of Ala 14 and that needed by MAESAL for flight testing.

As a general rule, one month before the course begins, the TLP headquarters communicates to the base the estimated fuel needs for all participating aircraft, which is not only limited to the students' aircraft, but also the fuel required by the transport aircraft supporting the deployment, which are usually large multi-engined aircraft such as C-130s, KC-135s, AWACS, Airbus 300s, Spartans ... etc, which represents an additional consumption of more than 500,000 litres.

According to the chief of the Operational Support Squad: 'The total consumption usually does not drop below 3,500,000 litres during a course.'

As soon as the fuel needs are communicated, the information is sent to Mando Aéreo General (Ejército del Aire (MAGEN) via Seguridad en las Comunicaciones (SECOM) so that forecasts can be made and delivered to the base in due time and the fuel tanks are full. Depending on the number of participants, an average of 600 refuellings are necessary, which requires the work of four people in two shifts during morning and afternoon, dedicated only to refuelling planes.

Runways Section and Foreign Object Damage (FOD) Team

At the Los Llanos Airbase deploy all types of aircraft, consequently it is necessary to carry out a more detailed study than one might think to design the parking plan. It is necessary to analyze the various air intakes and exhaust nozzles of all types of aircraft and according to the analysis, assign them an appropriate slot adequate to their particular conditions.

It is not the same as the downwards of big helicopters main rotors, nor the exhaust of a MV-22 with the big downwash of its proprotors.

According to the Sublieutenant José Diaz, Chief of the FOD team 'The F-16, due to the very low position of their air intake, must be pampered a lot. Any small stone can easily be sucked in, damaging an engine worth several million euros.'

This is taken very seriously, as the authors have been able to verify. Whenever a wheeled vehicle enters parking areas or runways, drivers should stop the vehicle and inspect the wheels to make sure that no stone is caught in the tread of the tires which may come off. Even photographers are not allowed to walk outside paved areas to avoid small stones sticking to the soles of their shoes.

To avoid problems, the F-16s are the first to be assigned a position in the parking lot, normally separate from the non-paved areas, and located in such a way as to minimize the risk of FOD considerably. On the first day of aircraft arrival, the Runways Section plays a fundamental role. All the aircraft are escorted one by one to their place assigned in the parking lot. This work is important because on most the occasions it is the first time for the pilots to land at the Los Llanos base. To park a formation of four aircraft usually takes half an hour since the 'Follow me' is done one by one, as mentioned and at a speed that does not exceeds that of a running man, as dictated by the operating procedures.

The first day is the most complicated: new planes of different nationalities arrive and the staff does not know what they will find. That day work begins at 09:00 and ends at sunset. It is hard, but when in the end all the planes are parked, the personnel gets the reward of seeing the E-2 platform, completely full and in which there is no longer room for a pin.

Sección de Apoyo al Transporte Aéreo (SATA – Air Transport Support Section)

The SATA Section deserves a mention, which plays a key role in the deployment and withdrawal phases of the TLP. Their numbers during a course, are equivalent to those of a base during a full year and that happens three or four times a year, if courses are not cancelled for reasons beyond the control of the organization.

The weight of equipment moved by staff during a course amounts to some 100,000kg and the number of transients reaches 800 people according to SATA data. All these amounts imply an extra workload that is concentrated especially on the days of deployment and withdrawal. The days prior to the end of the course are the ones that generate the most work for SATA. As is logical, all participants want to be the first to see their assets prepared and loaded to return home, so requests to SATA are made for 'the same day and the same time'.

To be able to attend to all cargo requests without making changes or delays to them, it would be necessary to triple the personnel and cargo machinery, so cargo shifts are established that are normally organized in relation to the take-off time of the respective aircraft of applicants. According to the ATOC (Air Terminal Operations Centre) Implementation Plan (AIP) the SATA staff's normal working hours are established from 08:00 to 14:30, Monday to Friday.

However, due to the peculiarities of the TLP, and the large amount of cargo that is handled, this is extended till sunset during the days of deployment and withdrawal, including weekends. Having said this, thanks to the effort of the staff that in less than three days all the Auxiliary Ground Equipment (AGE) necessary for the detachments of the different participating nations is loaded or unloaded.

EOD, Contra Incendios y Equipos de Rescate (Explosive Ordnance Disposal, Firefighting and Rescue Teams)

The safety of air weapons is one of the pillars of flight safety. In the case of the TLP, although live weapons are not used, it is important to know the details and peculiarities of the aircraft that will use chaff and flares during the missions. According to the Armament Security Officer: 'It is our responsibility to act correctly in the event of a hot flare'.

Subteniente Juan Carlos Castro describes the procedure followed.

> The Tuesday prior to the start of the flight course, we met with all the chiefs of the Detachments of the participating nations. The Fire Fighting Section also attends and all together they review the operational procedures and visually inspect the chaff and flare housings. of all aircraft, most, are already known, but it is our duty to ensure and inform foreign personnel of the base procedures related to weapons security.

The rescue team of the Fire Section is obviously essential for the rescue of pilots in case of emergencies, taking into account that some aircraft models are the first time that participates in a course, the EOD staff must know the procedures of the different ejection seats of all participating aircraft and their peculiarities, which is a complex task, but necessary for a good performance if need arises.

This is contemplated in the basic training plan, that includes all the procedures referring to the rescue of pilots, which prepares the personnel for almost any eventuality.

Seguridad en Vuelo (Flight Safety)

The Base Flight Safety Meeting takes place every month, usually the last Thursday of the month. The Oficial de Seguridad en Vuelo (OSV – Flight Safety Officer) of the TLP participates as a guest as a spokesmen member, and on many occasions, the Chief Colonel of the TLP also attends. From mid-2013 Major Cavil of the Greek Air Force played the TLP's OSV role. Currently this position is held by the Spanish Lt. Colonel A.F. García Masso (colonel at the present time)

The meetings are held in English and are discussed all the incident reports written by the pilots during the TLP course, the result of the hydrazine drill, which is a delicate element to deal with, is carried out in the first mission, FOD reports and any other news that both; the base and the TLP, consider that may have an impact on Flight Safety.

These meetings contribute considerably to improving the communication between the two units that coexist in the base and also to improve all briefings, coordination rules, incident reports, etc that are necessary for the proper functioning of the demanding courses that are teach in the TLP.

As an example, let's suppose that during a course, there has been a problem in an instrumental recovery of an aircraft formation and one of the pilots has written a Flight Safety report. This is studied first in the Board and normally, the conclusions are introduced directly in the briefing of local procedures that is given to the TLP's pilots during the theoretical sessions of the course.

As mentioned before, it is considered very important that any part of Flight Safety communicated by the TLP, be considered as if it were one of the EdA, that is, that solutions are sought instead of culprits.

La Oficina Meteorológica (The Meteorological Office)
A factor of central importance for the success of air operations is the meteorological information. Not only at the aircrafts' departing airbase, but also over the target area that is miles away.

Meteorology support is provided by Aeropuertos Españoles y Navegación Aérea (AENA) and civilian personnel who provide their services at the Albacete Airbase for Ala 14.

In the case of Albacete, a forecaster from the Meteorological Office is responsible for giving the meteorology briefings at the TLP, for which a good level of English is essential. The Head of the Agencia Estatal de Meteorología (AEMET) Office of Los Llanos base, comments on the matter: 'Bad meteorological information on the wind or clouds ceiling, can suppose that more than 30 aircraft may finish the mission in an alternative aerodrome.' He also adds that language is vital when working for the TLP and also that is necessary to be very precise in your predictions, because this is required by the type of missions carried out, since everything has to be planned and coordinated for a large number of aircraft. A significant failure in the weather predictions could ruin everything planned and with it the mission objectives.

Normally, the meteorology staff arrives at their office two hours before the start of the first TLP's briefing, in order to study the meteorological situation of the day and prepare the presentation to be made as a computer file.

Every course day, there are four briefings, plus an additional one depending on the mission of the day. The first briefing takes place between 08:45 and 09:30 with the mission chiefs, to assess whether the mission is feasible under the weather conditions foreseen during the flight window (15:00 to 18:00).

The second briefing is the general one and is carried out with all the participants of the mission attending. The third and fourth are done just before the pilots board their planes These are known as 'Step briefings' and are usually held around 14:00. It is necessary to point out that the predictions are for the flight window and for the specific area that will be used for the mission of the day. Is very important to be able to specify if there is any layer of the atmosphere, with a minimum thickness of 10,000ft (3,048m), in which the presence of clouds is not significant as to not prevent the development of the mission, since with so many aircraft in the same airspace, it is necessary to maintain visual conditions.

If favourable conditions are not met, the mission of the day could be cancelled. During the flight window in which the planes are in the air, weather monitoring is carried out. If any unforeseen phenomenon is detected or is considered important for the operation of the aircraft, it is communicated to the TLP for decision-making in this regard. The working day ends when the planes return to the base, around 18:30, but sometimes later, if the take-off time has been delayed for any reason.

La Torre de Control (The Control Tower)

The most difficult job, without a doubt, is the one performed by the Control Tower. In a standard mission, more than thirty departures are controlled in less than an hour, with the aircraft take-off with a separation of 2–3 minutes. However, take-offs are not the most complicated to manage. In all missions a taxi plan is made in advance, and the formations respect it to the maximum so the taxi is done orderly. One of the controllers' main concerns is, without a doubt, the recovery to Albacete (RTB). The return of all the formations is carried out according to a procedure. This means that since the first aircraft until the last of all has landed, have elapsed some 40 minutes.

To accomplish this phase correctly, it is essential a good coordination between the Ground Control Interception (GCI *Polar* or *Pegaso*) and Albacete APP (Approach). Normally the GCI transfers the traffic already sequenced, so Albacete only has to authorize it to make the approach, giving the pilots at the same time the updated meteorological information of the field. The problem occurs when traffic does not arrive in sequence from the GCI. In these cases, there is no other possible solution than to authorize them to wait in an orderly fashion, until the separation required by the Air Traffic Regulations is reestablished, which may mean that the recovery lasts for more than one hour. According to Second Lieutenant Juan Carlos Bonal:

> The level of training and instruction received by the controllers is very high. The proof of this is that teachers from the Matacán AB Air Traffic School, often come during the TLP courses to carry out practices and learn from the Albacete's staff, being this an unique opportunity for them. Always something is learn in all courses, but it is also a unique opportunity to see in real time, how is managed the recovery of more than 30 aircraft in just 45 minutes.

Occupational hazards

The transport of all the necessary material for the detachments, such as AGE equipment, APU, maintenance tools etc., arrives at the base by read, using heavy trucks that are sometimes military and other times civil. In both cases, there must be coordination for the prevention of occupational hazards between the civil companies or the corresponding

Air Force with the Office for the Prevention of Occupational Risks of the TLP and the Prevention Service of the Albacete Base to which the said office is attached.

This coordination is carried out in order to comply with Royal Decree 171/2004 on 'Coordination of Business Activities', which has been adapted by a specific procedure, at the level of the Ejército del Aire. Although it is a complex and sometimes tedious work, this is intended, on one hand to have an exchange of preventive information between participating units and companies, in order to minimize possible risk factors, and on the other hand, as mentioned above, to faithfully comply with said legal regulations on Occupational Risk Prevention. In agreement with this is the Head of the Prevention Service No. 11 of the Albacete Airbase: 'The reason for all this is as easy to understand, as everyone who accesses a third-party facility must have information available on the occupational risks at which may be exposed, as well as knowing how to act in the event of an emergency situation.' He states that: 'These people, in turn, must also report the activities they are going to carry out in the facilities, for if as a consequence of them, they can put other personnel present in the workplace at risk.'

Security

TLP does not has a security squadron as such. Security depends on the Albacete Airbase. There is an element/Support Group, which is in charge of the necessary coordination with the Base in this area, as well as many other things.

The work carried out by the Security Personnel in behalf of TLP simply masterful. The numbers speak for themselves, as an example in the course of TLP 1-2014 (lasting from 13 January to 7 February 2014) more than a thousand identification passes were made, and 160 rental cars for the benefit of the participating crews and 65 taxi entrances were managed, in addition to controlling the security of all personnel and planes. In this sense, during the courses the day and night security is reinforced, and periodic patrols are carried out to make sure that everything is in order and also to make sure that no aircraft has liquid spills, such as fuel, hydraulics or oil. It is logical to think that with so much movement there must be a problem at some point. However, thanks to the professionalism and disposition of the security personnel, they are always solved, passing the problems to the field of anecdotes.

We cannot conclude this chapter without mentioning Albacete's Maestranza (MAESAL), which is often used to carry out on-site repairs of breakdowns that would otherwise leave the affected aircraft grounded, awaiting a difficult and costly recovery to its home base.

The 'Persian Market'

When there is a course in progress, the area around the TLP´s hangar, looks like a 'Persian Market', completely littered with all kinds of auxiliary ground equipment for the different models of aircraft deployed, as can be seen in the collection of photographs that follows. (*All images Salvador Mafè*)

A portable engine bench for French Rafale SNECMA M88 engines. In the background can be seen the air-portable containers to safely transport the engines once removed from the aircraft. These are pressurized when the engine is being teletransported to avoid penetration of moisture and debris.

A portable engine bench for French Rafale SNECMA M88 engines with the protection cage for the upper part of the engine.

A French Azote compressed-air generator and its towing device, both easily air-portable.

A multi-purpose crane.

External fuel tanks ready to be used if the need or the mission demand their use in the aircraft.

Racks for aircraft loads wait to be used in case the need arises.

Spare auxiliary fuel tanks of a different model. Each air force brings their own.

Support for an AN-ALQ 131V pod. This pod is a different model from the other jamming pods in use. According to Northrop-Grumman, the AN/ALQ-131 Electronic Countermeasures pod is the most successful ECM system ever built. More than 1,600 pods of this model have been fielded. These use state-of-the-art technology to successfully protect aircrews and aircraft in every conflict since becoming operational.

One of the much-demanded towing tractors owned by TLP.

Rear view of the towing tractor.

An aircraft tow bar, also in high demand.

To avoid 'confusions and temptations' the TLP's ground equipment is clearly marked '**TLP PROPERTY**', like this tow bar.

Tractor and tow bar at work.

Another type of more capable tractor in service with the TLP.

Here we see a different type of tractor in service with a fork lift behind it. This is used to help loading and unloading heavy equipment from the cargo trucks and/or cargo aircraft.

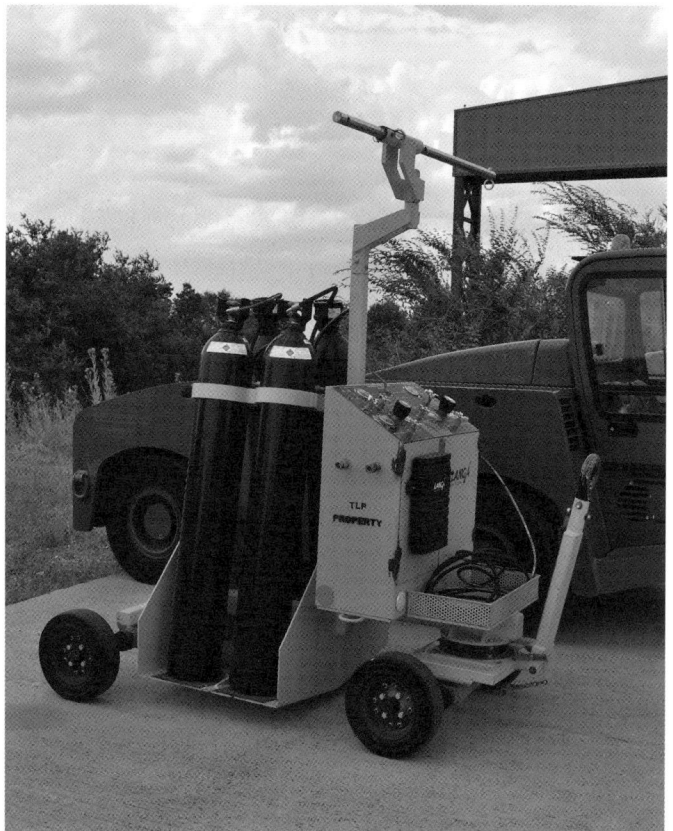

This yellow-painted trolley carries four oxygen cylinders used to refill aircraft crew oxygen respiration system. Given its 'convenient' size, it is also marked 'TLP PROPERTY'.

The oxygen trolley being towed to service one of the aircraft in the line.

The TLP's wheeled platform to carry practice missiles or similar loads.

A portable hydraulic bench for testing and/or repairing aircraft hydraulic systems.

Auxiliary Power Unit, popularly known as an AP, used to provide a source of power to aircraft for testing electrical systems .

Some of the wealthier air forces prefer to bring their own tractors to the TLP to avoid waiting, in this case a Bundeswehr Mercedes Unimog U-318.

A Polish F-16 being towed to the maintenance hangar for servicing by one of the TLP's more capable tractors.

Prior to the launch of a flying course or immediately after the landing of the aircraft, the refuelling cisterns can be seen busy refilling the aircraft tanks for the next day's mission. These cisterns nominally belong to the Albacete´s Air Base/Ala 14 and its effort and contribution to the success of the course is fundamental.

One of the many civilian cargo trucks that transport ground equipment for the aircraft taking part in TLP courses.

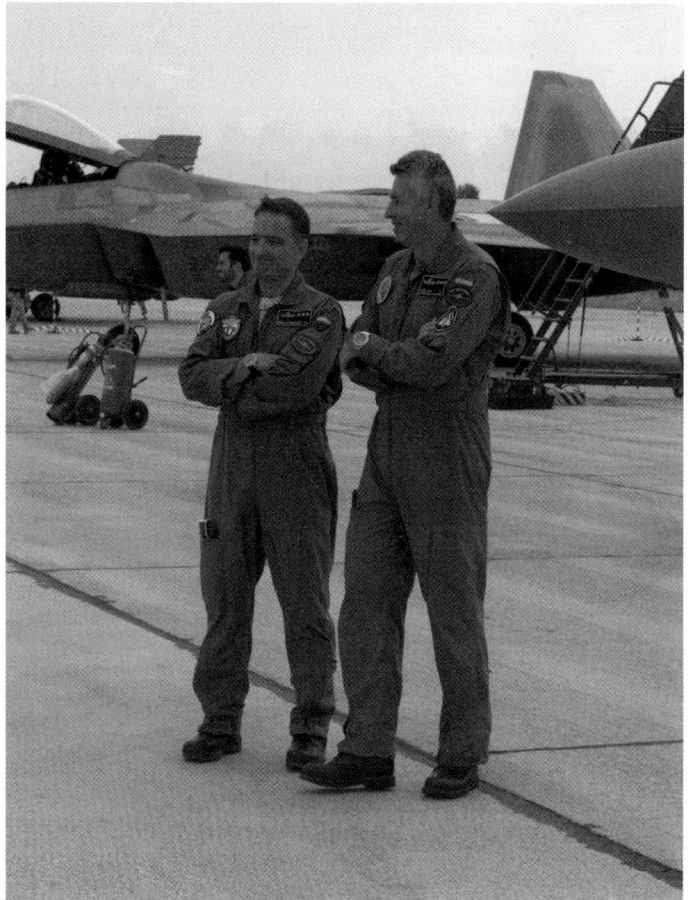

Colonel Andrés Maldonado (left), TLP commander, and Colonel Juan Manuel Pablos Chi, Ala 14 commander. Cooperation between both units is essential for the proper development of the TLP courses.

Suboficial Mayor (Chief Warrant Officer) Antonio B. Jiménez Zarantón. A true TLP veteran, having been at the programme from the very beginning. He has served under all the Spanish TLP´s Commandants until 2020. Has broad, first-hand insight into the courses and therefore his opinions are very well founded. During those years has been appointed Maintenance Manager. Also he escorted patiently the authors and other press representatives during the visits to the base, for which he must be fully acknowledged and thanked. After long years of service in the Spanish Air Force, he has recently retired with the rank of Lieutenant (OF-1) enjoying a well-deserved rest. (*R. Treviño*)

WO Antonio B. Jiménez Zarantón, holding the TLP´s flag during the change of programme command ceremony in 2018. (*R. Treviño*)

Chapter 10

'That others may live … and return with honour'

This is the motto widely accepted by the military units and organizations dedicated to Personnel Recovery (PR) activities.

Today world's paradigms are quickly changing, and we are spectators of these changes, without understanding too well the future consequences. These changes are affecting all the aspects of our societies, including military behaviours.

Probably we will not see a full-scale war as in the past, but as is notorious, we are surrounded by a myriad of small, never-ending regional conflicts that requires the implication of external powers to prevent its expansion and desirably, achieve its end. Meanwhile this happens, many people, either civil and military personnel, are involved and affected by these events, in some cases requiring to be rescued from difficult situations.

Colonel Andrés Maldonado, TLP Commandant. (*Salvador Mafé*)

Over the past decades, situations involving isolated personnel have had a profound impact on politicians and the general public. Because the availability of television and internet, people receive detailed information and remain gripped by more of these cases. There are many examples where isolated personnel or hostages have caused political embarrassment, and military operations even had been significantly altered or stopped, due to sensitivities related to public perception.

We can recall the numerous rescue missions of downed aircrews accomplished during the Vietnam War. Also can be mentioned the cases of pilot Major Gianmarco Bellini and his navigator Captain Maurizio Cocciolone of the Italian Aeronautica Militare, or the RAF's Flight Lieutenants Peters and Nichols, all four downed in their Tornadoes by Iraqi air defences during Operation Desert Storm, whose sorrowful images were widely broadcast on Iraqi television, or the more recent rescue mission by a CSAR team of Scott O'Grady, an F-16 US pilot downed in Bosnia, after six days stranded in 1995. The bad guys, knowing the deep impact caused by these events, have learned to exploit it for their own benefit and maximum dissemination of their ideas.

Thus, the recovery of so-called 'Isolated Persons' from these situations is becoming increasingly important, now that the consequences at national, international, political and military levels, are understood. While the significance of these matters is recognized, PR activity is developing slowly.

Definitions

We should begin with the definitions to clarify the meaning of many military operations that seem similar, but in fact incorporate substantial differences.

According to NATO's Joint Air Power Competence Centre (JAPCC), the term 'Personnel Recovery', defines 'the sum of military, diplomatic and civil efforts to effect the recovery and reintegration of isolated personnel'. This definition is widely accepted and is the proposed definitive description for both NATO and the European Union. This definition, as is notorious, does not include nor limit the resources that can be utilized during the recovery effort.

Continuing with the definitions, we will now review the concept of 'Isolated Person' (IP) that JAPCC defines as: The military or civilian personnel who are separated from their unit or organization in a situation that may require them to survive, evade, resist exploitation, or escape while awaiting recovery.' This is also proposed as the formal definition of the concept for both NATO and EU. It means that if a person or persons are unable to continue the mission and cannot return by means of the pre-planned arrangements, he or she may be considered an isolated person. This is most obvious in the case of aircrews who have been forced to eject from their aircraft 'behind enemy lines', but the list of personnel that can be considered 'isolated' is long.

In addition to his own nationals, NATO and EU forces, the force commander must also consider all those participants within the theatre of operations that are not subordinated

The use of the MV-22 certainly increases the 'Golden Ring' around the departing base and it is faster that an helicopter. We had some MV-22s participating in our Flying and Academic course. The fact is that if you want to use the Osprey for a PR mission you need a bigger landing zone, and this is not always available, (an Osprey needs at least 50m² to land and 100m between every MV-22 on the ground) and more time for the landing and take-off procedure (the MV-22 landing phase takes quite a long time). Ospreys belonged to SPMAGTF-CR-AF deployed at Morón airbase. (*USMC*)

to him, such as members of governmental and nongovernmental organizations, reporters, etc. Depending upon the number of those 'other' personnel and situations, the techniques and procedures and assets used to recover them may be different.

Thus under the umbrella of the common definition of 'PR', appear the more specialized missions as Search and Rescue (SAR), Combat Recovery (CR) and Combat Search and Rescue (CSAR) and their respective definitions, that in the NATO environment, have been developed in isolation and at separated times. The most generally accepted definitions are as follows.

Search and Rescue (SAR) missions consist of 'The location and recovery of persons in distress in an environment where hostile interference is not expected'. Examples are the missions launched to search for the persons on board a missing ship, not necessarily military, or people lost in the mountains during a weekend excursion.

Combat Recovery (CR) consists of 'the recovery of isolated personnel from a situation where hostile interference may be expected'. An important factor in those missions is that the personnel to be rescued is not trained in the CSAR Tactics, Techniques and Procedures (TTP) and consequently does not contribute too much to the rescue effort.

Finally and the most diffused and probably the oldest PR mission, is the Combat Search and Rescue (CSAR). Probably, this was the first type of mission which began to be developed with the purpose of recovering IP. Now it is defined as: 'The application of specific tactics, techniques and procedures by dedicated forces to recover isolated personnel

The Aeronautica Militare provided two HH139 CSAR helicopters assigned to 15° Stormo. (*Salvador Mafé*)

Ala 12 and Ala 15 EF-18Ms as well as Italian F-2000s from 4ª Stormo acted as Blue Air, and the former as Sandy, that is, close escort to the CSAR helicopters. (*Salvador Mafé*)

who themselves are trained and appropriately equipped to receive this support, from a situation where hostile interference may be expected'. Obviously, depending of the mission type, the assets to be employed will be different.

PR missions are complex in nature. A complexity which is added to by the different ideas and methods that each nation has to address the problem. Thus, all these definitions does not express, but are wishful thinking, in search of a common posture to address the problem internationally.

In Europe, only Belgium and France have national PR policies. Outside the EU, The US is the only nation that conducts national cross-governmental exercises dedicated to PR and jointly exercises between all military arms. Belgium and France have based their policies on the NATO's draft PR policy. Instead, US policy predated NATO's policy and was used as the basis for NATO's own policy development. Some other countries, like Italy, have only CSAR national policies, but all seven countries included within the European Air Group (EAG), are participating in successive iterations of the Combined Joint Personnel Recovery Standardization Courses (CJPRSC).

Today in Europe, the personnel who can be part of a PRCC in the Joint Force Air Component (JFAC) and intend to complete the specific formation in PR, have two courses recommended; the until now theoretical CSAR, course taught by the TLP in Albacete, and the PR course taught by the Centre d'Analyse et de Simulation pour la Préparation aux Opération Aériennes (CASPOA), in Lyon, France. These are the two courses that are, we could say, more aeronautically focused.

TLP's Rescue Mission Commander FC-1, 2024

The TLP School at Albacete AB developed an introductory PR (designated 'PR 101') intended for aircrews. This inaugural course successfully graduated in June 2010, but did not included flying activities, thus was a course of the Academic type. A further edition was planned in October 2011. Since then, in addition to the PR Academic courses, on every normal flying courses organized at TLP, there is one day that its dedicated to practising CSAR activities.

Now, with this new two-week specialized flying course, carried out between 29 June and 10 July 2024, purposefully educational courses have inaugurated to graduate tactical fast jet Rescue Mission Commanders in CSAR environment operations. According to TLP's Commandant, Colonel Maldonado, the intentions are to carried out such a course once a year at least, from now onward.

TLP's RMC FCs also aims to serve as the NATO-approved Combat Search and Rescue programme to train and upgrade RMC Instructors for NATO 'Salty' pilots, that is the NATO equivalent to the US 'Sandy' instructors. Once graduated, they can then return to their nations and instruct others as NATO CSAR experts.

Additionally, the RMC FCs are intended to improve the tactical interoperability of NATO air forces through the mutual exposure to the tactics and capabilities of other air forces and to provide a flying laboratory for tactical employments concepts between

No 8 Sqn RAF provided an E-3D Sentry, call sign MAGIC, which had a vital role during the CSAR mission. (*Salvador Mafé*)

participating nations,. The RMC FC also enables a free exchange of information on weapons, tactics and capabilities. The course provides an environment that encourages the discussion and development of multi-national tactics, allowing the participants to find the best way to employ different aircraft capabilities of the multinational forces in CSAR missions.

The lectures and missions are designed for the senior tactical aircrews or individuals with COMAO experience, with ranks of Captain or Major (OF2/3), with more than 1,000 flight hours, and with 500 hours of these spent as instructor on their actual platform.

The logical progression of TLP course attendance to become a RMC, begins with the Support Course, followed by the COMAO Synthetic Course, then the CSAR Academics course, the Flying Course and finally the RMC FC.

The secondary target audience is the support personnel likely to be involved in a CSAR in the future, including intelligence officers (INTEL), rescue vehicles and attack helicopters, fighter controllers (GCI), and Command and Control, Intelligence, Surveillance and Reconnaissance (C2ISR) operators.

Participation in these courses does not necessarily imply graduation. Each participant must meet basic mission capable status, determined by the Rescue Mission Commander IP with ultimate decision to CFB. After graduation personnel are presented with a proficiency certificate and will be referred to as RMC Instructor for European NATO

Two Mirage 2000B-RDIs from EC 2/5 'Ile de France' (call sign DEVIL) as well as one Rafale B from EC 2/4 'La Fayette' (call-sign VODKA) acted as Red Air during the 24 February CSAR mission. (*Salvador Mafé*)

Nations, a certificate that indicates their highest CSAR qualification, or a 'Salty' pilot, a much coveted qualification. Furthermore, a graduated RMC FC aircrew with current training, will be asked to act as Guesy Specialist to deliver and run future RMC FCs.

The TLP Plan of Operations (PoO) states that 'The ideal course will comprise twelve aircraft and crews, including eight in the air-to-ground (A/G) CSAR role, four rotary wing in the Rescue Vehicle role'. The ideal number of participants are: eight fighter jets (four pairs), four GCI/C2ISR participants and four INTEL participants. The minimum number of aircraft deemed necessary to conduct a RMC FC course is four fighter aircraft and two helicopters with their respective aircrews. Support units, such as AEW platforms and attack helicopters are integrated as much as possible. Also, non-combat ready or young combat ready aircrew are choose to act as IPs, in order to increase their CSAR knowledge on procedures by the SERE Specialist.

Support assets critical to the course are expert SERE instructors, UAVs, opposition forces with troops, vehicles and helicopters, Surface Based Air Defences (SBAD) systems, acting as tactical and mobile platforms (SA8 or decoy with TRTG/RWT, Mistral, Crotale or Roland). Slot allocations and procedures for non TLP's MOU participants are to be found in the latest version of the TLP PoO.

RMC FC Course Syllabus

This two-week long course uses a building-block approach through seven live missions: these step by step missions, teach the participant from the basics of CSAR, up to a variety of CSAR missions, including multi-survivor, non-conventional Search and Rescue, Immediate and on-call CSAR.

Each day, a different crew leads the mission as Rescue Mission Commander (RMC), or 'Salty 1' through all phases. Participants are exposed to Salty 1 to 4 specificities and responsibilities in low to medium intensity conflicts scenarios. Missions are flown from Albacete and use surrounding overland areas.

The RMC's duties

The RMC's responsibilities include: establishing communications, locating and authenticating the IP, prevent the CSAR team falling in a trap, and protecting the IP until the recovery assets arrive. The RMC controls all the assets assigned to the PR effort, including but not limited to rescue combat air patrol (RESCAP), suppression of enemy air defences (SEAD), additional strike aircraft, and the required aerial refuelling.

Based on the threat perceived for the IP and the recovery force, the rescue escort (RESCORT) is an integral part of the CSAR Task Force. RESCORT aircraft provide navigation assistance, route sanitization, and armed escort for the recovery vehicle(s). In increased threat environments, this assistance significantly improves the chances of a successful recovery.

Ideally, RESCORT aircraft should be tactical aircraft capable of operating in the same environment as the recovery vehicles. The RESCORT formations must be proficient

The Luftwaffe participated in FC 2024-1 with four Eurofighters, belonging to TAW 71 Wittmund and TAW 74 Neuburg, all within the Blue assets with the call signs VADER and BARON. Note the small Richthofen crest below the cockpit. (*Salvador Mafé*)

in rendezvous procedures, escort tactics at medium and low altitudes, and defence of the rescue vehicles during the mission execution. In the hands of qualified pilots, the A-10 is considered the premier RESCORT platform, based on its unique performance and capabilities.

In fact, Colonel Maldonado told us that he has tried hard to bring A-10 aircraft to participate in the RMC FC, but without success.

It is a pity, because the A-10s, usually associated with air-to-ground support activities, were not worthless adversaries in air-air activities.

According to veteran pilots who have participated in previous TLP courses with the A-10, even when these aircraft were not yet wired to use the Sidewinders for self-defence, they proved to be a formidable opponent due to their near-point manoeuvrability and its awesome 30mm GAU cannon.

Considering the effect of this weapon on tanks, it must have been terrifying to be within range of a slashing gun pass.

This capability took by surprise to many fighter crews and only the aggressive use of vertical manoeuvres eased the problem. To make things even worse, and just like in the Wild West movies, it was very hard to deal with a 'wagon wheel' defensive circle formed by four or six A-10s.

While the participation of the A-10 in the TLP courses is not possible, CSAR-qualified F-15E, F-16, F-18, AV-8 and AC-130 Spectre aircraft may be utilized as replacement for the A-10s. Rotary-wing escorts, such as the AH-64, AH-1 and MH-60L may be utilized as well but for the moment have not participated.

Recommended Capacities for RESCORT aircraft (*)

Communications
Sensors (FLIR, TDL, MIDS, SADL …)
Ability to fly at low speed and altitude.
Defence capability against ground to air threats.
Air refuelling capability
Low visibility
Capability to operate in darkness
Location equipment as ADF or LARS
Protection against EW
Armour protection
Firepower
Targeting Pods
Guided munitions

Source: JAPCC/Enhancing NATO JPR Capability Education and Training /May 2014

Concerning this matter, within the environment of the PR experts, assigning the RMC to a specific crew still generates some controversies.

The TLP, an institution that has been teaching TTPs for many years in its PR Academic courses, has done it with the help of personnel from A-10 units, but in the European theatre the A-10 is considered a 'rara avis'.

Then, in the absence of the Warthogs, other procedures have been adapted to aircraft that do not have the capabilities of the A-10 at all. The participating aircraft, such as the EF-18 and EF-2000 in the case of Spain, emulate the main tasks of the USAF A-10 units.

Until the institution of the RMC flight courses, the result was, that at best, only one of the crews acting as mission commander attempted to execute the same type of mission as the dedicated and perfectly trained crews.

Talking to one TLP graduate pilot of the TLP's neighbouring Ala 14, Captain Fernando Caballero, he says that the aircraft of the RMCs must be a 'comfortable aircraft', meaning that most of the flying time of the RMC is employed flying orbits over the rescue area coordinating the CSAR forces, as related. He describes that this job is done with the aircraft flying with a 25° bank, and also adds, for example, that the Mirage F-1 was not a good RMC aircraft because of its speed.

Another figure related to the CSAR Operations is the On-scene Commander (OSC). This is the individual who initiates the rescue efforts in the objective areas until rescue

An MV-22 of VMM-263 'Thunder Chickens' with the engine nacelles set at 90º for a vertical landing. The flight control system of the V-22 is of the full authority digital fly-by-wire type, still operational with two failures and driven by a redundant triple hydraulic system, of which two systems manage the aircraft in normal state and the third is a backup. The aircraft can be recovered with a single operating hydraulic system. The vectorization of the thrust is achieved by tilting the gondolas of the engines from the horizontal position or 0º, to fly in aircraft mode, up to 97º 30' (7º, 30' beyond the vertical), in helicopter mode. With the nacelles set between 0º and 30º is considered aircraft mode, between 30º and 84º is considered the transition mode and between 84º and 97,5º is considered helicopter mode. Flying with the nacelles set at 97,5º the aircraft flies rearwards or slows down. The flight system sets automatically the flaperons position accordingly. To change the incidence of the nacelles, the pilot has a control wheel in the Thrust Control Lever (TCL) that has two modes of operation; the *continuous* and the *discrete*. In continuous mode, the nacelles tilt up or down while the pilot acts on the control wheel. While operating in discrete, the nacelles move to predetermined positions with each pilot's action, these are 0º, 60º, 75º and 90º, in both directions, up and down. (*R. Treviño*)

forces arrive. Initially, the OSC may be any aircraft in the vicinity, including the wingman of the downed aircraft. The OSC's initial actions are to attempt to establish communications, locate and authenticate the IP, and pass the essential elements of information to the Airborne Mission Commander (AMC), the OSC role will be transferred to the RMC, or lead recovery vehicle upon arrival. After transferring OSC duties to the RMC, the original OSC may remain on station in a supporting role.

SERE

This acronym stands for Survival, Evasion, Resistance and Extraction. We have previously mentioned that the 'invitation' to the young pilots to act as IPs is done to increase their knowledge on SERE procedures and also that a critical asset for the RMC courses are the SERE instructors.

As mentioned before, the CSAR defined as the employment of specific TTPs by dedicated forces, to recover isolated personnel who themselves are trained and appropriately equipped to receive this support. Although reference to the aircrew survival equipment is made, the CSAR manual does not mention the type of training that personnel should receive. The issue about this matter was raised at the September 2004 SAR panel at which was agreed that a standard of SERE training would be beneficial. A validation proposal was drafted and in early 2005 and the MCASB formally tasked the SAR Panel to develop a SERE Training standard.

The resulting SERE training concept is based on three levels of training:

Basic training (Level A).
Intermediate training (Level B).
Advanced training (Level C).

As effective SERE training is considered an accumulative process, Instructors should progress through levels A, B and C with additional instructor training. The SERE training package combines generic functional and doctrinal training with SERE-specific continuation, theatre and reintegration training. Obviously a SERE-trained aircrew improves their chances to survive and be recovered as he or she can contribute actively to the rescue mission.

Speaking to a SERE-trained participant in the RMC FC-1 course, who spoke on condition of anonymity for being an actual active SOF member, they said that the SERE training 'is not a joke', and that some of the procedures applied to the trainee are the same used by the bad guys in case of being captured., adding that not all the participants in a SERE training week, can overcome it, despite knowing that they are not prisoners of the enemy, so realistic is it.

SERE Instructional Training Targets

Survival	Address the priorities of survival: protection, location, water and food. Maintain psychological and physiological wellbeing. Maintain normal body temperature. Maintain adequate hydration. Maintain sufficient caloric intake.
Evasion	Use locations aids. Avoid detection whilst static and mobile. Plan and execute an evasion plan of action.
Resistance	Assesses conditions of capture. Protect sensitive information. Mitigate physical and mental stresses. Maintain self and others (survive with dignity). Limit exploitation. Attempt to escape if practicable.
Extraction	Promote own recovery. Establish communications with friendly forces. Aid rescue/release. Carry out rendezvous procedures. Carry out recovery/pick up. Procedures.

Participating Units in RMC FC-1 of 2024

Blue Air

Aircraft Type	Unit	Country	Main Base	Call sign	Dates	Role
2 x EF-2000	14 Wing	Spain	Albacete	Jedi	Weeks 1 & 2	Multire
2 x EF-2000	11 Wing	Spain	Morón	Sabre	Weeks 1 & 2	Multire

Red Air

Aircraft Type	Unit	Country	Main Base	Call sign	Dates	Role
MV-22B	VMM-263	USA	Morón	Mig	6 & 7 July	Op For

Support Assets

Aircraft Type	Unit	Country	Main Base	Call sign	Part. Dates	Role
2xSuper Puma	48 Wing, 803 Sqdn	Spain	Madrid Getafe	Snail	Weeks 1 & 2	CSAR
2xCaracal	4 Reg. of SOF	France	Cazaux	Rocky	Weeks 1 & 2	CSAR
1xE2C Hawkeye	14 Flotille	France	Lann Bihoué	Damo	3 July	AWAC
1x Boeing E3C	'Berry' EDCA	France	Avord Airbase	Cyrano	6 & 7 July	AWAC
1 x KC-130J	VMGR-252	USA	Morón	Atlas	8 & 9 July	SLOM
2 x MV-22	VMM-263	USA	Morón	Globe	8 & 9 July	CSAR

* Slow Moving aircraft and Air to Air refuelling

Combat SAR at the Tactical Leadership Programme

As describe previously, the rescue of pilots downed behind enemy lines is one of the most important specialities in Western air forces, and to get ready for this task, each Flying Course at the TLP devotes one day to this subject. Rafael Treviño and Salvador Mafé interviewed Colonel Andrés Maldonado, current TLP Commandant, himself an experienced F-18 Hornet pilot, who participated in combat operations over the Balkans.

SMH/RT: We have noticed that in CSAR the exercises normally participate the transport helicopters with top coverage of jet fighters.

We would like to know why do not participate in such exercises attack helicopters, like the Tiger, Cobra, or Apache, which we believe would provide a more precise close support in case of needed during the personnel recovery OPS?

COLONEL MALDONADO: TLP is a centre of excellence born to teach the fighter pilots how to lead a COMAO in any possible scenario. We train the FC Participants to be not only Mission Commander but, also, Rescue Mission Commander. It is true that an attack helicopter can provide precise Close Air Support, but our scenario with medium to high threats are not always compatible with a rotary-wing escort. Most of the times, we have SBAD (surface based air defence) that could shot down everything below 15k

The Armée de l'Air participated with two Caracals belonging to EH 1/67 'Pyrénés'. (*R. Treviño*)

An 803 Squadron Super Puma, armed with a 12.7mm M-3M machine gun. (*Salvador Mafé*)

Spanish Air Force Special Forces operatives after the C-SAR mission. (*Salvador Mafé*)

feet, so we need assets that can overfly that threat, eventually suppress it and protect the most valuable asset of the mission: the Recovery vehicle and the ISOP. Surely, we are glad to integrate attack helicopters in our missions, but is not our final aim and there is other institutions, like EPRC covering that part with the APROC exercise.

SMH/RT: We would like to know if there is a significant difference if the Personnel Recovery Ops are performed with MV-22 instead of conventional helicopters, given that the Ospreys have a greater speed, range and air to air refuelling capability, can penetrate and extract much faster and consequently, remain less time in the contested areas?

COLONEL MALDONADO: The use of the MV-22, for sure increases the 'golden ring' around the departing base and it is faster that an helicopter. We had some MV-22 participating in our Flying and Academic course. The fact is that if you want to use the Osprey for a PR mission you need a bigger landing zone, and this is not always available, an Osprey needs at least 50m² to land and 100m between every M-V22 on the ground], and more time for the landing and take-off procedure [the MV-22 landing phase takes quite a long time]. Then you have to drop 20 to 25 marines, and this means more time and coverage needed. If you have a single little spot of 20m² with an injured pilot, a conventional helicopter is still the best option you have. He can also be easily diverted, to avoid any pop-up threat and protected by a fixed wing escort.

[NOTE: During this course, two MV-22s from VMM-263, Thunder Chickens, with base in Morón AB, have participated in the exercise playing the role of an strong OPFOR, each loaded with seventeen US Marines plus crew on board and air refuelled by an USMC KC-130J.]

SMH/RT: What are the main differences between Combat SAR and Personnel Recovery?

COLONEL MALDONADO: PR is like an umbrella that cover and include a broad range of possible operations: 'It is the sum of military, diplomatic and civil effort to effect the recovery and reintegration of isolated personnel' (AJP 3.7). This means that the JFAC would use any possible means to recover his personnel, from the connection that he as with the elder of a village to all of his assets.

When we talk about military effort to recover our personnel, we can have different methods as: CR (combat recovery), CSAR (Combat Search and Rescue), UAR (unconventional assisted recovery) and NAR (non-conventional assisted recovery). The main difference among all of these methods is, basically, the level of training of the ISOP (the personnel on the ground that we are trying to recover) and the PR Task force. We talk about CSAR when both, the ISOP and the PR TF 'are trained and equipped to receive combat search and rescue support'. This means that not only the PR TF can support the ISOP but also (and above all) the ISOP is trained and equipped to support his own recovery. He knows

Two VMM-263 'Thunder Chicken' MV-22B Ospreys deployed at Morón airbase participated in RMC FC-1. (*R. Treviño*)

how to use the CSAR Codes and the Radio, for example, he has an Evasion plan of Action to follow and he is able to survive outside, waiting to be picked up.

SMH/RT: Please elaborate on a typical CSAR mission, how it is planned, executed, etc.

COLONEL MALDONADO: We train our participants to execute a Deliberate CSAR mission [a CSAR mission that cannot be launched immediately because of threats, intel or planning limitations]. Like every other mission here at the TLP, a CSAR mission starts, in the morning with the target analysis [in this case the landing zone analysis made by the extraction team and the pilots of the recovery vehicles]. They study the landing zone, the possible approaches, the different ways of landing and recovery, in accordance with the last known information that they have about the ISOP. Then we have the weather briefing followed by the CONOPS [concept of operations] briefed by the General of the day [a TLP instructors that acts as JFAC]. At the end of the weather briefing we release the ATO [Air task order], with the established roles for all of the participants and we have the Intel briefing with the threats analysis that gives the participants the possibility to adapt their plan to the real threats that they have to face during the mission. After the briefing all the participants and the staff of TLP move to the main planning room for the next phase, the Brainstorming. During this phase the Mission Commander, using our 4Ts method [TASK, TARGET, THREAT, TACTICS], will lead the COMAO through a deep analysis of all the crucial aspects concerning the mission and its final planning.

At the end we have a deep analysis of the mission with a precise timeline, a map and a coordination card, that the COMAO use to execute the mission.

The execution is like a real CSAR mission, with all the assets playing their role, from the AWACS that acts as AMC (airborne mission coordinator) to the Extraction Team and the ISOP on the ground. Everything is monitored via link, GPS and radio, so the instructor are able to follow the mission and highlight any possible debriefing point.

Chapter 11

Hungarian Gripens in Spain

The TLP 2017-3 edition, which ran from 11 September to 6 October 2017, had the usual F-16s, F-18s, Typhoons, Tornados, E-3 Sentrys, etc, but something unusual arrived this time, and it was three JAS 39Cs from the 59th TFW of the Hungarian Air Force, as explained by Major Tibor Molnar.

1st Tactical Fighter Squadron 'Puma' at TLP 2017-3

For the first time, the Hungarian Air Force participated in a Tactical Leadership Programme flying course, deploying to Albacete-Los Llanos airbase three Saab JAS 39C Gripens (31, 34 and 35), six pilots and a GCI officer, plus thirty-six ground crew from the 59th Tactical Fighter Wing. During the course, the Gripens alternated between 'Blue Air' (call sign FADO) and 'Red Air' (TONIC). Major Molmar elaborated:

> TLP provides very high standard of training for NATO countries! The knowledge one can learn from TLP courses – whether it is an academic or flying course – is vital to be a leader on tactical level. It would be a boost for NATO if we would be able

1st Tactical Fighter Squadron 'Puma' JAS 39C Gripen 34, with its standard air-to-air load, comprising two AIM-9L Sidewinders and two AIM-120B AMRAAM missiles, and just in front of the port intake, can be seen the muzzle of the 27mm Mauser BK cannon with 120 rounds. (*HUNAF*)

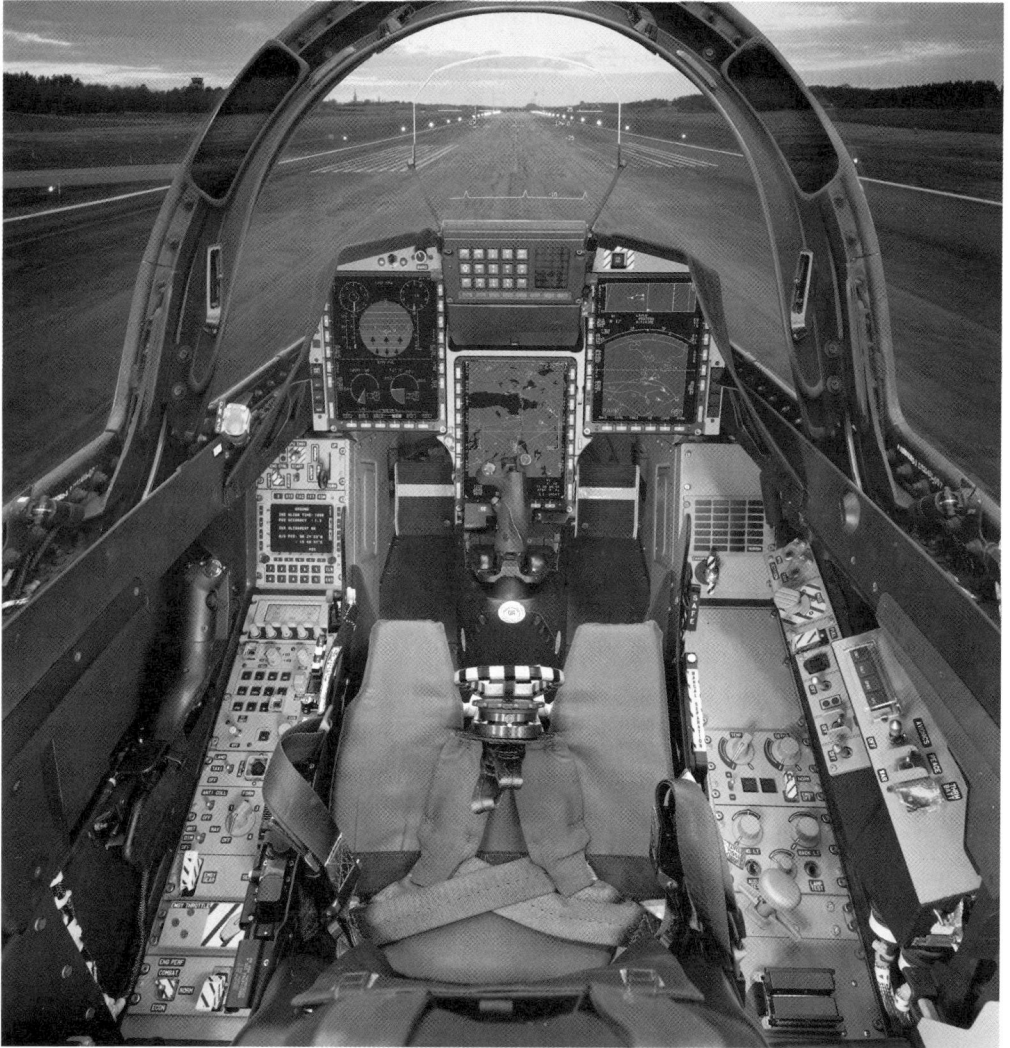

The JAS 39C cockpit dominated by the three large Mods and the wide-angle HUD. (*SAAB*)

to do our daily training at that high level. Also, it is a very nice commitment from TLP instructors that they are supporting large exercises like NATO Tiger Meet.

It is always a great experience to fight against another jet. But here in TLP we also get the chance to fight among them, which is the greatest possibility for getting to know the others capabilities, for team building, and good experience for the future if we have to go to an operation together. Also, the most modern aircraft is only as good as its pilot, and that is where TLP comes into the picture, because it will make you being one of the finest pilots on earth.

Concerning the main 'lesson learned' after this three-week TLP course, I believe we have learned tremendous amount of lessons here in TLP, but if I have to nominate

1st Tactical Fighter Squadron 'Puma' takes off from Albacete-Los Llanos Airbas on 3 October 2017, for a TLP mission. (*Salvador Mafé*)

This close-up shows the Gripen's tight-fitting cockpit. (*Salvador Mafé*)

Major Tibor Molnar from 1st Tactical Fighter Squadron 'Puma'. (*Salvador Mafè*)

Major Molnar is a highly experienced pilot with more than 1,700 flight hours logged, 900 in the Saab JAS 39C/D Gripen. (*Salvador Mafè*)

one then it would be teamwork. Our tasks here required a team led by a leader which could be you or your teammate, and he was only being able to achieve the commander's intent if we worked as a cohesive, efficient team doing our best and supporting each other!

An Experienced Fighter Pilot

Major Tibor Molnar, 41 years old, graduated as a fighter pilot in 1998, serving at 59th Tactical Fighter Wing at Kecskemét Airbase.

He has this to say about his career:

I have almost 20 years in service and I have had trained in five aircraft types, in different countries like Hungary, Canada, Sweden, Slovakia. I have been trained for Air to Air and Air to Ground roles from wingman up to four-ship lead. During my career I have collected almost 1,700 hours, from that 900 hours were on my current aircraft, the Gripen.

The JAS39 Gripen is a very modern, agile and sophisticated 4+ generation fighter aircraft. It was designed by a small country, providing a cost-efficient multirole fighter for their home defence, and has been updated for being NATO compatible when purchased by Hungary and later on by the Czech Republic. The Gripen is providing us a capable force to defend our country and to fulfil our NATO duties.

I have flown jet trainers like L-39 Albatros, CT-155 (Hawk 115), SK-60. Also, I had the opportunity to fly some missions in the backseat of the MiG-29 Fulcrum, and the F-16.

The Litening targeting pod fitted to the right chin pylon. (*Salvador Mafé*)

PUMA 12 – The vertical fin of a JAS 39C Gripen showing the low-visibility HUNAF national markings. (*Salvador Mafé*)

SAAB JAS 39C/D Gripen in Hungarian Air Force Service

Following Hungary's joining of NATO in 1999, there were several proposals to achieve a NATO-compatible fighter force. Considerable attention went into studying second-hand aircraft options as well as modifying the nation's existing MiG-29 fleet. In 2001, Hungary received several offers of new and used aircraft from various nations, including Sweden, Belgium, Israel, Turkey, and the US. Although the Hungarian government initially intended to procure the F-16, in November 2001 it was in the process of negotiating a ten-year lease contract for twelve Gripen aircraft, with an option to purchase the aircraft at the end of the lease period.

As part of the procurement arrangements, Saab had offered an offset deal valued at 110 per cent of the cost of the fighters. Initially, Hungary had planned to lease several Batch II aircraft; however, the inability to conduct air-to-air refuelling and weapons compatibility limitations had generated Hungarian misgivings. The contract was renegotiated and was signed on 2 February 2003 for a total of fourteen Gripens, which had originally been A/B standard and had undergone an extensive upgrade process to the NATO-compatible C/D 'Export Gripen' standard. The last aircraft deliveries took place in December 2007.

While the Hungarian Air Force operated a total of fourteen Gripen aircraft under lease in 2011, the country reportedly intended to purchase these aircraft outright. However, in January 2012, the Hungarian and Swedish governments agreed to extend the lease

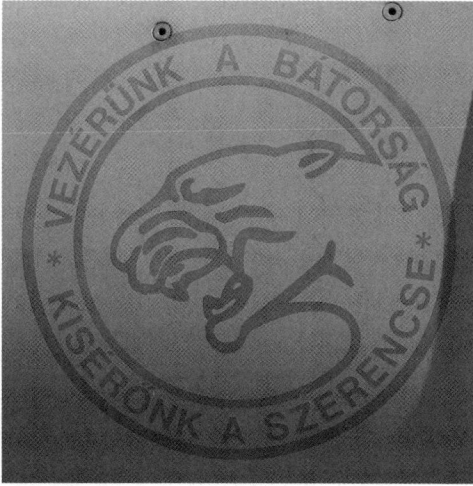

Puma Squadron badge as applied to both sides of the forward fuselage of 59th TFW Gripens. (*Salvador Mafé*)

75th anniversary Puma Squadron badge.

period for a further ten years; according to Hungarian Defence Minister Csaba Hende, the agreement represented considerable cost savings.

Two Gripens were lost in crashes in May and June 2015, leaving twelve Gripens in operation. Hungary will be back to fourteen Gripens with the signing of a replacement contract for a two-seater, and repairs to a single seater. On 9 May 2015, while landing at Čáslav Airbase, Czech Republic, JAS 39D number 42, overran the runway, but both crewmen (Brigadier General Ugrik and Major Grof) ejected safely with no injuries. The aircraft was heavily damaged with the nose section separated. On 10 June 2015, a single-seater JAS 39C number 30 performed a belly landing at Kecskemét Airbase, Hungary. The pilot, Major Sándor Kádár, ejected successfully but suffered spinal injuries.

Concerning the roles of the Hungarian Gripens, Major Molnar says:

The Gripen is capable to do a very decent job on every role. Even in reconnaissance, as Operation Unified Protector has shown, where the Swedish Air Force's Gripens were doing a big portion of the total reconnaissance needed to be done. Hungarian Air Force's Gripens are mainly performing Air to Air missions, but the aircraft is very capable also if we have to provide support to the ground troops as well, as that is our secondary task. In one word the best role depends on the operational needs, requirements.

Our task is to protect the sovereignty of Hungary's as well as Slovenia's airspace as part of NATO's collective defence. We are also providing support to the ground force commanders with Close Air Support.

The Gripen is quite easy to handle, with the triplex digital Fly-By-Wire Flight Control System the aircraft has an optimum combination of manoeuvrability, acceleration, and short-field performance. Gripen's sensor fusion gives the pilot high situational awareness and an efficient way to fight either in Air to Air or Air to Ground roles.

59th Tactical Fighter Wing

The SAAB JAS 39C/D Gripens are operated by two squadrons in the 59th Tactical Fighter Wing, these are the 1st Tactical Fighter Squadron (Puma Sqn.) and the 2nd Tactical Fighter Training Squadron (Dongó Sqn. Dongó is translated as Wasp in English). Both squadrons share the jets, while Dongó also has about ten Aero L39 trainers in strength. The 59th TFW operates from Kecskemét Airbase, about 80km from Budapest.

Major Molbar:

The emblem of the Puma Squadron dates back to 1938 and were moving from the former 1/3. Fighter Squadron to the 2/2. Squadron which became 5/1. Wing then finally officially transformed to the 101st Tactical Fighter Wing in 1944. The squadron has fought on the Eastern Front as well as defending Hungary against the large bomber fleets and their escorting fighters with their Messerschmitt Bf 109s in the last years of the war, sometimes facing 1 against 30 ratios. On the Eastern Front, during 1943, the Pumas were officially credited with the destruction of 70 Soviet aircraft, to which they added further 218 destroyed and credited during the Home Defence combats in 1944–5. They were credited with 64 American four-engined bombers, and 47 fighters of the USAAF Fifteenth Air Force in 1944.

The total number of victories credited against all opposing forces was thus 399. Relative to the small number of 'Puma' pilots, the losses were heavy. The 101. Wing bore the brunt of the fighting in the summer of 1944.

Badge carried by Close Air Support qualified Gripen pilots.

Major Molnar carries this badge, indicating he is a highly experienced Gripen pilot!

Between its creation in the spring of 1944 and the end of the war, the wing (and later, regiment) suffered 51 killed, 30 wounded, 21 MIA; seven pilots became POWs. After the war the continuation of the Wing was impossible. The image of Hungarian fighter pilots and aces, most of them very successful on the Eastern Front, was politically unacceptable to the communist leadership. The Pumas' insignia, motto, and traditions were reborn in 1988, when the 1st Fighter Squadron of the Hungarian Defence Forces 59th TFW took the name 'Puma' again. The Squadron has contacted surviving veterans of their World War II predecessor. The unit flew MiG-21 Fishbed, and later MiG-29 Fulcrum jet fighters. The unit is now operating the Swedish JAS 39C/D Gripen, and proudly serving under the motto of the squadron: 'Courage leads, luck escorts us!'

Chapter 12

Aegean Deltas: Hellenic Air Force Mirage 2000s at the TLP 2018-3 Flying Course

There were two different variants of the Mirage 2000 in Hellenic Air Force (HAF) service, the Mirage 2000EGM/BGM (replaced by the Dassault Rafale) and the Mirage 2000-5 Mk 2. The latter formed part of TLP 2018-3, at Los Llanos airbase in October 2018.

For information on these beautiful delta fighters, the authors interviewed a 331 Mira (Squadron) Mirage pilot who presented himself:

I'm Captain Spyridon Karelis. After finishing my training I jumped to the fighters. Initially I flew A-7E Corsairs and then I moved to M2000-5s. They are two totally different aircraft. A-7 is a 2nd-Generation aircraft while M2000-5 is a 3rd & half Generation aircraft. Moreover, both aircraft have different roles and different capabilities. A-7 could offer you all the A/G experience that you would require to

Captain Spyridon Karelis posing besides one of 331 Mira's jets, Mirage 2000-5 Mk 2 '550', during TLP 2018-3, Los Llanos airbase, October 2018. (*HAF*)

Mirage 2000-5 Mk 2, in the strategic attack configuration with the SCALP weapon, and a close-up of the same. (*HAF*)

reach an advanced level. It carried a very big weapons load and it had an extended combat radius. On the other hand M2000-5 is a state of the art aircraft. It's a multirole aircraft, with an advanced weapons system and some unique capabilities.

Tanagra AB, where both squadron are based forming part of 114 Combat Wing, is located approximately 70km northwest of Athens. It was built during the Second World War and served as a back-up military airfield. In the past few years, it has been reconstructed with the financial contribution of NATO and became a fully operational base of the Hellenic HAF. It has a single runway with direction 10-28 and two main taxiways, which can also be used as runways whenever needed.

The 114 Combat Wing was formed on 22 August 1956 and it initially consisted of three squadrons. The first F-104 Starfighters arrived at Tanagra AB in April 1964 and they remained operating from there until 30 June 1977. On 16 February 1967, the F-102 Delta Dagger arrived and stayed at Tanagra AB for almost 10 years until they retired at the beginning of 1977. The first French fighter for Greece, the Mirage F1CG, touched down for the first time on runway 10-28 on 4 August 1975 and ever since then 114CW has always operated Mirage fighters.

In March 1985, the Greek government announced the purchase of thirty-six single-seat Mirage 2000EGs and four two-seat Mirage 2000BGs in addition to the procurement of the F-16C/D Block 30. In 1989 the first Mirage 2000 aircraft were introduced into HAF service and delivered to two newly founded squadrons, the 331 Mira and the 332 Mira,

In air-superiority configuration with four of the excellent MICA air-to-air missiles. (*HAF*)

In early 2016 the Supreme Air Force Council approved the upgrade of the remaining seventeen single-seat Mirage 2000EGMs (the two BGMs are near the end of their structural life) to a standard close to the -5 Mk 2 standards. The Greek Mirage 2000 upgrade consist of three main aspects. The first is the replacement of the RDM-3 radar with the RDY-3, similar to the Indian Mirage 2000 upgrade programme. The new RDY-3 is a model based on the compact Thales RC400 first introduced in 1999 for lighter aircraft and used for the upgrade of the Moroccan Mirage F1CH/EH. The unit has 20 per cent less range than the RDY-2 of the Mirage 2000-5 Mk 2, but it is 50 per cent lighter, around 115kg. Combined with a bigger antenna possible on the Mirage 2000 the powerful transmitter still provides a range close to that of the RDY-2. The second aspect of the upgrade is a new mission controller. The most probable scenario is to acquire the Modular Data Processing Unit of the Mirage 2000-5 Mk.2 also used by the Rafale. The third aspect of the package is the upgrade of the existing self-defence suite ICMS (Integrated Counter Measures System) from Mk 1 to Mk 3 standard. (*HAF*)

The main visual difference between the Mirage 2000-5 Mk.2 and the Mirage 2000EGM/BGMs is the absence of the pitot tube on the nose cone of the 2000-5 Mk.2 because of the new RDY radome, which also has the antennas of the IFF interrogator. While initially the Mirage 2000-5 could also be distinguished by its hose-and-drogue aerial refuelling receptacle, this was later also added to the surviving EGM/BGM aircraft. Other visually notable differences are the four extra fuselage hardpoints on the 2000-5 for MICA missiles. The initial 40 Mirage 2000s were serialled 200 up to 240 (the two-seaters being 200–204), while the newer M2000-5 serials start from 500. (*HAF*)

marking the beginning of a new era for 114CW. On 30 June 2003, the Mirage F1CG was prematurely retired after 28 years of continuous service. From that point on, 114CW only consists of these two squadrons solely operating Mirage 2000 delta-winged fighters.

331 Mira 'Thisseas'

331 Squadron was commissioned on 18 April 1988 for the acceptance of the Mirage 2000 into HAF service. The squadron was named 'Thisseas' after the ancient Greek hero and its emblem shows Theseus pointing out a direction that two Mirages follow. The first aircraft landed at Tanagra AB on 27 April and at the same time all the training in different levels by French instructors had commenced. There were also a number of experienced pilots, who were selected from other HAF squadrons and had already been trained on the Mirage 2000 in France.

The main role of the squadron was all-weather interception. Despite the previous weapon of choice for the Mirage F1CG being the American AIM-9 Sidewinder, this time French missiles were selected for the French aircraft. Procured along with the aircraft, the short-range IR-guided Matra Magic IIs were initially the only missiles equipping the Mirage 2000s. In 1996 the capabilities of the Mirage were enhanced with the medium range radar-guided Matra Super 530D. These two air-to-air missiles in combination with the modern self-protection system ICMS (Integrated Counter Measures System) made the Mirage 2000 one of the best and more advanced fighters operated in the region at that time.

The differences in the state-of-the-art Mirage 2000-5 Mk 2 cockpit and the Mirage 2000EGM. (*HAF*)

In 1999, HAF officials decided to order a new anti-ship missile, the AM 39 Exocet. With the addition of this new weapon the Mirage 2000 gained the anti-shipping role, and for this reason the EG/BG were designated EGM/BGM.

In 2000, Greece signed a new contract with Dassault ordering fifteen new-built Mirage 2000-5 Mk 2 fighters. In addition to the new aircraft, ten examples from the existing HAF fleet were brought up to 2000-5 Mk 2 standard by Hellenic Aerospace Industry using upgrade kits provided by Dassault. These were all single-seat M2000s, the ten airframes being selected based on their lower level of fuselage fatigue compared to the other single-seaters. The two most important new systems of the 2000-5 Mk 2 were the RDY-2 radar and the ICMS Mk 3 self-defence suite. These two systems became the audit field of extensive testing of the Greek-French team IFEPG (In Flight Evaluation Program Group) which lasted three years starting from the Summer of 2003 in order to determine the compliance of these systems with their specifications. On 24 June 2003 Captain Leonidas Karanatsis became the first Hellenic Air Force pilot to fly the Mirage 2000-5 two-seater. The aircraft serialled 505 was a brand new Mirage 2000-5 Mk 2 used as the development aircraft for the Greek Mirage 2000-5 Mk 2 contract.

Concerning the behaviour and virtues of the Mirage 2000-5 Mk 2 as a combat aircraft, both in its multirole facets, i.e. air combat and in the attack on land and naval targets, Captain Karelis had this to say:

Within the Air Forces community we usually divide the combat by using as a reference the role, i.e. Air to Air, Air to Ground, Air to Surface role, etc. I think that the current trend is slightly different. We tend to use stand-off weapons either to shoot an Air to Air opponent or to shoot at a ground/surface target. This said, I believe that we can distinct the combat into two big categories: BVR and WVR. Even if these terms are coming from the so called Air to Air role, we can use them as well for Air to Ground/ Surface missions, based on the type of weapons that we use. Modern weapon platforms have swing roll capabilities. In other words a swing role aircraft can fight some Air to Air opponents before or while attacking some ground targets. M2000-5 is an aircraft with quite impressive swing role capabilities.

Both squadrons have Air to Air Role but the main difference comes to the secondary role: our squadron has the strategic attack role while 332 Squadron has an anti-ship role.

Concerning the fatal accident we had on 12 April 2018, we lost a brother in arms, Captain Georgios Baltadoros, a member of our squadron.

331 Squadron was selected to receive the new and upgraded aircraft, giving it a fleet of twenty-five aircraft from the initial batch of forty M2000EG/BGs that the HAF had acquired, after losses and accidents and minus the ten upgraded ones. So on 1 March 2007 the squadron handed over all its remaining older Mirages to 332 Squadron, so each would have twenty-five aircraft. 331 Squadron started to prepare itself for the upcoming

The differences between the Magic 2 and MICA air-to-air missiles are quite evident in these photos. (*Author*)

type. The new era for 331 began on 3 May 2007 when the first Mirage 2000-5 touched down on the runway of Tanagra airfield. Training followed provided by French personnel and the squadron became operational again almost a year later. The squadron received the last-ever Mirage 2000 built, which rolled off the production line on 23 November 2007.

According to Captain Karelis the Mirage 2000-5 Mk 2 is 'an amazing platform with some unique capabilities not only on the BVR arena but also in the WVR arena. The armament system, the aerodynamics characteristics, but most importantly the Man Machine Interface, make it a very capable platform.'

New and more sophisticated weapons arrived along with the new Mirages and these were the advanced air-to-air missile MICA in both radar-guided and IR-guided versions. Also for the first time in the history of the Greek Mirages, a new air-to-ground stand-off weapon, the

The excellent RDY-2 radar provides the Mirage 2000-5 Mk 2 with true multirole capabilities. (*HAF*)

SCALP munitions-dispensing cruise missile, was introduced to the inventory of the HAF. While it is compatible with the 2000-5 Mk 2, the Magic II missile is only being carried by the older EGM/BGM variants since the 2000-5 has the modern MICAs. While it was possible to integrate the Exocet anti-ship missile on the 2000-5, the HAF decided not to proceed with this option, since with the introduction of the SCALP the 2000-5 already has a secondary role.

The Mirage 2000-5 Mk 2, offers many tactical advantages compared to the Mirage 2000EG. The Thales RDY all-weather synthetic aperture radar offers increased capabilities compared to the previous RDI of the Mirage 2000EGM. It has the ability to track twenty-four targets and is capable of simultaneous launch of up to four missiles against multiple targets. It also provides the aircraft with air-to-ground radar capabilities.

Other enhancements to offensive systems include a datalink for the mid-course targeting of MICA ER missiles. Other upgrades included the addition of an on-board oxygen generation system (OBOGS), updated secure radio, and digital datalink for tactical information sharing. The Greek Mirage 2000-5 Mk 2 was also fitted with the updated ICMS Mk3 (Integrated Counter Measures System) suite. The Mirage 2000-5 cockpit has high resolution Multi-Function Displays for situational awareness and reducing the pilot's workload. The pilot has the ability to control most of the necessary functions of his on-board equipment with HOTAS, his hands not leaving from the stick and the throttle.

The main visual difference between the Mirage 2000-5 Mk 2 and the Mirage 2000EGM/BGMs is the absence of the pitot tube on the nose cone of the 2000-5 Mk 2 because of the new RDY radome, which also has the antennas of the IFF interrogator. While initially the Mirage 2000-5 could also be distinguished by its hose-and-drogue aerial refuelling receptacle, it was later also added to the surviving EGM/BGM aircraft. Other visually notable differences are the four extra fuselage hardpoints on the 2000-5 for MICA missiles. The initial forty Mirage 2000s were serialled 200 up to 240 (the two-seaters being 200–204), while the newer M2000-5 serials start from 500.

Concerning the air policing mission over the Aegean, Captain Karelis elaborated:

Initially I would like to talk about the historical and geographical frame of the Aegean Sea. It lies between the coast of Greece and Asia Minor (modern-day Turkey). It contains more than 2,000 Greek islands which were settled by the ancient Greeks more than 15,000 years ago. Ever since Greeks have a continuous presence, having established the world-known Greek culture and arts. The origin of the name 'Aegean' derives from the name of the King of Athens 'Aegeas', who drowned himself in the

AM39 Exocet anti-ship missile seen on a Mirage 2000EGM. (*Author*)

sea when he thought his son 'prince Thiseas' had died on his famous expedition to Crete to defeat Minotaur. Our Squadron's call sign is 'Thiseas'. This said, we are the grandsons of Prince 'Thiseas' and part of our Peace time mission is to assure the sovereignty of the national airspace along with the execution of Air Policing within Athens Flight Information Region. If you check on a map you will find out that a really big part of Athens FIR includes the Aegean Sea. So for us, being Greek fighters, this is what we do on a 24/7 basis across our area of responsibility, which is the Athens FIR. So, speaking about Aegean Sea we historically speak about the birth place of the Greek civilization, but we also refer to a very big portion of Athens FIR (including national and international airspace) in which Greece has the responsibility of conducting Air Policy and exercising its sovereign rights, IAW the international law provisions and ICAO documents, and while we mainly operate from Tanagra AB, we have some deployment bases along Greece, according to the operational requirements and the national plans of operations.

332 Mira 'Geraki'

About a year after the Mirage 2000 had entered service with 331 Squadron, the second squadron was formed on the 11th of August 1989. 332 Squadron was named 'Geraki' or 'Hawk' with its emblem depicting a hawk over a map of Greece with the Hellenic flag in the bottom right. The second Mirage 2000 Squadron mainly used the former 334 Squadron facilities at Tanagra, as 334 Sqn had relocated to Iraklion, Crete. 332 Squadron started with Mirages received from 331 Sqn along with pilots and mechanics, who trained the new personnel still inexperienced with the Mirage 2000. When 332 Mira reached full operational status on 15 July 1990, all personnel was redistributed between the Squadrons so that both could maintain the same level of knowledge and experience.

When 331 Squadron started to receive the new Mirage 2000-5, 332 Squadron received its remaining EGM/BGMs. The non-upgraded Mirage 2000 EGM/BGMs still had the capability of the Super 530D and to launch the Exocet anti-shipping missile. However, the Super 530D which lacks a CW (Continuous Wave) illuminator is outdated compared to the other medium-range missiles including the MICA-EM of the M2000-5, but also the AIM-120 AMRAAM of the F-16. Despite the complete differences compared to 331 Squadron's 2000-5 in terms of electronics, radar, systems, cockpit and of course capabilities, both are still Mirage 2000s.

All Greek machines (Mk 2s and EGMs) feature the Thales Totem 3000 inertial navigation system of the Mk 2 with ring laser gyroscope and GPS providing much greater accuracy, reliability, and shorter alignment time than the Mirage 2000 original ULISS 52 navigation system. The fuselage, engine, and many other components of the aircraft are also identical. This helps a lot in keeping both types fully operational as spare parts and similar components can be exchanged between the squadrons. During 2022, 332 started to replace its Mirage 2000s, with the much improved Dassault Rafale.

Greek Mirage 2000 upgrade: a real winner

In early 2016 the Supreme Air Force Council approved the upgrade of the remaining seventeen single seat Mirage 2000EGM (the two BGM are near the end of their structural life) to a standard close to the -5 Mk 2 standards. The Greek Mirage 2000 upgrade consist of three main aspects.

The first is the replacement of the RDM-3 radar with the RDY-3, similar to the Indian Mirage 2000 upgrade programme. The new RDY-3 is a model based on the compact Thales RC400 first introduced in 1999 for lighter aircraft and used for the upgrade of the Moroccan Mirage F1CH/EH. The unit has 20 per cent less range than the RDY-2 of the Mirage 2000-5 Mk 2, but it is 50 per cent lighter, around 115kg. Combined with a bigger antenna possible on the Mirage 2000 the powerful transmitter still provides a range close to that of the RDY-2.

The second aspect of the upgrade is a new mission controller. The most probable scenario is to acquire the Modular Data Processing Unit of the Mirage 2000-5 Mk 2 also used by the Rafale.

The third aspect of the package is the upgrade of the existing self-defence suite ICMS (Integrated Counter Measures System) from Mk 1 to Mk 3 standard.

Other improvements included in the planned package are:

- Updated cockpit layout along with new Multi-Function Display units.
- New communication package with Intraflight DataLink, new ECCM radios with Have Quick II and SATURN standards and Secure Voice capability.
- New IFF transponder.
- Ability to carry up to six MICA EM/IR missiles and the AM.39 Block II Mod2 Exocet anti-shipping missile.
- New mission planning and debriefing system; Thales SERPAM (Systeme de Enregistrement et de Restitution des Parametres se Mission).

If the upgrade programme is implemented, additional MICA missiles will not be necessary as the HAF already possesses 300 of these missiles in its inventory, giving a ratio of six to eight missiles per aircraft compared to the current twelve for only the -5 Mk 2 aircraft. In either case, the ratio is still larger than that of the AMRAAM for the F-16s and F-4E AUP Phantoms.

The upgrade programme does not cover the Inertial Navigation System (INS) as the newer Thales Totem 3000 INS with Ring Laser Gyroscope (RLG) had already replaced the old Sagem ULISS 52E on the Mirage 2000EGM.

Due to the financial crisis in Greece, the big question is when this upgrade programme will become a reality. The French side is putting a lot of pressure on Greek officials because the production line of the systems and other parts are currently open for the current upgrade programme of around fifty Indian Mirage 2000H/THs. Once the production lines are

Four Mirage 2000-5 Mk 2s (509, 547, 550 and 555) participated in the 3/2018 edition of the Tactical Leadership Programme at Los Llanos, which took place from 10 September to 5 October 2018, being tasked as 'Blue Air', with the TALOS and VELOS call signs. (*Author*)

closed, it may become financially impossible for the Greek Mirages to be upgraded to -5 Mk 2 standard.

There are rumours that Greek government wants to offer the remaining F-16 Block 30s for sale to other Balkan countries that are seeking affordable Western options to modernize their fighter fleets. Despite the fact that many HAF officials would totally disagree, the truth is that Greece has no other option to fund the upgrade of the Mirage 2000 and the younger F-16s.

The Future

The Mirage 2000-5 Mk 2s along with the F-16C/D Block 52+ and the Rafales are the most modern fighters in HAF service. If upgraded, the EGM/BGM aircraft that are now 25 years old will soldier on alongside them, but due to the financial crisis in Greece nothing is for sure. The recently-purchase eighteen Dassault Rafales are replacing the non-upgraded Mirage 2000s.

The personnel of 114CW do their best every day to keep each squadron fully operational and, for the Combat Wing in general, maintain the highest level of proficiency and professionalism. For the men and women one thing is certain, no matter what problems they, their own families, or their country faces, they must be ready to defend their homeland.

Chapter 13

Tragedy Strikes the TLP

U nfortunately accidents happen in aviation as in all human activities. On 26 January 2015 a Greek AF F-16 crashed during take-off during the flying activities of the 2015-01 Flying course then in progress. The following literal extract from the pertinent official Safety Investigation Report, gives the following information:

> The Hellenic Air Force (HAF) F-16D S/N 93-1084 (hereafter referred to as the mishap aircraft) of 341 Squadron (SQ), was the number 2 of a 2 aircraft (A/C) formation, taking off for a Tactical Leadership Programme (TLP) Flying Course 2015-1 mission from Albacete Air Force Base (Albacete AFB), Albacete, Spain on 26 January 2015.
>
> The mishap A/C crashed at 15:16 local time (14:16 UTC), approximately 7.8 sec after take-off on runway 27 (RWY 27). The aft seat pilot initiated ejection out of the seat safe ejection envelope. The mishap resulted in the fatal injury of both mishap pilots and the total destruction of the mishap A/C.
>
> The main causes of the mishap were:
>
> Mishap A/C was not properly trimmed for take-off as before TAXI, the yaw trim was inadvertently set to maximum right yaw trimming (12 degrees to the right), drastically affecting the aerodynamics of the aircraft during take-off.
>
> Pilot in command conducted the 'Before Takeoff' checklist actions in the parking area (ramp E2) approximately 20 min before take-off.
>
> After take-off, pilot stick commands and the resultant control surface outputs were insufficient to maintain the A/C in controlled flight.
>
> Impact and the post impact fire led to the destruction or damage of eight (8) additional A/C and caused fatal injuries to nine (9) French Air Force personnel, numerous injuries and significant damages to ground equipment and to Albacete AFB and TLP infrastructure in the vicinity of Ramp E2 and in front of the TLP hangar.

It was a real case of bad luck. If the plane had turned to port instead of turning to starboard, it would have crashed on the ground in front of the TLP facilities, which is empty with only trees and bushes, resulting in only the loss of the pilots and the plane.

An Ala 14 pilot provided this account on condition of anonymity:

> At approximately 15:15 hours on 26 January 2015, Captains Díaz Matas, Aybar and I were in the squadron, as the latter two had flown second period and had landed

Hellenic Air Force (HAF) F-16D S/N 93-1084. (*TLP Photo Section*)

about an hour earlier, as usual at that time of day. Díaz Matas and Aybar were in the 142nd Operations office and I had my back to the window at a desk, when I heard a loud continuous boom for several seconds. I turned around and saw a mass of fire coming at high speed from the D-4 and D-5 shelters towards the TLP platform and a huge fireball was being created. I quickly got up and told Aybar and Díaz Matas that a plane had just crashed. Instantly the emergency warning siren sounded and the three of us went out to the mechanics' line to see what was happening. Captain Aybar immediately went to the tower as he was the Flight Officer that day, and I went back into the squadron, seeing that I didn't have my mobile phone, to call my mother and tell her that if I saw anything in the press that had happened at the base, not to worry because we were fine, but that I had to hang up because we had enough trouble, and when I went back out to the line to continue watching what was happening, there was the ejection of several seats and other detonations of less intensity but with a greater cadence. At that moment, explosions of other aircraft began, one after the other, which had previously caught fire, causing an even bigger fireball than there had been initially. It was then that Captain Díaz Matas, on seeing the succession of planes on fire, gave the order to our mechanics and staff who were there to remove the 11th Wing planes that were parked in front of the Air Force building as soon as possible, as they had just stopped their engines when the accident occurred and the pilots had got out quickly. Díaz Matas and I lent a hand to the mechanics as much as we could, removing the chocks and putting away material and equipment that prevented the towing of any of the planes, while emergency crews were arriving at the TLP platform to try to put out the fire and control the situation, and little by little, during those minutes, more pilots from 142 Squadron who were eating at the base or in the vicinity of the Air Forces building were arriving. We were all watching helplessly from there as the events unfolded, and in the meantime a blue Mercedes Vito van appeared, driven by an American sergeant, calling for an ambulance. I approached him to tell him that there was no ambulance and he asked me for a hospital. There I realised that inside the van were three people with injuries of varying degrees of severity but all of them quite serious, to the naked eye. Several of my colleagues who were in the vicinity, including Captain Galán, Captain Moreno and Captain Díaz Matas, urged me to take the wounded to the hospital. Seeing that the American sergeant, Eli Gordon, would not know how to get to any aid station because he did not know the base, I set about getting into the van. The problem was that the wounded were seated, one in the front passenger seat, one behind the driver and one by the side door. I went to the back to get into the boot but there was a fourth person huddled there, totally immobile. Among the three injured there was one, François Combourieu, completely burnt by the flames and with only his boots on without the laces, I finally got in with them in the only place where I could fit, standing behind the co-driver, next to the side door, taking care not to move the person sitting there too much. And I showed the driver how to get to the first aid kit at the base. We went through the door of the first aid station and a soldier told us that no one was there, as they were all in the area of the accident. I continued giving directions to the sergeant to go straight to the Albacete General Hospital, entering by the Murcia road. It was 15:32 and Captain Aybar called me on my mobile and I told him that I was leaving the base with four wounded and we were taking them to the hospital. During the minutes it took to get to the hospital, the sergeant and I were talking to the wounded, asking them their names and nationality, and we kept talking to them, encouraging them as much as we could, but above all to keep them conscious. Of the three in the passenger compartment, the one sitting in the front passenger seat was the one who at first glance (from my almost nil medical knowledge) was the least seriously injured. Behind him sat Franck Poirot leaning over me, gesturing to me that he was fainting, but he remained conscious until he reached the hospital. His left hand was smashed and there was a lot of blood on the left side of his face. Next to him, behind the driver, was François Combourieu, who kept asking me to please call his mother. Minutes later, because of his suffering, he kept repeating the phrase: 'Please, kill me'. At the Repsol petrol station, François began to choke and cough, vomiting very frothy blood, an indication that he had a serious lung problem. But he also remained conscious until we got to the ER. I didn't know the hospital's ER entrance either, and as we went through the front door I saw a sign indicating that the ER was just around the corner. We turned and there I saw an entrance with lots of ambulances blocking the road and I assumed it would be there. I got out and ran inside to tell the staff but they told me that EMS was up ahead. I told the sergeant to follow me and ran down the street to the next corner

A destroyed French Air Force Alpha Jet. (*TLP Photo Section*)

of the hospital where I finally saw the entrance ramp to the ER. I told him to take the van right up to the front door of the building even though the street was in the opposite direction. I went back into the entrance hall asking for help: Please come out and help me, I have burns from a plane crash at the base! To which an employee (I don't know if she was a nurse, auxiliary, orderly, doctor …) answered me: But … what happened? Please hurry up and get a move on because these are the first four of many who are going to start arriving. Clearly, they were not informed of what was coming to them. It was 15:39, because that's when Capt Moreno called me to ask me how things were going with the wounded. Initially, three or four women and I went out to the van. When I opened the door, several of them were literally in 'shock' when they saw the wounded. One covered her face, another burst into tears and another asked me what to do. I guess she wasn't a specialist in medical care either and was perhaps one of the reception staff.

Bring whatever you can, stretchers, wheelchairs, sheets, …but we have to get them out of the van now! There was a large ambulance blocking the entrance to the building, and I told the American sergeant to get back in the van to bring it as close as possible to reception while the staff brought the stretchers in and I moved the ambulance, which had the driver's door open but no one in it, out of the way as the stretchers were brought in. First we took out the co-driver, who almost got out on his own, but with help. I then indicated to Franck that he was next but he said he couldn't, pointing to his feet. In addition to the serious injuries to his left hand, both his ankles had open fractures and his feet were almost dangling. Sergeant Gordon and I took him in our arms and put him on the second stretcher. The next thing to do was to get François out, who, due to his burns, was very difficult to get out as he was almost immobile and the severity of his burns made it almost impossible to grab him. When we finally got him out of the van and onto the stretcher, the medical staff who had arrived laid him down and I told them to get him up, otherwise he was going to suffocate, as he had been choking for several minutes due to internal bleeding. Finally, I went to the back and opened the boot to get the fourth casualty out. To my surprise, he was also conscious even though he had not said anything during the drive to the hospital. I asked him his name and he told me his name was Luc and that he was French. The American sergeant told me that his right leg was broken, which Luc himself confirmed. The sergeant grabbed him by the fabric of his trousers and I grabbed him under his armpits, noting that his right hand was amputated and that he hadn't even realised it. He had a tourniquet on that arm. We left him on a stretcher in the hands of the hospital staff and then I approached what I thought might be the most qualified of those there and I told him the name of each of the wounded we had taken and the most significant thing they had so that they could identify them. When we finished, Sergeant Gordon asked me what else we could do and I told him that we had to get back to base quickly for whatever we might be needed for. He asked if I would please drive. We got into the van and drove back to the base. We parked behind one of the hangars next to the TLP platform, I got out and tried to clean the inside of the van a bit in case someone had to use it later, so that the inside wouldn't be so stained. Captain Moreno saw me, came towards me and accompanied me to the Air Force bar to isolate us a bit from all that, as there was little else we could do. As we were leaving, I saw Major Daza and I also gave him the names of the French TLP comrades we had taken to the hospital in Albacete. That was all.

Chapter 14

5th-Generation Fighters at the TLP

95th Squadron 'Boneheads' Raptors visit the TLP facilities in Spain

United States Air Force F-22A Raptors from the 95th Fighter Squadron, 325th Fighter Wing, Tyndall Air Force Base, Florida, refuelled and trained with a pair of Spanish Eurofighter Typhoons and a Hornet an during an F-22A forward deployment to Albacete, Spain, on 16 August 2018.

Thirteen F-22A Raptors and airmen from the 95th Fighter Squadron at Tyndall AFB, Fla., deployed to Spangdahlem AB, Germany, on 8 August and would remain in theatre for several weeks, US Air Forces in Europe announced.

During the deployment, which was funded in part by the European Deterrence Initiative, the Raptors will forward deploy to operating locations in Germany and other NATO nations 'in order to maximize training opportunities' and deter regional aggression, according to USAFE.

USAFE boss Gen. Tod Wolters said in late July the aircraft will 'work with US and allied forces already in Europe to build on …previous deployments.'

Col. Jason Bailey, commander of the 52nd Fighter Wing there, told the authors the wing is committed to providing full spectrum airpower to the European and African theatres, and its ability to 'receive, support, operate, and integrate forward deployed forces' is key to that. 'We previously had three fighter squadrons here. Now we're down to one,' which means 'we now have the real estate' to support theatre security packages and other forward deployed forces, said Bailey. 'We've done that in the past from F-22As to A-10s to F-15Cs, and we're actually putting in specific infrastructure here that enables us to be postured for 5th Generation integration,' he said.

For example, Spangdahlem is spending $18 million to build a 25,000ft^2 low observable composite repair facility that will allow maintainers to do repairs on F-22As. The facility will include one bay with room for a fourteen-strong administrative staff, paint tools, and other things needed to work on the Raptor's highly specialized composite material. Another $2.7 million of EDI funds will go towards the upgrade of seven existing third-generation hazards at Spangdahlem to accommodate the F-22A.

F-22As from the 1st Fighter Wing at JB Langley-Eustis, Va., visited the base last year as part of the Air Force's flying training programme.

F-35As departing Los Llanos for the afternoon mission on 10 June (*Tono Fernández*)

The two Lightning IIs that arrived at Los Llanos in the morning of 10 June were part of the twelve fighters belonging to the USAF's 421st Fighter Squadron, 388 FW, that coming from Aviano where had deployed on 23 May to take part in Exercise Astral Knight alongside with USAF B-52 bombers and other Italian AF aircraft including their F-35s. (*Tono Fernández*)

The Arrival at Los Llanos-Albacete AB

On 16 August 2018 a joint advanced aerial training exercise that included the participation of two USAF F-22A Raptors (CLASH 01 and CLASH 02), 05-088 and 05-91 5th-Generation jets and Spanish Air Force's Eurofighter Typhoon and F-18s took place at Los Llanos-Albacete Airbase.

It has been an excellent opportunity to evaluate the capabilities of Los Llanos-Albacete (Ala 14) and the TLP, to host an exercise that has the participation of a 5th-Generation jet, as are the F-22A of the USAF.

Exercises of this type represent an excellent opportunity for instruction and training that allows a joint assessment of the capabilities of the aircraft, two of American manufacture and one European in this case, in a demanding tactical environment.

The exercise consisted of two independent missions to each other in the assigned flight zone, in the areas known as D-98 and D-131/132 after carrying out the F-22A of the American Air Force a refuelling mission in flight from the companion KC-135R (QUID 424 80094 from the 100th Air Refuelling Wing.

After the initial take-off of two Eurofighter Typhoons (CE.16-31/14-01 and CE.16-12/14-71) from Ala 14 from Los Llanos, they carried out a mission with one of the

F-22As. Already in the work zone, dissimilar combat manoeuvres were carried out, that is, between fighters of different characteristics.

At the same time, an F-18BM (CE.15-12/12-74) of Ala 12 took off from Torrejón Airbase to meet in zone with the second American F-22A and perform the same type of mission.

Then the two Eurofighters of 142 Escuadrón in the air police mission, located the trace corresponding to the F-22A and made interception manoeuvres for their subsequent identification. In the event of any offensive action of the attacking plane, they made defensive and coordination manoeuvres in pairs to maintain the enemy's control zone.

Once the work was done in the sector, each American F-22A met with the couple of Spanish fighters assigned and proceeded to land at Albacete Airbase.

The training involved F-22As receiving mid-air refuelling from a USAF KC-135 Stratotanker assigned to the 100th Air Refuelling Wing, RAF Mildenhall, England. After refuelling and entering Albacete airspace, the F-22As trained with Spanish Eurofighter Typhoons and a two-seat Hornet from Ala 12 by practicing various dogfighting scenarios and manoeuvres.

'It was very good training,' said Captain Antonio Juarez, a 142nd Squadron Spanish Eurofighter Typhoon pilot. 'It was the first time we trained with this platform, and it's good for us to fly with different squadrons and aircraft to see the movements in the air, in fact the Raptor did things that we have never seen in dissimilar air combat scenarios!'

Following training, the aircraft landed at Los Llanos Airbase where the pilots from each aircraft spoke to media about the training. Afterwards, Spanish Air Force pilots and military personnel from NATO allied nations attended a brief held by the US Air Force on the capabilities of the F-22A.

In the briefing, we went over what the Raptor can do, why we have the Raptor, and what support it can provide to our NATO partners in the fight,' said US Air Force Major Michael Frye, an F-22A pilot and 95th Fighter Squadron weapons officer, and a graduate of the Fighter Weapons School. 'It would be great to repeat this training again in the future,' Juarez said. 'We both have interesting platforms and I look forward to an even more challenging scenario.'

Flight Course TLP 2019-02, the first with USAF F-35s

TLP's Flight Course 2019-2 took place in Albacete Airbase, between 27 May and 14 June 2019. During those days, more than 350 people have participated and 16 pilots, two Intelligence Analysts and six Air Controllers have been graduated. The participant countries were Belgium, Greece, Italy, Poland, Spain and the United States with two USAF F-35As, that became the stars of the day.

The Blue Air contingent, have been formed by Greece, Poland and Spain. The Red Air contingent has been formed mainly by Spanish aircraft that have provided two C101s and two F-5Ms playing the role of low speed OpForces to train the fast jets in dissimilar combat mode.

On 16 August 2018, two F-22s from the 95th Fighter Sqdn visited the Albacete airbase. The reason was to check with an exercise, the state of readiness of the base to operate with 5th-Generation aircraft. (*Salvador Mafè*)

As usual, the flight crews participating in the visit to Albacete took the 'family photo' as a souvenir, including the Spanish and USAF crews. The fourth officer from the left is Colonel Andrés Maldonado (TLP Commander) and the last one, is Colonel Juan Manuel Pablos Chi (14th Wing Commander). (*Salvador Mafè*)

The Red Air side was constituted by twelve aircraft and nine pilots have been graduated in the TLP OPFOR Program. One AWACS belonging to the 2 SQN NAEWC has played the role of Air Controller.

The class included nine flight missions, three sessions of academic formation and another three of simulator. In all, 26 aircraft have participated having flown 291 sorties, amassing 391 flight hours. Other participant assets have been a Spanish Mixed Regiment of AA Artillery

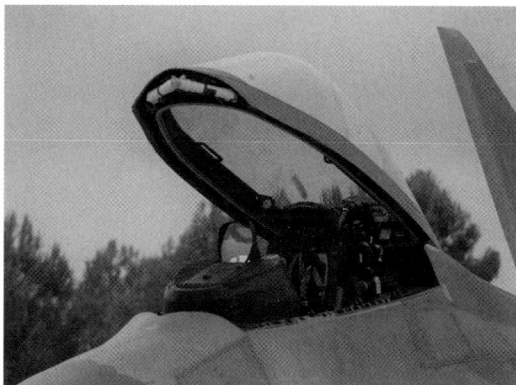

Close-up detail of the F-22 cockpit. (*Salvador Mafé*)

(RAMIX 30), two Italian helicopters with two extraction teams from the 15th and 16th Stormos of the Aeronautica Militare, an F-100 class Aegis frigate of the Spanish Armada and two Belgian SETE 10W TAC Instructors.

High-Profile Presentation

In contrast with the reserves and secrecies of the previous day, on 11 June, the following day of the F-35s' visit to Albacete, what was called 'Informative and Distinguished Visitors' Day' took place, plus an important presence of national media. The day was dubbed as an important milestone in the history of the TLP.

As a measure of the importance assigned to the event was the presence of very high-ranking personalities of both the Spanish and US Air Forces, and even a diplomatic representative of the US Embassy in Madrid. From the Spanish side attended Lieutenant General Cesar Simón López C.O. of the Mando Aéreo de Combate (MACOM), Major General Major Francisco González-Espresati Amián, MACOM's second in command, and Major General Ignacio Bengoechea Martí, Director de Sustainment and Support of the Logistic and Support Command.

The American presence was provided by Major General Greg A. Semmel, ANG Adviser to the Commander-in-Chief of the USAFE and the Minister Counsellor Benjamin G. Ziff of the US Embassy.

Mr Ziff gave a brief speech and presented Colonel Maldonado with a small and symbolic coin that was adorned with the legend: 'Integrity, Excellence in everything we do and Service above our personal needs'.

The TLP is in Evolution

The interesting fact of this Flight Course has been the participation of two USAF F-35As. These aircraft are part of the twelve fighters belonging to USAF's 421st Fighter Squadron, 388 FW, that came from Aviano where they had deployed on 23 May 2019 to take part in Exercise Astral Knight along with USAF B-52 bombers and other Italian AF aircraft including its F-35s.

Reportedly, the squadron arrived in Europe as part of a rotatory Theatre Security Package (TSP) that would last around six months until a new unit replaces this one. The TSP is funded through the European Deterrence Initiative, that has the dissuading purpose for the potential adversaries and to assure partners and allies the US commitment to regional security.

This is the first deployment of the 421st that was then the newest F-35A unit of the USAF equipped with the multi-role stealth fighter. They will establish during this time its home base at Spangdalem. From there it is planned to participate in other training exercises with European air forces.

The two aircraft arrived at Albacete on the morning of 10 June, half an hour in advance of schedule, performed three exhibition circuits above the base and landed. Both aircraft arrived armed with two Sidewinders carried in underwing pylons, that is, in 'visible' configuration.

Colonel Andrés Maldonado in the centre, posing with a Spanish pilot, and another American. With the exception of the colonels, none of the American pilots wore rank emblems, only the name, and the Spanish pilots wore it hidden. (*Salvador Mafé*)

Under American request, during the first day of its process, the press was strictly forbidden to take photographs of the parked aircraft.

Both jets took part in the afternoon flight exercises and then was permitted the photographs during the take-off runs. Later on the return to base the press was moved to the taxi runways that direct the aircraft to their parking and again we were forbidden to take photographs. The two aircraft stayed overnight under cover inside the TLP's maintenance hangar.

This visit to the TLP, more than an 'exotic' or goodwill gesture, is part of a planned road map that has as a goal integrate the aircraft of the so-called 4th Generation with those of the 5th.

Possibly this visit has some connection too with the previous visit of two F-22s to Albacete during the 2018 summer as an initial contact between both generations. Given the international political situation and tensions, one of the main concerns of the Western air powers is the integration and interoperability of the two generations of aircraft, which does not seem an easy job, given their different capabilities.

These plans are not new. The previous TLP commanding officer, Colonel Luis Villar, already mentioned in 2017 that the TLP was aiming at and looking for ways to manage

The F-22 arrived at Albacete escorted by Spanish EF-2000s and F/A 18 Ms. Here we see one of the Eurofighters landing and the rear-seat crew member saluting the photographers. (*Salvador Mafé*)

that integration. Now these plans are plainly confirmed by the current colonel, Andrés Maldonado, who during the press conference held in the base as part of the F-35's introduction said:

> The maximum priority of the TLP is to integrate, or better said, lead the integration of the fourth generation with those of the fifth. The main reason is because in very short time or even right now, six of the ten nations that forms the TLP are bound to be users of fifth generation aircraft.

The F-22s are thirsty birds. The two that visited Albacete AB arrived accompanied by a KC-135 to refuel them in flight. (*Salvador Mafé*)

As an example, the Netherlands will be a user only of fifth-generation combat aircraft. Therefore for the TLP Programme is vital or even existential, being able to integrate those aircraft in our courses.'

To achieve this goal, we are working in five lines of actuation that are the strategy we have identified for finally arrive to the point of being the European reference program on which we could integrate those aircraft and come through that every year they come to train together.

We are working on infrastructures.

We are working on the airspace. Although we have a great airspace, we must improve it and we are working on this.

We have changed the format of the courses. Previously the courses lasted four weeks and have been reduced to three, but we have incorporated the synthetic simulation, which improves the training and reduces the flying weeks.

Obviously, this reduction of a week in the duration of the courses has and economic impact for the attendants. He continued, adding:

We are designing and working so that the scenarios become more complex. Is what are called the Contested Degraded Operations (CDO) in such way that the scenarios be very demanding for those aircraft of very high capabilities.

Finally and possibly the most important step, is that we are working on Doctrine. As you know Doctrine is one of the mission of the TLP. Innovate in air Doctrine for the NATO. In that sense we are leading the preparation of a chapter of the Doctrine Manual that rules all the NATO's air operations.

Following the visit of the F-22s, the following year, a pair of F-35s from the 421st Fighter Squadron participated briefly in a TLP course. (*Salvador Mafé*)

Then Colonel Maldonado handed over to Major Holly Schmidt, one of the F-35 pilots who was very topical in his speech. After thanking to the host colonel and to the audience, basically he explained that 'the main differences are that our stealth capabilities permits that we are detected at a later stage than the aircraft of the fourth generation; and our sensors and systems allow us to see them long before they see us'. He also spoke briefly about the multirole capabilities of the F-35.

The presentation of the two F-35s had a high profile and included the presence of diplomatic representatives from the US embassy in Madrid.

Question Time

Once the Press Conference finished, came the question time. Most of the questions were addressed to Major Schmidt who again was very politely evasive in his responses.

The two F-3s5 visiting Albacete with serial numbers 17-5239 and 17-5252, belonged to the 421st FS, that received its jets on 12 December 2018, so is one of the latest if not the last USAF's squadrons to receive Lightning II jets.

Being so new, this magazine asked Major Schmidt if he would provide details about the Automatic Ground Collision Avoidance System (AGCAS) and if the two aircraft had already received this software upgrade. He responded not being technically qualified to talk about the AGCAS, adding that 'we are working on this system' and confirmed that the two aircraft present did not have it yet installed. The AGCAS is aimed to automatically prevent aircraft crashing inadvertently into ground obstacles.

Statistics elaborated with the compilation of years of flight data show clearly that is very rare that pilots crash because they fly too close to the ground. It is in those circumstances when pilots are more concentrated on their work. Is more frequent this happens because pilots become disoriented by bad weather, spatial disorientation, losing consciousness because manoeuvring aggressively at day or night or even because they are working concentrated inside the cockpit and losing the situational awareness of his external environment.

The system uses inputs from the GPS, terrain data and situational or spatial

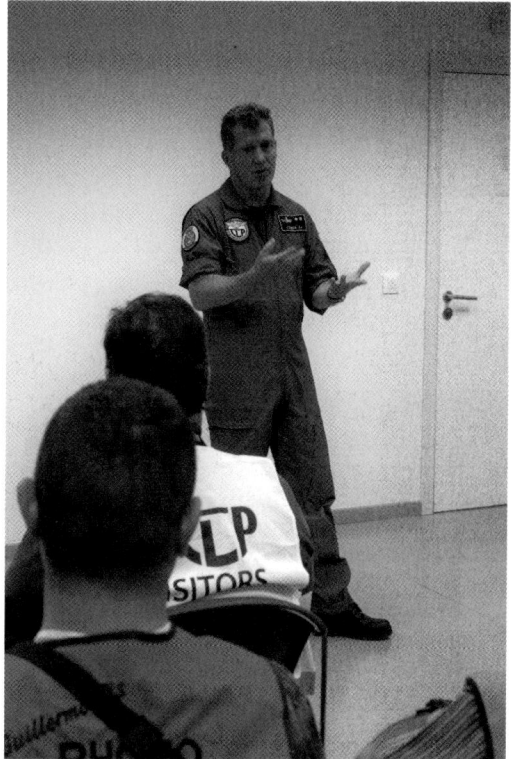

Lt Col César Lardies, TLP's Chief Support Unit during the Flying Course press briefing at the Flying Course 2019-2. (*Salvador Mafé*)

An F-22A Raptor pilot getting ready for take-off from Los Llanos-Albacete airbase. (*Salvador Mafè*)

awareness to identify when the aircraft is heading toward the ground, a mountain or even another aircraft. Using as a base for its calculations the aircraft speed, trajectory, and no inputs from the pilot, the systems modifies the trajectory to avoid the impact without damaging the aircraft structure. The system has an internally-predetermined safety height which is considered as the point when is too late for the pilot to react and pull up. Reached this height the system takes the authority and pulls the jet upward on his own before returning the control to the pilot.

The AGCAS safety point is established at 2,300ft. During tests Lockheed added a safety cushion of 10.000 additional feet to that floor in such way that the test F-35 when reaching 12,300ft would react by pulling up but without compromising test pilots' safety allowing to retake control in case of system failure.

The test have been conducted by the 461st Flight Test Squadron home based in Edwards AFB and with the cooperation of a wide range of pilots and engineers from the Air Force Research Lab., the Defence Safety Oversight Council, the F-35 Joint Program Office, Lockheed-Martin and NASA's Armstrong Flight Research Centre. The 412th Test Wing has recently published its technical report on the F-35 AGCAS and has recommended it for fielding, with seven years ahead of schedule.

Once initiated the process, the upgrade will be very fast. According to Billie Flynn Lockheed Martin experimental pilot: 'is as easy as updating an I-Phone Operating System'.

Since autumn 2014 the AGCAS has been already satisfactorily fitted to the some 600 F-16 Block 40/50s.

About Infrastructures

Another question raised to Colonel Maldonado was: Which infrastructures have been built and which are pending?

He responded at length.

> We started in July 2018. The Americans offered to come here and make a Safety Survey. That's to say; to recognize all the base to identify all the logistic needs and aeronautical safety requirements that may prevent the deployment of the F-35. A second survey come in November led by Major Schmidt. They were studying the safety distances needed for parking the aircraft, the communications needs. With all their findings it was written a report and the base started to work to comply with the requirements.
>
> Lately, in February 2019, there was a third more important visit formed by 20 people from Safety that analysed all the capabilities of the base, in relation with the security distances communications and even the drillings of the runway.

Apparently, the safety distance was an important issue as was mentioned several times by Colonel Maldonado. Possibly the Americans, habituated to their super-bases feel a bit uncomfortable with the size of European bases.

Colonel Maldonado continued:

> Three months ago, in March 2019, we received the final very comprehensive and complete report with the conclusions that Albacete was prepared for the deployment of thirteen F-35As, supported by a Deployable Debriefing Facility (DDF). This is just like a container connected via optical fibre to an Internet web that allows connection with the Logistic System ALIS in USA that is also of a very advanced generation.

The DDF containers are frequently seen in Albacete brought by some of the participants in the FC, the case of the F-35 is special because of its dependency of the ALIS System.

> One of the infrastructure examples we have accomplished has been the extension of our optical fibre net from TLP's Headquarters that we have extended surrounding the platform were usually are parked the participants, up to an adjacent platform hat complies with the safety distances requested and the connections needed and that will be dedicated to the F-35s. Additionally we have installed security cameras.
>
> Also will have provisions to extend the optical fibre to other platforms or positions that comply with the safety distances in order to provide the service, just in case there is more than a squadron of F-35 deployed. The infrastructures go in that direction.

Now there is nothing important pending, and we can say that by now the base is prepared to receive the F-35s.

Finally Colonel Maldonado put emphasis on the following:

> The TLP is NATO's Doctrine's Laboratory. We organically do not belong to NATO's structure, but we are related by an agreement with them and they provide us the doctrine that is the base of what we are doing here. We put it in common to allow all the air forces speak the same language
>
> With the fifth generation there is like a doctrinal void because of the confidentiality that has surrounded the programme since its beginnings. By now there is nothing written that can be distributed among the allied countries that not form part of the JSF.
>
> Here at the TLP we have initiated to elaborate the texts that will be available with the security restrictions and would be used in the TLP courses to integrate both generations during the next five years.

In coincidence with the F-35 visit, the Spanish national 'non-specialized' press the previous day distributed a notice with a delicate or perhaps yellowish nature, according to which, in an attempt to bring back the TLP to Italian soil, 'Italy' without a specification who was 'Italy', would have declared that Albacete was not prepared to conduct operations with the F-35.

In this respect colonel Maldonado denied knowledge of these comments and affirmed that 'Italy is a friendly country and a fundamental member of the TLP, that is solidly established in Albacete 'by signed agreements' during the next ten years or so I think'. Even he recalled the previous TLP 2018-04 held in Amendola during November-December 2018, home base of the Italian F-35s, saying one of his purposes was to test 'if we see the F-35 in our systems and how do we see them, as part of the roadmap leading to the integration. As I have said, this was first step or a first approach to help us to learn what was needed for the integration of which we are talking about.' AMI declared the IOC of its F-35 in coincidence with its participation in the TLP course deployed specifically in Italy.'

Given all these statements the next question addressed to colonel Maldonado and Major Schmidt was: When the US F-35 will deploy to Albacete?

Colonel Maldonado responded that the TLP goal was to count with the F-35s beginning in 2020: Probably he was referring to the European F-35, as put that until 2021 will not be US F-35 permanently deployed in Europe. Major Schmidt said: 'I cannot make promises. We are looking for every opportunity to integrate fourth generation aircraft with those of fifth and this is a great opportunity.'

Do you want to talk to me?

Future Force Projections reveal that in 2030 70 per cent of the combat aircraft will be 5th Generation but a remaining 30 per cent of 4th-Generation aircraft will still be serving among the NATO ranks; consequently both generations still will need to live together during some time.

In telecommunications science a data link is the means of connecting one location with another for the purpose of transmitting and receiving digital information. Then the integration of both generations has to do with the way aircraft, or other military assets communicate among them.

As it is known, the F-35 uses the Multifunction Advanced Data Link (MADL) that is a fast switching narrow directional communications data link. MADL works with Ku band, which is the portion of the electromagnetic spectrum in the microwave frequencies ranging from 12 to 18 gigahertz (Ghz).

With its integrated and fused sensors the F-35 is capable of obtaining an holistic picture of the battlespace and automatically share the data with other pilots or ground and naval stations using 'the most modern data links'. And here is the problem; not all friends or allies enjoy the benefits of the advanced data links and are not compatible with the MADL.

The B-2 bomber is MADL-compatible and probably some of the new unmanned systems too, but ironically, the F-22 Raptor is not. In spite that the Office of the Undersecretary of Defence for Acquisition, Technology and Logistics directed the Air Force and Navy to integrate MADL among the F-22, F-35 and B-2 fleets, the plans to integrate in the Raptor were scrapped in 2010 by the Air Force, citing technology maturity risks and being expensive and cumbersome.

Most of the 4th-Generation aircraft and other ground and naval systems are using MIL-STD-6016 data link 16, which is widely diffused among the US and allied forces.

Ln addition to the MADL The F-35 also uses Link-16, but the problem is that not all the information of the battle space gathered by the Lightning II, that is often defined as Tier 3, can be shared with Link-16 users, that receive Tier 1 data. So there is a wide working field.

The Exercise

The new paradigms since the release in 2017 by the US National Security Strategy and signed by President Trump, are the 'Multidomain Operations in Contested and Degraded Environments'.

Those concepts still are not clear and have sparked a wide range of almost philosophical discussions, papers and lectures within the US Armed Forces, trying to find a definition that satisfies everybody for a physical application in the battlefronts and the technological resources required.

A definition of 'Domain' that has some acceptance is: 'A region distinctively marked by some physical or virtual feature(s)'. Another is 'A domain is a space in which forces can manoeuvre to create effects.'

In modern military parlance there are five domains, some think tanks define some more, but the basics are: Land, Maritime, subdivided in Surface and Subsurface, Air, Space and

Cyberspace and is the responsibility of the military to work in multidomain environments and its seams between.

The challenge comes when in the NATO parlance the concept has a very different meaning. The NATO uses the term 'multidomain' in reference to the Political, Military, Economic, Social, Infrastructure and Information Systems, all collected in the acronym PMESII.

The concept CDO refers to the operations in environments where in the past the US and allied forces enjoyed an uncontested superiority, but now the new technologies, missiles, communications, asymmetrical threats, space and cyberwarfare, denies the past freedom of action.

All this together, implies that in the current situation 'the ways US and allies build its military forces integrates its planning and synchronizes its operations must change and it must change quickly.'

Not much detailed information is released about the TLP's courses, but from the battle order of the participants we can deduct that they are addressed in the direction of the multidomain battlespace.

In the last course have seem the participation of AA artillery (RAMIX 30, with a Mistral SAM battery), naval (an Aegis frigate) and the Air units, configures an almost three domain battle space, which enters in the multidomain definition.

The exercise that received more attention was a Personnel Recovery operation. The recovery of a shot-down pilot behind enemy lines. We asked which had been the role of the F-35s and Lieutenant Colonel César Lardiés, TLP's Chief of Support, said that in the Recovery exercise, the Lightnings were the first to enter the battle space to neutralize 'enemy defences', using their superior capabilities, thus allowing the 'good guys' penetrate with the helicopters to recover the downed pilot.

We asked if the neutralization of the enemy defences was 'dynamic', using bombs (simulated) or 'passive', using electronics, The response was: 'Both'.

During the exercises in Spain for safety reasons in a somewhat congested airspace, both F-35s flew with their transponders 'on' to enhance their visibility.

Chapter 15

Polish MiG-29 'Fulcrums' at the Tactical Leadership Programme. The Perfect 'Red Air'

The MiG-29s of the Polish Air Force have participated three times in the TLP's Flying Course, always acting as 'Red Air', in which role they are excellent. In a few years, the 'Fulcrums', as well as the Su-22 'Fitters', will be replaced by F-35A Lightning IIs.

Major Piotr Iwaszko, Commander of the 1elt (1st Fighter Squadron) describe for us what the role of this Russian fighter is.

Of course, the MiG-29 is still a good platform for aerial combat, which is its main role, although it has some limitations. It lacks, for example, some modern elements, such as air-to-air TACAN, in-flight refuelling capacity, multifunction screens and some other elements, but it maintains its great qualities such as its perfect aerodynamics and good thrust/weight ratio, this aspect is very important in air combat.

On the other hand, its avionics and weapons control system is highly optimized

Major Piotr Iwaszko, Polish squadron leader and commander of the MiG-29 1 Squadron, in the cockpit of his plane. (*Salvador Mafé*)

for air combat, especially with the HMS (Helmet Mounted Sight) used in combination with R73 light infrared guidance missiles.

In short, our aircraft lacks capabilities and avionics adequate for long-range combat, but in close combat, within a range of 10 miles, it is a dangerous and highly capable opponent that is really difficult to defeat.

As I pointed out before, on the one hand, excellent aerodynamics, good weight/thrust ratio and very good handling throughout the speed range. In addition, the avionics are designed and optimized for close combat. Another important advantage is the ability to use the HMS in combination with the infrared 'Archer' missiles.

Another of its advantages is its powerful 30mm cannon. capable of taking down an enemy fighter with just five shots. It is also a quality its double power plant that guarantees its survival in combat and finally, the best of its qualities: It is the most beautiful combat aircraft in the world.

In the TLP we play the role of what is called 'Red Air', that is, we are the opponents for the pilots participating in the course.'

The Poles with their MiG-29s captured much of the attention during the Flying Courses. (*Salvador Mafé*)

The sleek lines of the MiG-29 can be appreciated in this photograph. (*Salvador Mafé*)

The MiG-29 'analog' cockpit. (*Salvador Mafé*)

Full afterburner take-off: this image really shows the raw power of this fighter. (*Salvador Mafé*)

Close-up of the short-range IR R73 'Archer' air-to-air missile. (*Salvador Mafé*)

Nice air-to-air images of Polish 'Fulcrums'. These iconic fighters will be replaced shortly in the Polish Air Force by the 5th-Generation F-35A Lightning II. (*Salvador Mafé*)

Chapter 16

The Tactical Leadership Programme and the Pace of Change

C hange is often associated with necessary actions, associated with positive effects, in politics, in aesthetics, in life. But this statement is not necessarily true if the changing subject is already a relevant model of success. Altering the pillars and structures of a well-established work programme can inadvertently have unexpected negative impacts in some of its areas, so every change must be processed, analysed and managed through an unbiased and contrasted decision process.

This is exactly the case with the Tactical Leadership Programme. The TLP is overseen by a multinational headquarters based at Los Llanos Airbase, Albacete. It is composed of personnel from the 10 NATO member countries participating in the programme. Its main objective (mission) is 'to increase the effectiveness of allied tactical air forces through the development of leadership skills, mission planning, briefings, tactical flying and briefing/debriefing skills and doctrinal/conceptual initiatives' (TLP Memorandum of Understanding. Section 1, 1. (2009), p. 7).

Throughout its 43-year history, TLP has become the focal point for NATO allied air force tactical training and associated leadership knowledge and skills. These skills are considered fundamental to NATO's ability to effectively meet today's tactical air challenges. This has been, is and will continue to be achieved through the effort, dedication and professionalism of TLP personnel of yesterday, today and tomorrow, a diverse and talented workforce. TLP has navigated well through the various strategic, tactical and technical stages of the past decades. The pattern of change has been based not only on the technological advances of modern systems, but also on additional dynamic needs, such as the consolidation and growth of mutual trust and the willingness of its members to operate together.

Operation Allied Force, the International Security Assistance Force (ISAF) Mission, Operation Unified Protector and multiple air operations under various campaigns are a testament to how TLP graduates bring undeniable value to the Alliance or any international coalition when it comes to integrating Tactics, Techniques and Procedures (TTP), judgement and effort. This is the product of a shared methodology, curriculum and camaraderie that enables the 'plug & play' effect that so accurately represents one of the key defining characteristics of NATO air forces. Combined with technological superiority, all of these facets are crucial to maintaining the Alliance's strategic advantage.

Without the implementation of an effective strategy, an accelerating pattern of change can lead to erratic decisions. A strategy is a plan comprising interrelated actions to achieve

The recently opened Modern Air Combat Environment (MACE) flight simulator. It consists of more than thirty combat cockpits and ground control interception (GCI) positions so that virtual training can be conducted by pilots and controllers, all seated in the same room. MACE also includes modes related to 5th-Generation aircraft and a wide variety of platform, threat and weapons modelling options. (*TLP*)

TLP platform in a photograph taken some years ago, with a pair of French Mirage F1CRs in the foreground. (*A Cárceles*)

a long-term goal. The TLP has designed and is currently implementing its own strategy to ensure that change enhances the success of its leadership programme, which is fast approaching its 50th anniversary.

The TLP strategy

The most recent TLP strategy is based on its stated mission, and was proposed to the approved members during the Steering Group (SG) 2020 meeting. The ultimate goal of the strategy is twofold: to remain relevant to the needs of its members, while aligning with the latest challenges and changes facing TLP. These challenges, which adjust the operational tempo at which the TLP wishes to train, include: technology, infrastructure, doctrine, participants and, crucially, scenarios and opponents.

The TLP's strategy is also based on several assumptions:

- The airspace enjoyed by the TLP, already established in the Aeronautical Information Publication (AIP) Spain, is suitable for the envisaged activities to be performed in terms of size, meteorology and allocated land and sea legs.
- The integration of Future Combat Aircraft System projects to include connectivity.
- Systems procured by NATO nations will be in various stages of development.
- Budget constraints will continue.

The impressive Italian HH101A of the 9th Stormo dedicated to COMBAT SAR. (*A. Jails*)

During TLP 2021-3 a civilian Learjet of the German company GFD Bmbh participated as electronic 'aggressor'. (*Salvador Mafé*)

A pair of Eurofighter Typhoons taking off from Los Llanos on 21 September. These two were assigned to Blue Air. (*Salvador Mafé*)

- Core air power functions, as defined in NATO's Allied Joint Publication (AJP) 3.3 (B) (NATO Standard AJP 3.3. Allied Joint Doctrine for Air and Space Operations. Edition B, Version 1. Published by the NATO Office of Standardisation (2016): p 1.8 1.17) for the Air and Space series, will remain a solid reference.
- Information and data-sharing limitations, national security requirements, caveats, restrictions and limits will be present and will require management in fora similar to the TLP.

Recognizing these preconditions, five Lines of Operation (LoO) have been developed to operationalise this strategy, i.e. to act in each area in a particular way but in a coordinated manner across the board. These LoOs and their associated milestones correspond to the inferences of a deductive planning process, in other words, the things that can be done sequentially to achieve the objectives. All LoOs are interconnected, all converging towards the execution of TLP's mission and the realisation of TLP's vision, which clearly states that TLP will remain aligned and relevant.

LoO 1: Integration of 4th- and 5th-Generation Aircraft Operations

Doctrinal initiatives at NATO level, related to the integration of 4th- and 5th-Generation platforms, gravitate between several options. Some are provided through information

The 59th Tactical Fighter Wing of the Hungarian Air Force took part in TLP 2021-3 with two JAS-39C Gripens. (*Salvador Mafé*)

integration solutions, which in turn have been merged with integrated sensors. Others are based on the reorganization of conventional Command and Control (C2) structures, which may, in some tactical contexts, consider 5th-Generation aircraft as a C2 sub-node. The sharing and orchestration of different generation platforms, manned and unmanned, is one of the challenges facing the TLP, which represents at the tactical level the perfect Live, Virtual, Constructive and Live-Virtual laboratory for the Alliance to consolidate this integration process. in a multinational context.

The current decade represents a transitional period in which the initial coexistence of 4th- and 5th-Generation platforms will continue to expand. Some nations will continue to design interim processes in which, at the national level, 5th-Generation assets will replace 4th-generation ones. The TLP will improve the level of instruction provided to its mission leaders, helping to bridge the gaps between the training requirements of these two generations and helping to avoid potential fractures within these two training communities, which should certainly be a single struggle. Furthermore, through its various curricula and, in particular, through opportunities that will open up in terms of virtual and live-virtual training, the TLP will represent an unbeatable and optimal opportunity to assist nations in their transition to the new generation of aircraft.

Shortly after inspection and evaluation by the United States Air Force in 2019, Albacete Airbase has been certified for the operation of 5th-Generation aircraft. Currently, the milestones (decisive conditions) included in this LoO mainly concern infrastructure, such

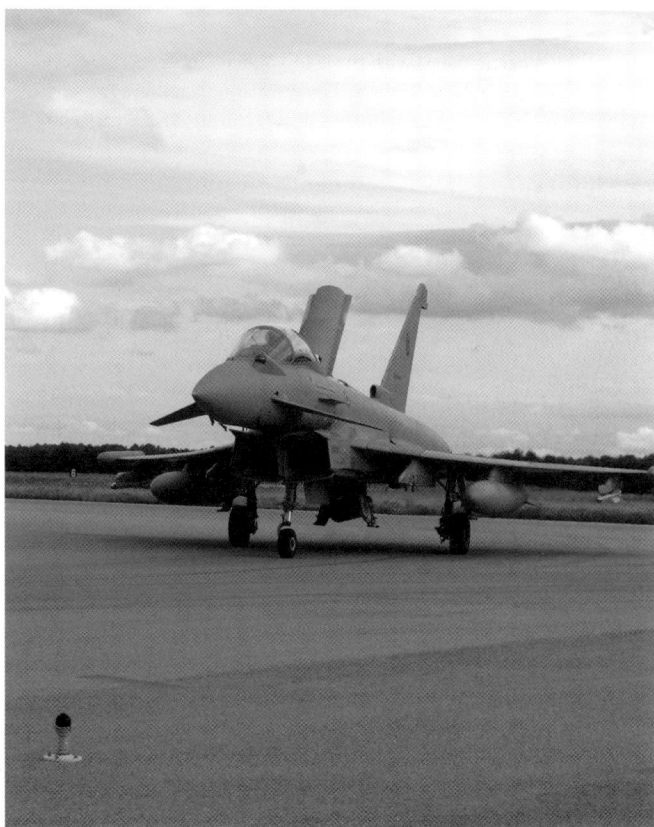

EF-2000 of the 37th Stormo, AMI. Their way of greeting the photographer is to deploy the aerobrake. (*Salvador Mafé*)

Czech L-159 ALCAs are not often seen on flying courses, but on this occasion three were deployed at TLP 2021-3 to act as Red Air. (*Salvador Mafé*)

The USAFE participated with three F-16CMs (including a reserve) from the 480th Fighter Squadron/52nd Fighter Wing, SEAD specialists. The numerous bombing missions in which this Viper has participated, over Afghanistan, Iraq and Syria, including six strafing sorties, are shown. (*Salvador Mafé*)

as the provision of a new Deployable Debriefing Facility (DDF) with the required physical security elements. The DDFs will be distributed throughout the TLP infrastructure to enhance the regular and safe operation of 4th and 5th Generation aircraft detachments. Work is also underway on the installation of an approach radar to speed up the recovery phase of missions with large numbers of aircraft, thereby improving flight safety. This Airport Surveillance Radar (ASR) is expected to enter service in 2022.

LoO 2: Agile Combat Employment (ACE)

The USAF defines ACE as a 'proactive and reactive operational scheme of manoeuvre executed within threat timelines to increase survivability while generating combat power'. TLP scenarios will incorporate those ACE actions that combat air assets can employ to protect personnel, equipment and facilities before, during and after an attack and thus continue to generate combat power from locations other than their primary operating bases.

ACE-related concepts have been addressed and trained in other formats and forums. Since the Ample Train series of exercises in the 1990s, allied nations have striven to increase logistical flexibility at the tactical level. Notably, the European Air Group (EAG) collaborates with the TLP by basing its Eurofighter Typhoon Interoperability Programme (ETIP) in Albacete as part of TLP flight courses.

Including ACE as an LoO brings an agile combat culture among the participants. A first step is to include the ACE concept in the supporting academic courses, followed, as a second step, by the introduction of ACE-related injections and cross-service maintenance practices within the flight courses.

Czech L-159 in a peculiar pixelated camouflage. (*Salvador Mafé*)

The French Aeronavale participated in TLP 2021-3 (13 September/1 October) with seven Rafale Ms belonging to the 17 Flotille de Landivisau, four in Blue Air (callsigns 'Paris' and 'Lion') and three in Red Air (callsigns 'MiG' and 'Vodka'). (*Tono Fernández*)

LoO 3: Virtual and Live-Virtual Training

This LoO is the most transformative and addresses all the changes that will be introduced with the use of this new tool: the Modern Air Combat Environment (MACE) flight simulator.

This simulator consists of more than thirty combat cockpits and Ground Control Interception (GCI) positions so that virtual training can be conducted by pilots and controllers, all seated in the same room. MACE also includes modes related to 5th-Generation aircraft and a variety of options for modelling platforms, threats and weapons. MACE, as a laboratory for complex tactical air missions, will allow the processing and definition of a multitude of new possibilities directly related to and replicating the integration of all types of systems being played in virtual and mixed Live-Virtual environments.

Tactical synergies detected in the real world can be further modelled in the virtual world and reciprocally, whether it be cooperative interaction between 4th- and 5th-Generation aircraft, between different platforms, weapons, sensors and air power roles, as well as between other capabilities currently being introduced, such as miniature air-launched decoys, electromagnetic pulse weaponry, Tomahawk-type ground attack missiles, and others. Virtual maritime and land platforms can be introduced to enrich the tactical context of Blue (friendly) Forces. In addition, both the TLP and participating nations will be able to use the MACE tool to model and execute mission or scenario-specific 'war games'.

This new simulator incorporates connectivity with C2 systems to provide some degree of Live-Virtual training. MACE will be the alternative tool to be used in case of bad weather or other limiting factors. In addition, it is already possible to fly virtual blue and red (enemy) routes, inserted into live flight scenarios from the simulator cockpits via the Link-16 network. The first Live-Virtual event (real blue fighters plus virtual blue fighters versus virtually generated routes, both in the air and on the ground) took place in June 2021. The TLP, in coordination with the Host Nation (HN) (operator of the C2 system and responsible for airspace management), will determine the levels of ambition that will enable both safe operation of the systems and optimal training.

Once MACE capabilities are properly analysed, the TLP curriculum will be reviewed to propose new options to its SG. These options will mainly be a product of combining or blending live and virtual training.

LoO 4: Degraded Operations

The TLP deploys live ground and airborne threats during its flight course. Many other regional stakeholders (European Defence Agency, EAG) are looking for medium-term solutions regarding Red Air provision.

Live Red Air is provided by the different participating countries in accordance with the TLP Operations Plan, while Live-Virtual Red Air can now be fed by virtual traces

An Ala 14 Typhoon during an offensive counter-air mission. (*Nando Caballero*)

The latest unofficial badge created by the TLP is this one depicting The Mandalorian, an F-35 and his famous saying 'This is the Way'. (*TLP*)

operated in real time from the MACE simulator or from future simulation facilities that can be integrated into the HN C2 system.

With regard to Red Surface-Based Air Defence (SBAD), the MACE intelligence generator will be the perfect tool to introduce complex orders of battle, including appropriate SBAD configurations of opposing forces based on movement patterns and emission control procedures. Simulation of enemy SBAD at an appropriate level of information classification (TLP has just incorporated a NATO Secret Wide Area Network (SWAN), so the simulator supports classified information) will allow the reconstruction, in the virtual environment, of specific tactics observed in various scenarios, particularly those typical of access area denial scenarios. The addition of a broadband joint threat emitter, planned for 2022, will significantly improve the quality of such tactical contexts.

The TLP and HN have supported several site studies of participating nations to identify potential unpaved airstrips that can be used in missions that require them (such as Slow Mover [SLOWMO] or Personnel Recovery [PR]). These types of operations enrich scenarios that already include emitters, inflatable decoys and other live ground-based air defence support elements (NASAMS, Patriot, Crotale, Mistral).

LoO 5: Linking All Domains

Air combat platforms will be networked and orchestrated with other land and maritime platforms while executing complex missions. The cyber domain will provide cross-domain and/or cross-component connectivity features, resulting in complementary C2 architectures parallel to those of each component command.

TLP's cooperation with JAPCC aims to introduce relevant cyber and space aspects affecting the planning and execution of 4th- and 5th-Generation COMAO, as well as to update the joint part of TLP's tactical scenarios incorporating JAPCC's lessons learned from its participation in the Trident Juncture series of computer-assisted exercises.

Note that this level of complexity may not be adequately replicated during the standard execution of the Flight Course or COMAO Course, as the TLP Mission states that the primary objective is to increase the effectiveness of Allied Air Forces. Consequently, an overload of joint operations across all domains (JADO) may obscure this mission. In addition, manning constraints are a relevant limiting factor, as TLP trainers focus on the aforementioned air-centric tactical mission. Therefore, additional personnel would definitely be a great asset to enhance this step towards JADO. However, once MACE is ready to take a step further with regard to joint scenarios, it could offer TLP participants a joint battlefield-focused introduction, which they may encounter in the future, while operating within the Air Component Command in sync with other active joint forces.

Conclusion

TLP's vision demands that it remains aligned and relevant. Throughout its history, TLP has successfully adapted to meet strategic, tactical and technical transformations to effectively enable NATO allied air forces to meet relevant and demanding challenges. To continue to successfully navigate this path, and based on TLP's stated mission, these five intricately linked LoOs will ensure that TLP continues to achieve its long-term goal.

Chapter 17

The Commandants

Since the Tactical Leadership Programme was established at Los Llanos-Albacete airbase in southeastern Spain, six Ejército del Aire Colonels have led it:

- Ignacio Bengoechea Martí: 1 August 2009–27 July 2021.
- Enrique Martínez Vallas: 27 July 2012–3 July 2014.
- Cándido Antonio Bernal Fuentes: 3 July 2014–6 July 2016.
- Luis Villar Coloma: 6 July 2016–3 July 2018.
- Andrés Enrique Maldonado García: 3 July 2018–10 July 2020.
- José Carlos Presa Díaz: 10 July 2020–July 2022.
- Luis Alberto Martínez Ruiz: July 2022–July 2024.
- César Oscar Acebes Puertas 4 July 2024–present.

Colonel Ignacio Bengoechea Martí.

Colonel Enrique Martinez Vallas.

Colonel Cándido Antonio Bernal Fuentes.

Colonel Luis Villar Coloma.

Colonel Andrés Enrique Maldonado.

Colonel Carlos Presa Díaz.

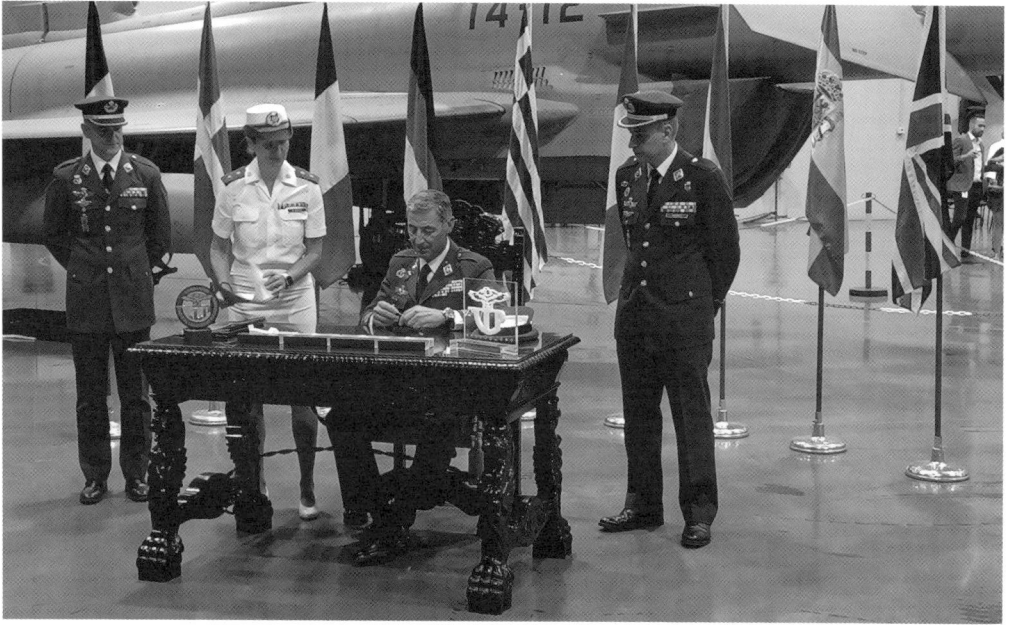

Colonel Oscar Acebes Puertas, signing the document as the new TLP Commandant, 4 July 2024.

Colonel Luis Alberto Martínez Ruiz (left) and Colonel Oscar Acebes Puertas (right), Air Combat Command CO General Espressati is in the centre.

Index